T.

ENGLISH HISTORIANS

WITH AN
INTRODUCTION
BY
A. J. GRANT

KENNIKAT PRESS
Port Washington, N. Y./London

ENGLISH HISTORIANS

First published in 1906
Reissued in 1971 by Kennikat Press
Library of Congress Catalog Card No: 73-118472
ISBN 0-8046-1221-8

Manufactured by Taylor Publishing Company   Dallas, Texas

PREFACE

Any attempt to illustrate the characteristics of English historians by a series of extracts can attain at best to a very limited success. Much more than any other volume in this series it must recall the classical wiseacre who carried round a brick as a sample of the house that he had for sale. At first it seemed to me impossible to devise anything within the limits imposed which could be of service to serious students of literature; but, upon deliberation, it seemed that something might be done by a double and to some extent parallel series of extracts, the first illustrating the aims and motives of historians, mostly by their own utterances with regard to their craft; the second exhibiting their style and method of composition by passages of some length drawn from their most important works. I have convinced myself during the progress of the book that the study of the development of historiography offers a promising and little-worked field, from which valuable results might come both for philosophy and history.

The volume is concerned only with works in English. This limitation gives a certain unreality to all that part which deals with the centuries before the sixteenth. For six centuries at least all that was most important in English thought found expression in Latin; and we miss some great names in English historiography when we give exclusive attention to those writers who discarded these classic robes for English home-spun. But it was necessary either to do this or to leave the earlier centuries untouched; and I hope that the extracts from the *Anglo-Saxon Chronicle*, and from Capgrave, may at least serve to give perspective to my subject.

I must make grateful acknowledgment for help received to Professor Herford, the editor of the series; to Mr. H. W. V. Temperley, now of Peterhouse, Cambridge, formerly my colleague; and above all to Mr. T. Seccombe, who has given me much valuable assistance, both in the Introduction and the selection of the extracts. The many shortcomings of the book would have been more and more serious if I had not been able to appeal to his remarkable knowledge of historical literature.

My thanks also are due to those publishers whose permission to print passages from works of which they hold the copyright has made this book possible. I am indebted to Messrs. Longmans for this permission with regard to the extracts, in Parts I and II, from Gardiner; to Messrs. Macmillan for the passages drawn from the Inaugural lectures of Professor Seeley and Lord Acton; and to the Syndics of the Cambridge University Press for the extract from the Inaugural lecture of Professor Bury.

A. J. G.

CONTENTS

INTRODUCTION

THIS book is an attempt to exhibit the different forms that history written in English has assumed at different periods in the history of English literature. It is thus a small contribution to an important subject—the history of historiography in England.

History is a word of such wide and indefinite meaning that it is necessary to define the way in which it is used here. There is nothing that cannot be regarded in some sort as the material of history: there is no narrative, professedly relating to the actual past, to which the name of history may not fairly be applied. "*Quicquid agunt homines*" is more and more the theme of the historian; nothing that concerns humanity is outside his province. In the following pages, however, the common usage of the word will be followed: by history will be meant the orderly record of the life of some considerable section of the human race in its main features. Thus, on the one hand, mere lists of events, chronological summaries, and genealogical tables are excluded;[1] and, on the other

---

[1] These are rejected as being rather aids to the writing of history than history itself, though the modern student of history will be far from accepting Bacon's view of *Epitomes* as being "the mere corruptions and moths of history, the use of which deserveth to be banished,

hand, memoirs (though often so closely related to history) and all sectional histories, as of literature, music, art, or social customs. The object of the book may indeed be defined as an attempt to exhibit the views which at different times have been taken of the past of man and the different methods that have been adopted in describing it.

I. The earliest phase of historical writing in English reveals to us, on the one side, a bald chronicle-narrative of events with little connection or sense of their relative importance, and, on the other, the heroic poem or saga, in which the chief object is to glorify nation or king without much effort at the accurate statement of the facts or incidents of the narrative. The Anglo-Saxon Chronicle illustrates well both these forms of historical writing. Side by side with the baldest records of comets, floods, pestilences, marriages, harryings, battles, come bursts of saga-like poetry, telling of heroic battles or the saintly lives of kings. Both are illustrated in our extracts, and echoes of both styles may be heard in our later historical literature. It is clear that at this time History was not conscious of herself, and could not have answered any question as to what was her special mission and object. If she amuses, interests, and incidentally instructs, that is enough; she has not yet asked in what the interest or in-

as all men of sound judgment have confessed, as those that have fretted and corroded the sound bodies of many excellent histories and wrought them into base and unprofitable dregs ".

struction that she provides differs from those provided by other departments of literature.

The historical literature of the Middle Ages is almost exclusively in Latin, and does not therefore fall within the scope of this book. The Latin writers, it is now generally admitted, do not deserve the contempt that was once generally poured upon them. But history, whether in Latin or English, did not emerge from the atmosphere of chronicle and poetry until the Renaissance, and the mists were slow to disperse even then. It has been remarked by Professor Bury in his Inaugural Lecture, that " it would be a most interesting investigation to trace from the earliest ages the history of public opinion in regard to the meaning of falsehood and the obligation of veracity ". And much of the historical literature in English that precedes the Renaissance is interesting from this point of view, as well as for the information contained in it with regard to the events contemporary with or slightly preceding the times of the writer. It would serve no good purpose to give here a list of the historical works published in English prior to 1485, but it will be well to notice the characteristics of a representative example.

The *Chronicle* of John Capgrave is the earliest historical work of any pretensions in English after the Anglo-Saxon Chronicle expired in 1114. John Capgrave was born at King's Lynn in Norfolk in 1393, and lived most of his life in a friary of that town. He was the author of many works, historical and theological, in Latin, but the *Chronicle* is written throughout in English. The book is not a good specimen of what the Middle Ages could do in the way of describing events and commenting on them, but deserves note as illustrating some general characteristics of the mediæval chronicle. In true mediæval fashion Capgrave begins at the beginning. "Anno Mundi 1. The first man Adam was mad on a Friday, withoute modir, withoute fader, in the feld of Damask; and fro that place led into paradise to dwell there: after dryvyn out for synne. Whanne he had lyved nyne hundred yeres and xxx he deied, byried in Hebron: his hed was lift with the flood and leyd in Golgatha." His narrative then flows on in annalistic form through channels well worn by the classical and ecclesiastical guides of the Middle Ages. Most of the early part of his book is devoted to Greek, Roman, and Jewish rather than to English history. The first mention that is made of Britain comes under the date "Anno 4084", and a few short extracts from the neighbourhood of this year will serve to show the general character of the first part of this entertaining book.

"Anno 4044.—This yere deied Samson with deceyt of a woman; whech was the Juge of Israel xx yere. His strength passed alle men. He rent a leon. He brak the bondis that he was bound with. The gates of a town, and the postis, he bore them away. And at the last, be stering of the Holy Goost, he pullid down too postis, where a hous fell, and oppressed him and mech othir puple.

"In this same time Ascanius, the son of Eneas, in the third yere aftir Troye was distroyed, biggid a town, Alba, whech stod upon the flood which had the same name, but now it hite Tibir, and that same town is now a part of Rome."

"Anno 4084.—This yere deied Hely the preest of the tabernacle that was in Silo, undir whom Samuel first was mad a ministir of the same tabernacle. This Heli, for his necligens, that he correated not his sonnes of her insolens, fel down fro his chaeyer where he sat in the tabernacle, and, thus punishid with temporal deth, scaped, as we suppose, the deth that is evirlasting. In the time of this same Hely was the arke of God take be the Philisteis, to her grete confusion. For whan it was sette in her temple her god Dagon fel down and was al to broken. The peeple eke was smet with grevous sores, as the first book of Kynges makith mynde.

"In this same Hely tyme, Brute, that was of Eneas, Kyng, cam into this lond, and called it Britayn aftir his name. Whan he deyid he departed his kyngdam to his thre sones. The first hite Loegrius; and to him he gaf the land fro Dooyr onto Humbyr. The second son hite Albanactus; and to him gave he al Scotlond onto Humbir. The third hite Camber; and to him gave he alle Walis."

His narrative has considerable historical value as it approaches his own times. His account of Henry V's siege and capture of Havre is given in our extracts as a favourable specimen of what he could do in the way of narrative.

II. The reign of Henry VII not only saw the

opening of a new era for politics in England, but
also the first stirrings of the Renaissance, which
was destined to exercise a profound influence on
the writing of history as well as on other branches
of English Literature. Many forces were tending
to push the spirit of man on to untried paths. The
breakdown in the Papal power had been visible
since the beginning of the fourteenth century, and
soon the Reformation came to turn the neglect of
Papal and Catholic authority into decided opposition and contempt. This brought with it a neglect
and contempt for all things mediæval, from which
the nineteenth century only with difficulty escaped.
Geographical discovery and new conceptions in
astronomy played their part in quickening men's
imagination and inclining them to the acceptance
of new ideas. Yet the present cannot really cut
itself adrift from the past, or navigate the unknown
seas of the future without assistance derived from
experience. And the late fifteenth and sixteenth
centuries, though they were ready to consign the
mediæval centuries to oblivion, turned with passionate and often unreasoning admiration to the
example of classical antiquity. Not only the poets
and philosophers, but also the historians of Greece
and Rome, became the most cherished possession
of the reading world of that century. Now English writers might learn from Thucydides that the
work of the historian may be of practical use to
the statesman; and from Polybius the obligation
of veracity and the difficulty of achieving it.
But the sixteenth century set little store by any
suggestions which the classics contained as to

methods of historical research. It would be difficult to show that Thucydides or Polybius had any influence on English thought in the sixteenth century: the men of that age found more to their taste in the efforts of Herodotus "not to let the notable deeds of men of old perish"; they admired the fluent story-telling of Titus Livius, and cared little that he avowed his equal fondness for the plausible and the true; above all, the charming narrative gift of Plutarch, and his high but always human morality, appealed to Shakespeare's century, and influenced the thought of the time more than any other classical historian.

The historical product of the sixteenth century does not reach a very high standard. It is seen at its best in historical biography, as in Cavendish's *Wolsey* and in Roper's *More*. The more elaborate historical works have not shaken off the characteristics of the mediæval chronicle. They are rambling, uncritical, anecdotal — anything rather than sober and accurate. Sir Walter Raleigh's *History of the World* bears the impress of the Renaissance in the style of certain splendid and renowned passages, but its subject-matter shows no advance on *Giraldus Cambrensis* or Matthew Paris. Its five books only reach to the first century B.C., and much of the early books is taken up with questions as futile as ever puzzled the brain of a mediæval scholastic. Chapters III and IV, for instance, are concerned with the site of the garden of Eden and the nature and size of the tree of life. Raleigh shows considerable knowledge of the scholastic comments on the early chapters of *Genesis*; and here, as often in the book, he takes pleasure in bringing to bear the experience of his own travels on the problems in hand. He criticises the view that the tree of life was the *Ficus indica* by relating his own adventures among them "in the inner part of Trinidado", where "I have travelled a dozen miles together under them". There is visible throughout the book a desire to exhibit the writer's own knowledge and the extent of his reading; but in spite of the vast amount of various information that is to be found in its pages, it cannot be held to mark any real advance in the art or science of historiography. Holinshed's *Chronicles* (1586), Stow's *Chronicles* (1525–1605) and *Survey of London* are far less pretentious, less definitely works of the Renaissance, but convey more authentic information. The sieve of the modern critical historian finds in them much of value, but they do not show any great advance in method or outlook on the works of the earlier centuries. Camden's works (1551–1623) are written for the most part in Latin, and must not therefore be dealt with here; but his *Britannia* and his *Annals of the Reign of Elizabeth* (the first a topographical work, the second a narrative of contemporary events) were based upon a life-long study and a critical accumulation of material. His biographer, writing in 1691, claimed that they "tasted more of the truth and plenty that may be gained from the records of the kingdom" than any earlier work. He professes to follow in his writings the austere maxims of Polybius, and reaches a higher standard in his work than had been reached under the Tudors by any English historiographer.

But, if the age of scientific history was not yet, the materials were being accumulated out of which scientific history would one day be written. The Cotton (founded by Sir Robert Cotton, 1571–1631) and the Bodleian (1602) Libraries both belong to this age, and the prominent men of the time, such as Cecil (1520–1598) and Walsingham (1530–1590), were accumulating books and manuscripts with emulous zeal.

III. The seventeenth century was for the most part so busy with the making of history that it had little time to devote to calmly considering it or writing of it. But the century had passed through its first quarter before its decidedly revolutionary character showed itself, and during this period of comparative quiet the name of Bacon cast glory upon the annals of English thought. Bacon has touched every department of human thought, and in the matter of history, as elsewhere, he may claim to be the prophet of a far-distant future. Considerable passages from the *Advancement of Learning* (published in 1605) are printed in the first series of extracts, and it is therefore not necessary to give here a full account of the views there advanced. But it is a striking testimony to the wide sweep of Bacon's genius that no century earlier than the nineteenth would have been able to appreciate the meaning of his advice, or could have attempted to act on it. Here, as in so much of his work, he surveys the promised

land from afar; but it was left to distant generations to enter upon it.

No one before had ever taken so comprehensive,
so synthetic a view of history as Bacon; no one
before had ever conceived of it as being of such
direct and general human advantage. There is
little in common between the genius of Bacon and
that of Carlyle; and yet if the extracts from the
Advancement of Learning be compared with those
from Carlyle's *Essay* (also printed in this volume),
there is a striking resemblance in certain parts of
them. Both lay the greatest stress on biography.
"For Lives I do find strange," says Bacon, "that
the writing of Lives should be no more frequent."
And it was Carlyle's constant theme that history
is the essence of innumerable biographies. Again,
Carlyle's insistence on the history of religion as
the core and explanation of history in general is
paralleled, in fact though not in phrase, by Bacon's
sense of the importance of ecclesiastical history,
and his desire to see the growth of "literary"
history, by which he means the history of opinion.
The phrase in which he recommends these two
departments of thought is a striking one: "It is
not St. Augustine's nor St. Ambrose's works that
will make so wise a divine, as ecclesiastical history
thoroughly read and observed; and the same reason
is of learning".

It may be doubted whether there is any historical treatise produced during the rest of the
century that does not bear the marks of partisanship, or that does not aim at defending or attack-
ing some religious or political party. But it must

be noted that the very character of the Revolution
was itself an incentive to historical study of a
certain kind.   The contest between King and
Parliament was not founded (like the French
movement of a century later) on an appeal to
first principles or *a priori* conception of right.
The Bible, and such political ideas as could be
derived from it, played an important part; but
above all, the champions on either side appealed
to the traditions and precedents of the actual
historical past of England.   There was, in consequence, keen search made into the historical and
legal antiquities of the country.   Now for the
first time *Magna Carta* came to be regarded as
the impregnable basis of English liberties, and
the men of the Long Parliament found in the
Lancastrian period weapons well adapted for their
struggle against the Stuarts.   Among the legal
antiquaries of the period John Selden (1584–1654)
is far the greatest.   He appeared as counsel for
Hampden, and held that the first and most important thing for the Parliament to do was to
"reassert the ancient laws of the country by which
the liberty of the subject was secured"; and many
of his numerous works contributed powerfully to
this end.   The names of Sir Roger Twysden (1597–
1672) and Thomas Madox (1666–1727) deserve
mention, along with Selden, as legal antiquaries
who did much to illuminate the constitutional
past of England.

If we turn to historians of the more ordinary
type, the most notable name is that of Clarendon.
His work suggests a comparison with Thucydides,

in that he was himself a prominent actor in the events that he describes; and there are, especially in his character-sketches, passages that will bear comparison with the great Athenian master. As with Thucydides, too, banishment from his native country gave him an opportunity for calm and detached contemplation of the events through which he had lived. But there the comparison ends. The inner spirit of the two men is entirely different. Neither his double exile nor advancing years brought philosophic calm or intellectual fairness to Clarendon. He writes now as a partisan of the monarchy, now of the Church, now of his own administration, and the later books are mainly autobiographical. But none the less Clarendon's work is epoch-making in the development of English historical writing. Here the nation's story is told by a man of practical knowledge, in language well suited to the subject, and in a tone of honest conviction.[1] For a century and a half it fixed the ideas of Englishmen with regard to the prominent actors in the great Puritan revolution. Its prestige was destroyed, as by a sledge-hammer, by the publication of Carlyle's *Cromwell*; but the book remains one of the foremost of English historical classics.

But the contemporary and autobiographical

---

[1] He has said himself in one of his Tracts: "It is not a collection of records or an admission to the view and perusal of the most secret letters and acts of state that can enable a man to write a history, if there be an absence of that genius and spirit and soul of an historian which is contracted by the knowledge and course and method of business, and by conversation and familiarity in the inside of courts, and with the most active and eminent persons in the government".

character of Clarendon's *History* makes it of little value for understanding the way in which the seventeenth century contemplated the past and tried to obtain a knowledge of it. A glance at Milton's *History of England* (published in 1670) may be of service from this point of view. It extends from the "first traditional beginning" and is continued to the "Norman conquest", and is described as being "collected out of the ancientest and best authors thereof". Milton expresses his belief that the authorities from which he draws are of differing and doubtful authority; he knows that there are some who "admit that for proved story" which others "explode for fiction"; but he concludes that it is best to put all down, "seeing that ofttimes relations hitherto accounted fabulous have been after found to contain in them many footsteps and reliques of something true, as what we read in poets of the flood and giants little believed, till undoubted witnesses taught us that all was not feigned; I have therefore determined to bestow the telling over even of these reputed tales, be it for nothing else but in favour of our English poets and rhetoricians, who by their art will know how to use them judiciously". We pass, therefore, in the first book through all the story of Brutus of Troy: "certain or uncertain be that upon the credit of those whom I must follow; so far as keeps aloof from impossible and absurd, attested by ancient writers from books more ancient, I refuse not as the due and proper subject of history". We have, therefore, the narrative of how "Brutus with an easy course arriving at Totnes,

in Devonshire, quickly perceives here to be the
promised end of his own labours"; how "Brutus
in a chosen place builds Nova Troja, changed in
time to Trinovastum, now London, and began to
enact laws; Heli being then High Priest in Judæa;
and, having governed the whole isle twenty-four
years, died and was buried in his new Troy".
Without going farther, it is plain that the critical
spirit as applied to historical records leaves no
traces in Milton's work, and that even his mighty
intellect had no sense of the importance of determining the true relation in which the present
stands to the past.   Milton's work naturally improved, as his authorities improved; but a passage
at the end of the second book deserves quotation,
to show how difficult the polemics of the age made
the writing of history.   At the end of the Roman
occupation he writes: "Henceforth we are to steer
by another sort of authors; near enough to the
things they write, as in their own country, if that
would serve; in time not much belated, some of
equal age; in expression barbarous, and to say
how judicious I suspend awhile.   This we must
expect—in civil matters to find them dubious re-
laters, and still to the best advantage of what they
term Holy Church, meaning indeed themselves; in
most other matters of religion blind, astonished,
and struck with superstition as with a planet; in
one word, monks."   It is, in fact, mainly in dealing
with contemporary events, as in May's *History of
the Long Parliament*, that the historical writing of
the age has value, and such writings are inevitably
rather in the nature of memoirs than of history

properly so-called. Sir Richard Baker in 1643 published his *Chronicles of the Kings of England.* It has been called the "last of the Chronicles", but the true historic spirit is not to be found in it. Sir Richard Baker's *Chronicles* was long a popular work; Addison makes it the favourite reading of Sir Roger de Coverley. But its entirely uncritical spirit soon removed it from the list of serious histories.

Nor can the remainder of the century be said to have produced a work thoroughly historical in spirit—that is to say, painstaking and conscientious in its search for the facts; careful and unbiased in its presentation of their relations to one another. There was historical work being done in France of the most valuable kind. Tillemont's work on the Roman Empire dates from the year 1690; Bossuet's *Discourse on Universal History* was published in 1681; and Mabillon's *Treatise de Re Diplomatica* (1681) laid, in the opinion of some, the foundation of historical criticism. But though the influence of France was to have so great an effect later, for the present the fury of ecclesiastical and political contentions left no space for the contemplation of the past. John Strype (1643–1737) was accumulating with somewhat unscrupulous zeal valuable material for the period of the Tudors and the Reformation, but the time had not yet come for those materials to be properly used. The chief name in historical literature that meets us before the reign of Queen Anne is Gilbert Burnet, the famous Whig Bishop of Salisbury. Both his *History of the Reformation of the Church*

of England and his *History of His Own Times*
have played an important part in moulding the
opinion of England concerning the events described. Both owe their origin to the contests of
the time, and are indeed projectiles fired in defence
of the Whig and Protestant interests. The *History
of the Reformation* (published in 1679) was a defence of the establishment of the Anglican Church,
called out by the many dangers, internal and external, with which the church was threatened, and
especially by the temperate, and therefore all the
more dangerous, attacks which were being made
upon the Protestant position by the various treatises of Bossuet. Burnet's book has been generally
commended for its fairness and clearness, and it is
noteworthy that the narrative is supported by a
considerable array of illustrative and justificatory
documents. English literature had perhaps seen
no fairer or more sober treatment of the past on
anything like the same scale; but it is clear that it
belongs to the controversies of the time in spirit
and purpose: it is essentially polemical, not historical. And the same thing must be said of the
more famous and more interesting *History of His
Own Times*. There is no need to enter into the
controversy as to the *bona fides* and accuracy of
the book. It is enough for our present purpose to
point out that it, quite as much as the History of
Clarendon, falls into the category of memoirs and
autobiographies rather than of history.

IV. The writing of history, in the sense in which
we now use the word, began in England with the

eighteenth century.   That is a fact which a survey
of the earlier attempts in that direction brings out
with especial clearness.   Somewhat suddenly history
ceased to be written, as with Froissart, to rescue
the acts of brave men from oblivion; or, as with
Milton, for the judicious use of English poets and
rhetoricians.   The truth at length is seriously sought
after, and is presented with all the grace indeed of
style that the author may chance to possess, but
with a serious desire to show events in their true
relationship, and to disentangle the action of cause
and effect.

It is, as a rule, difficult to determine the genesis
of a literary movement.   " The wind bloweth where
it listeth ": and the conditions that stimulate literary
production are far from accounting for the appearance of genius.   But the great attention paid in
the eighteenth century to the study and writing of
history stands in clear relation to certain influences
which it is important to summarize.

The era of religious contention had long passed
its zenith.   The theologians still wrangled, but
their struggles no longer occupied the centre of the
European arena.   The year 1648 and the Treaty
of Westphalia close the period of the Reformation for Europe.   In England the Revolution of
1688 and the Hanoverian Succession in 1714 had
decided the victory of official Protestantism, but
had not exterminated Catholicism.   In England
as in Europe differing faiths would live side by
side, and only stupidity or fanaticism would
imagine that one could hope to exterminate the
others.   But while the tempest of religious con-

troversy sank into something approaching a calm,
philosophy in England, as in France, had begun
to make great strides. Hobbes (1588–1679) and
Locke (1632–1704) had devoted their great intellects
to the solution of political and social problems.
They and their followers asked: What is the origin
of civil society? Upon what basis does government rest? What is the relation of the State to
the Church? They turned from the theological
disputes of the earlier age to man and the mind
of man, and considered all problems, religious,
political, and social, in relation to man's welfare,
rather than from the point of view of Scriptural
texts and rival schemes of theology. This movement was not at first inclined to pay much attention
to history. Neither Hobbes nor Locke imitated
their contemporary, Leibnitz, in the attention which
he paid to the actual historical past. But the movement, of which they were representative, could not
fail to lead to the careful and scientific consideration of the facts of man's past. If Hobbes traces
the origin of society to one kind of "social contract", and Locke to another, it was inevitable
that the records of the past should be scrutinized
to see what support they gave to one view or the
other. The movement of the eighteenth century,
especially when its pace quickens as it approaches
the revolutionary whirlpool, is often said to be
unhistorical, or even to amount to a rejection of
the lessons of history. But this is only super-
ficially true. It does, indeed, especially on French
soil, despise the Middle Ages; it often affects to
regard the inheritance of the past as a burden from

which men must extricate themselves. But its preoccupation with human problems made a study of the human past inevitable; and the importance of the issues involved made the study serious and scientific.

But the eighteenth century was far advanced before our islands saw the appearance of any great historical work. In England, though to a far smaller degree than on the Continent, work preparatory to historical writing was being accomplished. Documents were being edited, collections formed, a number of private libraries devoted to various branches of erudition were already in existence, and led up to the foundation of the British Museum in 1753. But it was not until the third quarter of the century that any historical narrative was produced which holds a place in the history of English literature.

There is a book, however, of a much earlier date that deserves careful note, as indicating how the current of thought was running in the direction of history, and as doing perhaps something to direct it: Lord Bolingbroke's *Letters on the Study and Use of History* bears the date 1735, and was written during the time of his exile in France. Henry St. John, Viscount Bolingbroke (1678–1751), had played a great part in the history of English politics. He had struggled and intrigued for the restoration of the Stuart dynasty, and the accession of the Hanoverian dynasty in 1714 had overthrown his hopes and relegated him to a private station for the rest of his life. No one has ever ventured to call him a great man or a noble character. It must be

admitted that he was vain and superficial, and
that something of the charlatan runs through all
he writes as well as through his actions.   But
none the less he was one of the formative influences
of his time.   His influence on the literature and
political thought of his own and the next generation
is well known: the later Toryism was largely of his
making.   And his "Letters on History" mark at
least the chief lines on which the history-writing
of the century was to proceed.   When he comes
to consider the purpose for which history should
be studied, his ideas differ very widely from those
which we have hitherto found expressed.   He
dismisses in the opening paragraphs of the first
letter those who would write or read history for
amusement, or for purposes of conversational and
rhetorical display.   He speaks, too, of the labours
of erudition, compilation, and scholarship with a
curious and quite unmerited contempt.   He re-
cognizes, indeed, the value of the work that has
been done by those who have devoted themselves to such tasks: "they grow neither wiser
nor better by study themselves, but they enable
others to study with greater ease and to purposes
more useful".   He admits that it is difficult "to
avow a thorough contempt for the whole business
of these learned lives, for all the researches into
antiquity, for all the systems of chronology and
history that we owe to the immense labours of a
Scaliger, a Bochart, a Petavius, or Usher, and even
a Marsham".   But he thinks that the material on
which such scholars must work is quite limited
and nearly exhausted, and, in fact, that the work

preparatory to the writing of history has been done. " The same materials are common to them all; but those materials are few, and there is a moral impossibility that they should ever have more. They have combined these into every form that can be given to them; they have supposed, they have guessed, they have joined disjointed passages of different authors and broken traditions of uncertain originals, of various peoples, and of centuries remote from one another as well as from ours. . . . They deserve encouragement, however, whilst they continue to compile, and neither affect wit nor aspire to reason." Such is the contemptuous treatment accorded by Bolingbroke to a class of men who in our days have claimed the exclusive right to the title of historians. His view that the scholars had already exhausted their material sounds strange indeed when we remember that more than a century and a half later Lord Acton could still speak of " the incessant deluge of new and unsuspected matter ". In the second letter, which is printed in this book, he gives his own ideas as to the purpose and aim of history. There is much of affectation and patronage in the manner, and lack of clearness in the presentation. Its conclusions would have to be restated to satisfy the twentieth century; but it is a notable and a fine utterance. He finds in the study of history no longer a graceful accomplishment or a useful help to the rhetorician and the poet, but something of direct practical human utility. History, he says, quoting from Diogenes Laertius, is " philosophy teaching by examples ", and as such is necessary to the states-

man and the citizen.   Besides this it has an invaluable ethical influence: it emancipates the mind
from narrowing prejudices, and ennobles it by a
wide knowledge of mankind.   In later letters he
deals sensibly with certain objections to the study
of history, and with a good deal of originality urges
that it is modern history, dating from the end of
the fifteenth century, which will most repay study.
He meets the arguments of those who urge that
history is not deserving of study because absolute
certainty can rarely or never be obtained.   A passage deserves quotation.   " But it is time I should
conclude this head, under which I have touched
some of those reasons that show the folly of endeavouring to establish universal Pyrrhonism in matters
of history, because there are few histories without
some lies, and none without some mistakes; and
that prove the body of history which we possess,
since ancient memorials have been so critically
examined, and modern memorials so multiplied,
to contain in it such a probable series of events,
easily distinguishable from the improbable, as force
the assent of every man in his senses, and are
therefore sufficient to answer all the purposes of
the study of history.   I might have appealed, perhaps, without entering into the argument at all, to
any man of candour, whether his doubts concerning
the truth of history have hindered him from applying the examples he has met with in it, and from
judging of the present, and sometimes of the future,
by the past?   Whether he has not been touched
with reverence and admiration at the virtue and
wisdom of some men and some ages, and whether

he has not felt indignation and contempt for others?"

The third quarter of the century saw the publication of works by the triumvirate who at last relieved the annals of English literature from the charge of lagging far behind France and Germany in the production of historical works of importance. Hume published the first volume of his *English History* in 1754; Robertson's *History of Scotland* saw the light in 1759, and his *Charles V* in 1769; Gibbon's *Roman Empire* came in 1776, but he had already published minor and almost - forgotten treatises on historical subjects. These three names are so far above the rest, that the eighteenth-century school of history can be adequately studied in them alone.

It seems at first strange that it should be possible to class them together, for they were widely separated from one another in social circumstances, in cast of mind, and in their relation to the political and religious controversies of the day. Hume's (1711–1776) historical work was an interlude in his vast philosophical elaboration, and he united opinions in philosophy of a strongly negative type with a strange championship of Tory principles in church and state and an admiration for the Stuart monarchy. William Robertson (1721–1793) was Principal of Edinburgh University, a thorough Whig at every point. He was Moderator of the General Assembly of the Church of Scotland, and his orthodoxy was sincere though circumspect and tolerant. Edward Gibbon (1737–1794) was a man of means, possessed of no important official post; sceptical in matters of religion, but without zeal for any social or religious movement, a *bon vivant* and a man of the world. But their work, though strikingly individual, is stamped with certain common characteristics. They are all typical men of their century, and, without knowing it, standard-bearers in the intellectual movement that leads up to the Revolution. It is instructive, and important too, to notice how closely all three are connected with the philosophic movement of the time. Montesquieu, Voltaire, and Rousseau had some part in moulding the opinions of all; for even the orthodox Robertson lived on terms of familiarity with such sceptics as Hume and Adam Smith. The serious study of history was in England born from the desire to understand the human problem in its widest aspects.

By what characteristics, then, is the work of these men marked off from the historical writers of a preceding age? By their critical and discriminating spirit, in the first place: the record of the past is regarded by all three as the story of something that really happened, where truth must be sought for and distinguished from the plausible and the interesting. And next, underlying the work of all three, there is an attempt at some sort of political and social philosophy: events are not merely arranged in chronological sequence or described so as to make interesting pictures. The relations of events are studied. The philosophy is often tentative, and in Gibbon's case even self-contradictory, but it is there; and it is a clear mark of the eighteenth-century spirit. It should be added that none of the three joined in Bolingbroke's contempt for the preparatory work of erudition, compilation, and scholarship; though Hume made less use of these than either of his great contemporaries.

Hume's history is now little read, and when read it is rather for the light which it casts on the author's opinions and powers than for its contributions to knowledge. It was written from printed materials only. Hume knew of the existence of manuscript and unpublished records; he is said to have contemplated making use of them, but to have desisted, in alarm at the extent and character of the material. But Hume's history, especially that part which deals with the Stuart period, is eminently readable and worth reading. It has been said that a historian should write "well but not too well", and Hume's style exactly answers to that description. It does not, as is the case with the styles of Carlyle and Macaulay, fatigue the reader by the brilliancy of its episodes: Hume is always conscious that he has a long journey before him, and travels smoothly and at a brisk pace. Nor can the comments of such a genius as Hume lack a certain interest. It is specially noteworthy that he, catching the idea perhaps from the French encyclopedists, gives to social matters an attention not previously bestowed by any English historian.

Robertson, far inferior to Hume in intellectual power, has nevertheless obtained a higher rank among historians. History was his main occupation, and he could devote a larger amount of time to the examination of sources than was possible to Hume. Of his three works (*Scotland, Charles V,* and *America*), the second stands highest; but his treatment of Scotch history during the period of the Reformation had a considerable influence on men's thoughts about the great problems of that time. The style is ponderous and somewhat colourless, but readable in spite of all; and one may say of Robertson, what can be said to a much greater extent of Hume and Gibbon, that he provokes thought and leaves a permanent impress on the mind of the reader. The introductory chapters to his *Charles V* form the most remarkable part of his work. They give a general sketch and a critical estimate of the political and social transformations of the Middle Ages; and their wide and lucid survey still renders them valuable, though modern research has done much to modify their conclusions. No survey of so wide a kind, conducted in so serious a spirit, had previously been attempted in English.

But Gibbon is without question the great historian of the period. His *Decline and Fall of the Roman Empire* is a classic of English literature. It is a century and a quarter old; it deals with a period that has been more ploughed and harrowed by historical research than any other; many positive mistakes in the work have been discovered. Yet it is probably read now as much as it ever was. Alone among English histories it is constantly republished with notes and additions, as though it were an original authority, instead of a secondary work. No book of Macaulay or Carlyle holds its place with such security against competitors.

It is important to grasp the causes of this phenomenon. They relate partly to the matter and partly to the style of the book. For in the first place Gibbon's history was the product of profound research, pushed as far as the circumstances of the time allowed. It is written, too, with a wonderful absence of prejudice and bias. The contrary is sometimes held; but the truth is that his own prejudices and prepossessions did not intrude very much on his historical judgments, as his chapter on Julian clearly testifies. But an accuracy even greater than Gibbon reached, and the most passion-less impartiality on men, politics, and religion, would not have procured his work immortality. It lives mainly because of its literary qualities. The style is far from faultless; its dignity is disfigured by artificial antithesis; there are passages that are bombastic. But it is always clear, and, above all, always interesting and singularly well fitted for the long narrative which the author had in hand.[1] Fur-ther, he is never buried in detail; he sees his period steadily and sees it whole; the book conveys the exhilaration of the first view, gained from some commanding mountain-top, of a country hitherto unknown. The experience of many is that from Gibbon for the first time they learn the meaning of the phrases about the continuity and indivisibility of history. His philosophy of causation is often

---

[1] Gibbon has himself told us with what care he polished the style of his history. "The style of an author should be the image of his mind, but the choice and command of language is the fruit of exercise. Many experiments were made before I could hit the middle tone be-tween a dull chronicle and a rhetorical declamation. Three times did I compose the first chapter, and twice the second and third, before I was tolerably satisfied with the effect."

strangely thin and unsatisfying, but the book itself implies a philosophy. And yet when this is said, more remains to be said. The secret of Gibbon's permanence lies in his personality. There is no other history that reveals the writer as this does. Most historians try to get out of the way and let the events speak for themselves. The events speak for themselves in Gibbon, but the historian's personality is everywhere too, in the style, in the arrangement, in the allusions, in the occasional irony and innuendo, in the foot-notes, which are themselves a wonderful piece of art and humour. Gibbon's is assuredly the only great modern history over which the reader is constantly amused.

There is a wide gap between the publications of these three men and the appearance of the next considerable historical work in English literature. The reason is not far to seek. Robertson and Gibbon both lived to see the French Revolution break in tempest over Europe; the Napoleonic wars followed hard on it; and Britain was again so busily concerned with the making of history that there was little time for contemplating and writing it. The Revolution, too, made it impossible that history would ever be written again quite in the mood of Gibbon or Hume. The passions and fanaticisms of the Revolution were a strange ending to the "Age of Reason". It was plain that there were still elements in human nature which earlier writers had thought non-existent or almost outworn, and the historian would for the future have to take account of them. The writing of history (in our country especially, and such part of it as comes under the cognizance of literature) has always stood in close relation to the political and philosophic movements of the time; and the Revolution, in the widest sense of the term, left its mark on historical composition. Meanwhile, if little was done in the writing of history, thought on social and political questions was active. Burke's speeches and letters were giving men, among many other precious gifts, a clearer notion of the organic connection of the present with the past, and the efforts of the Revolutionists to tear themselves free from the past only made it clearer that such an operation was impossible, and that, in the words of a later philosopher, " progress must be the development of order ". Moreover, among the forces that moulded the future of history-writing in England, the general influence of the Romantic school, and especially of Scott, must not be forgotten. The attitude of cold superiority, when not of contempt, which the eighteenth century had adopted towards the Middle Ages was for ever at an end. The influence which the Waverley Novels had in this direction has been often commented on, but still deserves emphasis. It is not that, in Great Britain at any rate, this period brought much fresh knowledge of the Middle Ages. Gibbon knew far more about the centuries, from the third to the sixteenth, than Scott. What is new is the attitude of mind, the sense of relationship between the past and the present. And while thus the movement of events and the movement of literature were forcing on a more comprehensive and organic view of history, the criticism of the

documents on which historiography is founded was
producing results of wide-sweeping consequence.
In 1797 Wolff published his *Prolegomena to the
Study of Homer*, which Professor Bury, in his Inaugural Lecture at Cambridge, declared to be "one of
half a dozen books which in the last three hundred
years have exercised most effective influence upon
thought". This famous book subjected the text
of the *Iliad* to a close scrutiny, and declared the
poem to be the work of many hands; but it is to
the inauguration of a method rather than to the
particular conclusions of Wolff that Professor Bury
alludes in the above, perhaps exaggerated, phrase.
Niebuhr's *Roman History* appeared in 1811, and,
after a careful criticism of the legendary history
of Rome, attempted to construct the beginnings
of Roman history on a rational basis. The method
employed by both these scholars roused bitter
feelings here: they seemed to many to be laying
hands on what was almost sacred, and in the vain
pursuit after accuracy, to be depriving men of a
great source of noble and ennobling enjoyment;
further, many saw that the methods used in the
study of secular and classical literature must shortly
be applied to Biblical literature as well. In the
opinion of the present writer some of the early
antagonism to these books was justified, and the
praise of the methods employed has often exceeded
sober limits; but it is certain that they, and the
methods which they employed, were destined to
exercise an abiding influence on all historical
compositions for the future.

Between the death of Gibbon, in 1794, and the

end of the Napoleonic wars, in 1815, no historical
work of the first rank was produced in English.
But hardly had the storms of the Napoleonic wars
died down before historical works of great importance began to issue from the press. In the year
1818 appeared Hallam's *Europe during the Middle
Ages*, the completion of Mitford's *History of Greece*,
and James Mill's *History of British India*, and in
the next year came the first volumes of Lingard's
History of England. None of these is a work of
quite the highest order, but three of them are
typical of the change which had passed over English thought since the days of Hume, Robertson,
and Gibbon. Mitford (1744–1827) indeed owed
the idea of his book to a suggestion of Gibbon's,
but it has none of the qualities of permanence
possessed by its great example. It succeeds in
being eminently readable by virtue of its decisive
opinions. Mitford walks with the utmost self-
confidence through a subject where now even the
strongest writers proceed slowly and with hesitation. His marked hostility to the Athenian democracy and his anti-popular opinions generally
reflect the feelings of England during the struggle
with the Revolution, and furnished him with a
ready-made ethical judgment on every phase of
Greek politics. His work performed a great service
in provoking Grote to answer it, but its pages are
now very rarely turned. Hallam's (1777–1859)
book is evidence of the new interest that was being
taken in the Middle Ages, though it may be noted
that he deals almost entirely with the fourteenth
and fifteenth centuries, which belong rather to the

modern than the mediæval world. The book still
lives. It is based on a long study of such authorities as were accessible in print, and is written in a
tone of the most absolute fairness. The style is
dry and didactic, though Hallam is capable of
passages of dignified eloquence when the subject
specially appeals to him. Lingard's (1771–1851)
work is a notable one, and marks a real epoch
in the intellectual emancipation of the Roman
Catholics in England. For Lingard was a Roman
Catholic, and was trained exclusively by Roman
Catholics. Until the publication of his work
in 1819 the story of the Middle Ages, the
Reformation, and the deposition of the Stuarts
had been told in England by Protestant writers
as a rule, and in no case had the views of a
Roman Catholic managed to reach the public ear.
When Catholic writers had dealt with controversial points it was usually in a tone of bitter
invective, and often of misrepresentation as unscrupulous as they encountered on the other side.
Under such circumstances Lingard's achieve-
ment was really remarkable. He pleased indeed
at first neither Protestants nor Catholics. His
treatment of Cranmer and of the Massacre of St.
Bartholomew was specially denounced on the one
side, while on the other he was declared to be "a
dangerous enemy of the rights of the Catholic
Church". It is now universally admitted that his
work shows conscientious research and great fairness in presentment. The revelations of new documents have shaken the credibility of his narrative
in certain points, but his *bona fides* is unquestioned.

It may be suggested that if the work were eoited by some competent scholar it would again assume a place on the book-shelves of the student of history.

V. During the whole of the nineteenth century the stream of historical composition neither ceased nor slackened. And until the middle of the century was reached and past there is no general change in the character of historical composition. The great works of Milman, Grote, and Macaulay stand in immediate connection with the ecclesiastical and political movement in England, and they aim not only at discovering and presenting the truth, but also at presenting it in a manner that shall be generally intelligible and interesting to a wide circle of readers. One and all would have agreed that written history was a part of literature, and that a knowledge of history was so important to the general public that it ought to be told in such a way as to reach the general public. On the Continent, meanwhile, a movement had begun which was destined to have a great influence on the writing of history in England.

As early as 1824 Ranke had published his *History of the Latin and Teutonic Nations from 1494 to 1519*, a work which has been acclaimed as " inaugurating the critical period of historiography ". Ranke, said Lord Acton, is " the real originator of the heroic study of records and the most prompt and fortunate of European pathfinders ". " It is through his accelerating influence ", he adds, " that our branch of study has become progressive, so that the best master is generally distanced by the better pupil." As early as 1821 there had been founded in Paris the *Ecole des Chartes*, for the study of archives in general, and the national collections in particular. Its beginnings were humble; but perhaps no institution has in the long run more directly modified the writing and teaching of history. But until the middle of the century was past this tendency had little influence on the popular writers of history in England.

Macaulay died in 1859, and that date may, because of his own great importance and for other reasons which will shortly appear, be taken as a dividing line in the history of English historiography. The chief writers of history from 1819 to 1859, exclusive of those already mentioned, are Milman, Arnold, Thirlwall, Grote, Napier, and Macaulay himself. Lingard and Hallam were also continuing their work during this period.

Let us take first the group of writers who concerned themselves with the history of the classical world. Dr. Thomas Arnold's (1795–1842) is a great name in the culture of the nineteenth century. He has been called the creator of the modern public school system, he was a powerful influence in the religious life of England, and his historical writings have a place of their own in English historical composition. History-writing was not the central thought and aim of his life: rather, like most of his contemporaries, he was drawn to history by his interest in the current politics of church and state. He was appointed Regius Professor of History in the University of Oxford in 1841, but the teaching that was required was but slight, and he did not abandon his post as head-master of Rugby in which he had won his fame. His chief historical works are: (1) an edition of *Thucydides*; (2) three volumes on the *Early History of Rome* (1838–43); (3) his *Lectures at Oxford*. His lectures are altogether lacking in depth of research, if judged by the standard of university lectures in Paris or Berlin. His Roman history is his chief work, and its importance is largely due to the fact that he made himself for English people the interpreter of Niebuhr. Niebuhr had died in 1821, but his opinions were still fiercely decried and little understood. Apart from this service, Arnold's work is noted for the lucidity and dignity of its style. There are passages that rise to a very remarkable height of restrained eloquence, and his account of the second Punic War is one of the finest descriptions of a war in the English language. Arnold does not intrude contemporary politics on to his history; but it is plain that parallels with English history are rarely absent from his mind.

Connop Thirlwall (1797–1875) was from 1870 Bishop of St. David's. He was a man of profound learning, a student and a translator of Niebuhr, and a man of independence of judgment, who possessed to the full the courage of his opinions, as he showed when, alone among the bishops, he voted for the disestablishment of the Irish Church. His one great historical work is his *History of Greece*, at which he laboured from 1835 to 1847. It was his great misfortune that it appeared almost contemporaneously with Grote's work on the same subject, and the

latter work has almost monopolized the attention of
the reading public. Yet Thirlwall's work has certain high qualities which Grote's can hardly claim.
Its narrative is more even, its judgments more
balanced and serene; and there are passages of real
beauty such as cannot be found in his rival's work.
Moreover, he shows a truer historic judgment in
prolonging his narrative beyond the death of
Alexander the Great, where Grote stops short;
rightly judging that Alexander widened the influence of Greece, even though he deteriorated the
quality of it, that he was the expander not the
destroyer of Hellas.

The work of George Grote (1794–1871), which
has undoubtedly effaced Thirlwall's, began to be
published in 1846, and was not completed for ten
years after that. It is a work very characteristic of
England in the middle of the nineteenth century.
The universities had not yet taken up the study
of history in a serious fashion: and this great work
of erudition and argument, on topics which might
seem remote from the current of modern life, was
written by one who had not been to an university
at all, who was at the head of a great banking
business in the city, and who, as an advanced
radical, occupied for many years a seat in the
British House of Commons. Foreign observers
have expressed their amazement at this, but there
is none of the historians of the middle of the
century who does not approach his subject to
some extent as a man of the world and an
amateur: and if there is loss, there is also considerable gain in the absence of the academic

atmosphere. Grote's huge work has lived in spite of its style. It has often the attraction which comes of a strong logic dealing lucidly and forcibly with questions hitherto obscure; but there is not a passage which has any charm or grace of style, hardly a sentence which admits of separate quotation. It was Mitford's history that produced Grote's. As a disciple of Bentham, a radical and a philosophical democrat, he was offended by Mitford's assumption of the invariable baseness and falseness of the actions of a democracy. The main thesis of his book is a defence of the Athenian democracy from the charges of fickleness, corruption, injustice to its great men, and the like. We need not here discuss how far he has succeeded; certainly the charges of Mitford will never be repeated in the form in which they were made. Grote's interest in contemporary politics, his knowledge of the actual working of the English constitution and the money market, has allowed him to reveal certain features of Greek life which were necessarily obscure to the mere scholar. On the other hand, it may be held that he identifies the problems of Athens far too closely with those of England, and does not admit to his imagination the vast gulf that separates ancient from modern democracies. The sound knowledge and the vigorous thought which are visible on every page will still procure for it many readers, and men's thoughts on Greek history will always bear traces of its contentions. If it no longer seems now, as it seemed a few years ago, the inevitable avenue to a knowledge of Greek history, that is partly due to the progress of modern research, partly to its too great preoccupation with modern problems and its exclusively political tone, and partly to the absence of that fine literary quality which would keep Gibbon alive even if he were proved guilty of far greater errors than are laid to his charge.

W. F. P. Napier (1785–1860) and Henry Hart Milman (1791–1898) may be somewhat rapidly dismissed, as introducing no new quality of great importance into the writing of history. Napier's *History of the Peninsular War* (published between 1828 and 1848) gave the world a vigorous military narrative, which is still read, and will continue to be read. Napier had himself been through the greater part of the Peninsular war, and was an intimate friend of Wellington's. His narrative thus has a certain affinity with that of Clarendon, but as it does not touch on such highly controversial matters, it has been generally accepted as a fair treatment of the subject, just equally to French and English, but unfairly contemptuous of the services of the Spanish. From the point of view of style, there are few finer battle-pictures in English literature than those which its pages afford. Milman's chief work, *The History of Latin Christianity*, covers almost exactly the same ground as Gibbon's history, but treats the period from the point of view of a broad-minded Anglican churchman. Milman's fairness, now generally recognized, subjected him to charges of heresy in his own day. The book is an illuminating survey of a subject which lies at the very centre of an understanding of universal history. If it fails to hold its own as the representative book on the subject, it will be because the advance of research leaves it behind, and its deficiency in knowledge will not be made up for by any special individuality in the style or clearness in the general conception of the subject.

In turning to Macaulay (1800–1859), we approach the second greatest name in English historiography, if Gibbon's is the first. No writer of historical narrative in the English language ever equalled his popularity, or is likely to equal it. His essays were a mine of gold to the Reviews in which they were published, and his *History* more than realized his ambition of producing something that would supersede the last fashionable novel. His work is so important in itself, and its influence on literature and the writing of history was so great, that it is important to mark its characteristics.

Occupied though Macaulay was in politics and administration (he was a member of the Supreme Council of India from 1834 to 1838, and member of Parliament for Edinburgh from 1838 to 1847, and again from 1852 to 1856), he nevertheless was singularly out of touch with the intellectual currents of his day. His reading was so prodigious that it would never be safe to affirm of any book that he had not read it, but it is certain that German scholarship and research left no mark upon his thought or style. His *History* has three chief aims: he desires to reveal the truth about the events he handles; he desires to uphold the policy of the Whig party, though the extent of his partisanship has been much exaggerated; and he has the artist's desire to impress and please his audi-

ence. The close alliance of literature and history,
so much discussed and criticised of late, in him
reaches its zenith. He made no pretence of writing only for the learned world, or of caring only
for the applause of *savants*; he prided himself on
never having written a sentence that was not intelligible at the first reading, and he took the popularity of his books as sufficient evidence of their
success. " I shall not be satisfied ", he wrote, in a
letter that is sometimes unfairly quoted against
him, " unless I produce something which shall for
a few days supersede the last fashionable novel on
the tables of young ladies "; and he always expressed a frank delight in the success that had
attended his efforts in this direction. His style
was universally admired and generally imitated;
it has left a permanent impress on the journalism
and popular literature of England.

No one will deny that he is, for the general
reader, the most interesting of all historians. Both
in the essays and the history he can hold the
reader's attention even when he is dealing with
topics which another writer would have made dry
and uninviting. The secret of his success is not to
be looked for in any subtlety of mind or sudden
revelations of the deep cause of things. He does
not thrill us like Tacitus, or expand our horizon
like Gibbon. But he floods every topic that he
handles with a dazzling rhetoric and a wealth of
apposite illustration. He is never above the head
of the average reader; he never assumes that the
reader understands his point; he has the orator's
temperament, and he employs the orator's method

of iterating and reiterating his points with such
dexterous variation of phrase and illustration that
he does not weary even the most critical reader.
But there is not only information and pleasure,
there is very valuable teaching to be got from his
books; not, indeed, on the deepest things that
concern the life of states and humanity, but on
things that lie next to those. Constitutional questions, questions of finance and coinage, find in his
history a treatment more illuminating and con-
vincing than can be found in any other writer.
Lastly, as we have maintained of Gibbon, so we
may maintain of Macaulay, that his personality is
a very large element in his success. He was in
many respects a typical Englishman of the mid-
century, clear-sighted within limits, vigorous, effective, somewhat superficial, a little blind to the deep
causes of things; and his generation found its own
opinions interpreted and restated in his writings.

It is unquestionable that Macaulay taught the
age a great deal of history, of Continental as well
as of English history; his work made powerfully
for culture in the middle classes of the English
people. What is there that has been urged on the
other side? We need not concern ourselves with
his style, its occasional artificiality, its lack of
warmth and depth. But against the matter of his
historical work the following points may be urged:
(1) The political partisan is present throughout,
though in his *History*, as distinguished from the
essays, he is a partisan rather of William III than
of the Whig statesmen of the time. (2) Prodigious
as his reading was, he did not avail himself of the

latest critical methods in handling his authorities;
the records of the different European capitals had
still much to reveal when Ranke began to work at
the same period; he is held, too, to have accepted
somewhat uncritically the evidence of ballads,
broadsheets, and other ephemeral literature. (3)
Of the three main departments of history, political,
social, and religious, he only really understood the
first; his handling of social movements was always
superficial; the nature of religious movements he
hardly understood at all. This is a serious limitation to his greatness, if it be true that social forces
are more important than political in moulding the
destinies of states, and religious causes more important than social. (4) The scale on which the
history is written is so large, that it was impossible
for him to achieve his aim, which was to bring the
history of England down to the nineteenth century.
A long lifetime would not have sufficed for such a
task if the whole history were to be on the scale of
the portion actually accomplished. The five large
volumes only take us from 1685 to 1700 with any
fulness. And this implies something more than a
mere criticism of style. It means that he tends to
lose sight of the main features of history in super-
abundant detail, that he does not allow his readers
to see the wood for the trees, that he is lacking, in
fact, as Mr. Cotter Morison asserts, in general and
synthetic views.

We have spoken mainly of the history; but
among those who love and admire Macaulay, it is
always a question whether the history or the essays
should be regarded as his chief claim to fame.

Without expressing an opinion on this point, it is necessary to remark that the essays contain far the more serious of Macaulay's blunders—serious errors of fact in his essays on Frederick the Great and Warren Hastings, serious errors of judgment in his essay on the Popes and on Bacon—and that there are passages of rhetoric in them of a showy and tinsel description. Macaulay himself always spoke in depreciation of them, and desired posterity to judge of him only in the light of the history; but the fact that the essays were written for publication in reviews secured them from the redundancy that sometimes disfigures the history, and they reveal a sense of historical perspective which does not always appear in the larger work. As an instrument of popular culture they have probably been more valuable than the history, and many persons would admit that their first impulse to historical study came from Macaulay's Essays.

Macaulay would not have heeded the criticisms that are advanced here, nor any others. He aspired to show the world that history was interesting, to blend, as he himself said, poetry and history; and his success on these lines is far the most striking in English literature.

VI. The death of Macaulay in 1859 may be taken, as we have already said, as the dividing line in the historiography of the nineteenth century. No stress must, however, be laid on the exact date, and certain important and significant events happened a year or two previously. Buckle's *History of Civilization in England* began to be published in

1857; and the same year saw the inauguration of the series of State Calendars and mediæval document bearing on English history, which is usually known as the "Rolls Series". Without, however, laying undue stress on any particular year, it is clearly true that, shortly after the middle of the century, historiography in England entered on a new phase, and was subject to new influences. European politics played their part as at the end of the eighteenth century; Europe was seething with revolutionary thought and action from 1848 to 1852, and historians were driven to strike deeper and wider in their survey of the human record and their estimate of its formative forces. European thought was occupied with the social problem in its widest significance. The new thought was no longer merely sceptical, as in the eighteenth century; vigorous efforts were being made, especially in France, to develop a constructive policy for the future, and, with a view to guiding the future, the thinkers of the time were anxious to explain the past. Saint Simon's social speculations had been published before 1825; Comte's *Positive Philosophy* was completed in 1842; his *Positive Polity* in 1854. Nor did the social question wait for the philosophers and theorists to solve it. All over Europe practical experiments were being made, and the existing social order was seen to lack the elements of finality. If the French Revolution made Gibbon's treatment of history impossible, it may be said that the events of the years 1848–1852 made those whose minds were receptive of the new impulses incapable of treating history with the political

dogmatism of Macaulay.[1]   Along with wide variation in detail certain general tendencies in the new
thought are perceptible.   It seeks for the widest
survey of the history of man, and endeavours to
pierce through the outward political forms to the
inner life of the people, to their social, economical,
and religious condition.   The idea of the organic
connection of all parts of the life of a people or of
humanity grows; a deeper philosophy of causation
is adopted.   The historical thinker for the future
will have to take a wider and a more synthetic
view of his subject.

On the other hand, it is necessary to notice that
while the historical survey was growing more extensive, the study of documents and the scrutiny of
authorities was becoming more intense.   We have
already said that on the Continent this movement
was no new one.   Ranke had for a long time past
been pouring out works for which he ransacked the
public records of Europe.   The *Monumenta Ger-
maniæ Historica*—a vast compilation of the authorities for mediæval German history—began to
appear in 1826, and this was only one of the many
similar collections that indefatigable Germany
brought forth.   Similar work was being done in
France, where diplomatic documents, inscriptions,
and ancient manuscripts were being edited under
the direction of such men as Mignet and Guizot.
The same kind of work, too, had at last been begun
in a systematic fashion in England.   The year

---

[1] Macaulay was living, thinking, and writing during these years; but
his opinions had been formed and fixed long before. His vigorous
intellect shows little sign of development.

1857 saw the beginning of two series: (1) the
"Calendars of English State Papers", and (2) the
"Rolls Series", as the mediæval books published
under the presidency of the Master of the Rolls is
usually called. Somewhat later (1869), the Historical Manuscripts Commission undertook to explore private collections and to publish whatever
was likely to be of value to the historian. Thus at
last the vast accumulations of English state documents began to be made available for purposes of
research: the action of the state stimulated the
action of private individuals and societies. The
documentary age of historiography had fully come
in England as well as on the Continent.

Another important influence was the action of
the universities with regard to the teaching of history. Both at Oxford and Cambridge Regius
Professorships of Modern History had been established in 1724. At neither university have the
holders of the office in the eighteenth century left
any mark upon the historical literature of England,
but during the nineteenth century noteworthy
names begin to appear. We have seen how at
Oxford Thomas Arnold was appointed to the
chair in 1841; Goldwin Smith held it in 1858, and
yielded it to Stubbs in 1866. At Cambridge, during
approximately the same period, the list includes
William Smythe, Sir J. Stephen, Kingsley, and
Seeley—all men of mark, though Kingsley owed
his appointment to quite other causes than his
knowledge of history. But the structure and system of the English universities is such that the
zeal with which a subject is pursued depends more

on the examinations than the teaching. An Honours degree in Jurisprudence and Modern History was instituted at Oxford in 1853; and at Cambridge History formed one of the subjects for examination in the Moral Science Tripos instituted in 1851, and soon afterwards a special Historical Tripos was instituted. The effect of these changes was not visible at once; but though, most fortunately for English historical literature, the statesman and the man of business still continued to interest themselves in the study and the writing of history, the number and importance of academic historians rapidly increased, until, by the end of the century, the greater number of historical works was produced by men who were professionally occupied in the study and the teaching of history.

Thus we shall be able to discover in the historical work of the future a double tendency. On the one side its philosophical outlook is more comprehensive and more serious, and on the other hand the minute and scientific study of the authorities has begun which was destined to divorce so many books on history from all alliance with literature.

Since the death of Macaulay the study of history has been unceasing and increasing. Somewhat remote from the path of literature proper, English scholars have been editing texts and documents and producing monographs in considerable numbers, though not quite in such volume as has flowed from the printing-presses of France and Germany. At the same time historical narratives have been constantly appearing, continuing the literary tradition of Gibbon and Macaulay, and

deserving a place in the history of literature. The
chief names in this department for the last forty
years have been Buckle, Carlyle, Froude, Freeman, Green, Lecky, Creighton, Seeley, Gardiner,
Hodgkin; while the works of Seebohm, Maine,
and Maitland, though excluded from our survey
as containing no direct narrative of events, are
nevertheless among the most important products
of the modern English historical school.

These historians may be arranged in two classes
(widely different in size), according as their chief
interest and motive lies in the deductions that they
draw from history and the theories they found on
it, or in the discovery and record of the facts. The
division is a rough one, for the commentators of
history are in some cases the authors of very
vigorous narrative; and in the list I have given
there is no narrator of history who does not find
some meaning or lesson in it, or one to whom it is
merely a tale "full of sound and fury, signifying
nothing". In the first list may be placed the
names of Buckle, Carlyle, and Seeley: the other
names will form the second list; it is doubtful to
which category the work of Froude ought properly
to belong.

Henry Thomas Buckle (1821–1862) published
his *History of Civilization in England* in 1857 and
1861. This work is an effort not merely to narrate
the history of English culture, but to penetrate and
reveal the causes which have governed it: his object, as he himself defines it, is to "discover the
principles which govern the character and destiny
of nations". He deplores the absence of broad

generalizations in ordinary histories in a passage
that is quoted in this volume, and, boldly claiming
that the phenomena of history reveal the working
of fixed laws, declares that it is pre-eminently the
historian's business to discover and declare them.

The very title of his first chapter will illustrate
the daring character of his enterprise. It reads:
" Statement of the resources for investigating history, and proofs of the regularity of human actions:
these actions are governed by mental and physical
laws: therefore both sets of laws must be studied,
and there can be no history without the natural
sciences". He did not live to complete his work,
but, as it stands, the title is misleading. It is far
from being a national history, either in aim or
execution. Generalization, above all, was what
Buckle aimed at, and he devotes as much attention to Scotch, French, and Spanish affairs as to
English. But the book, as published, is but a frag-
ment of the great conception of its author.

Buckle's book has found more detractors than
champions, but it is unquestionably one that has
had an influence upon the mind of England. The
vast reading of the author, coupled with a style of
great conviction and clearness, though at times
over-rhetorical in its methods, make it one of the
most readable of philosophical works. Among the
theses contained in his book are the following:—
" That human actions are governed by laws as
fixed and regular as those which rule the physical
world; that climate, soil, food, and the aspects of
nature are the primary causes of intellectual progress; that the advance of European civilization

is characterized by a continually diminishing influence of physical laws and a continually increasing influence of mental laws; that human progress has been due, not to moral agencies which are stationary, but to intellectual activity which has been constantly varying and advancing; that religion, literature, and government are at the best the products and not the cause of civilization; that the progress of civilization varies directly as scepticism and inversely as credulity ".[1]

It is impossible here to enter into any discussion of these principles. Buckle's contentions have not, as a rule, found acceptance with historians and critics, though they have still their capable and eager defenders. The book remains alone in English literature: later historians have not dared to generalize in such a fashion, and later philosophers have not possessed Buckle's knowledge of the facts of history.

The most prominent figure in English prose literature since the death of Macaulay is Thomas Carlyle (1795–1881). He was no mere historian, but the greater part of his work consisted of historical narrative or comment; and history was at the back of all his thought as the chief criterion of truth and the chief court of appeal. He produced three important historical works, *The French Revolution* (1837), *The Letters and Speeches of Cromwell* (1845), *The Life of Frederick the Great* (1858–1865), besides many essays on historical subjects. These

[1] I take the statement of these theses directly from Professor Flint's article on Buckle in the *Encyclopædia Britannica*.

dates show that he was a contemporary, though a
younger contemporary, of Macaulay; but as his life
and literary activity was prolonged until 1881, and
as his whole cast of mind is far more modern than
that of Macaulay, it seems most fitting that he
should find treatment here.

Extracts from Carlyle's *Essay on History* are
printed in this volume, and it is a characteristic
production, giving us, as it does, the summary of
his views on history and the method of writing it.
Here we may see, as we see all through his historical work, his fondness for definiteness in the
narration of fact and for indefiniteness in the construction of theory. He desires to proceed from a
narration of facts to the construction of a philosophy
of them, but he doubts the possibility of such a
procedure. " The whole meaning lies beyond our
ken; yet in that complex manuscript, covered
over with formless inextricably entangled unknown
characters . . . some letters, some words may be
deciphered; and, if no complete philosophy, here
and there an intelligible precept, available in practice, may be gathered: well understanding that
much still remains to be interpreted; that history
is a real prophetic manuscript, and can be fully
interpreted by no man." The inter-relation of the
different parts of human life is clearly set forward
in this essay, and was always realized by Carlyle:
he stands in this respect far in advance of Macaulay
in historical insight.   The history of Religion is to
Carlyle the central thread of history.

Carlyle had never heard that the historian should
have no dealings with the literary artist; or, if he

had heard, he paid no heed.   Like Gibbon and
like Macaulay he writes his histories in a style that
is a true mirror of the man.   But it may be questioned whether it is as well adapted as the style of
Gibbon or Macaulay for the purpose of historical
narrative.   In sheer artistic beauty it reaches heights
greater than either of the others can touch, but it is
better fitted for a detached picture than for a long
narrative; and there are places where the striving
after artistic effect has induced him unconsciously
to modify the facts.   But, as with Gibbon and
Macaulay, the literary and personal history of his
books seem likely to preserve them: the compli-
ment of being edited with criticisms and additions
is paid to him along with the two others.   There
are no other historical works in English, except
those of Gibbon, Macaulay, and Carlyle, where
scholars have been content to give additional information in foot-notes and appendices without re-
writing the whole story.

His *French Revolution* shows his writing at its
best, and of all his works is probably that which
has been most widely read.   There is no book like
it in English literature.   The blending of poetry
and history that Macaulay desired is here achieved
indeed.   Of true poetry there is more in a few
chapters of Carlyle than in all that Macaulay has
left.   The siege of the Bastille, the flight to
Varennes, the condemnation of the king, the fall of
Robespierre—these are achievements in literature
that deserve to stand by the very highest.   His
reading and researches had been conducted, too,
with great assiduity and sincerity; the general

accuracy of the work, after all that has been written on it, stands remarkably high. Yet it is not history as Gibbon or Macaulay or Ranke would understand the word. It is a rhapsodical sermon; a series of pictures seen in the flashes of a thunderstorm, and commented on by a Hebrew prophet.

His *Letters and Speeches of Cromwell* takes higher rank as history, and performed a great service for the proper understanding of the seventeenth century. Until the publication of this book Cromwell had generally been regarded as tyrant, impostor, and hypocrite. Carlyle's book banished that view for ever from serious historical literature. The documents have been edited with the greatest care, and the comment shows as much insight as eloquence. His *Life of Frederick the Great* hardly deserves such high praise. It dispelled the view of Frederick that had been made current by Macaulay's famous Essays, but Carlyle wrote a great deal of it strongly against the grain: there is some admirable writing in it, and good history, but it lacks the spontaneity and irrepressible flow of his early books.

Carlyle has been classed among those who used history as a vehicle for teaching. What, then, was the teaching that he desired to convey? It is characteristic of the man that it is hard to answer this question. He preached vehemently, but his doctrine was somewhat nebulous. His chief doctrines, however, are that democracy is illogical and self-destructive; that the great need of the age is an increase of reverence for human greatness, that shall allow of the placing of government into the hands of some strong " heroic " man. In the more strictly historical domain he showed little interest in a knowledge of the world of classical antiquity, and had the strongest prejudices against the mediæval church and all that belonged to it. The two great revolutions in modern European society—the Protestant Reformation and the French Revolution —were the *foci* to all his thought; and, though he constantly declaimed against a policy or philosophy of negation, his deepest sympathies were with the spiritual revolutionary. He saw more clearly in history the processes of destruction than of construction, and the political and religious efforts of the modern world failed to gain his sympathy or assent. Later thought has failed to support many of his judgments, and his reputation as a historical thinker would probably have stood higher if it had rested only on the *French Revolution* and *Cromwell.*

The name of Sir John R. Seeley (1834-1895) may seem hardly worthy of mention along with those of Buckle and Carlyle; but his work demands attention as illustrating an interesting experiment in the writing and teaching of history. His earliest studies were classical, and he occupied at one time the chair of Latin in University College, London. He became Professor of Modern History in Cambridge in 1869. His writings include a work on the *Life and Times of Stein*—a study in the development of Germany during the Napoleonic age; *The Expansion of England*; *The Growth of British Policy*; and Lectures on political science. It is no one of these books, but the general aim of his whole work, that it is important to notice. He conceived of history as occupying itself exclusively with politics, or with other subjects only as subordinate to politics; and he regarded the task of the historian as being the instruction and guidance of the statesman. The closing words of his Inaugural Lecture, from which considerable passages are quoted in the body of this book, give the key to the remainder of his life-work. " History the school of statesmanship! This was what I began with. It is a maxim which to many practical men sounds, I know, somewhat hollow. To give it another sound, to vindicate it as a sober maxim in this university, is a task to which I feel very unequal; nevertheless it is what I understand myself to be called on to attempt. If I succeed in any measure I hope to do so by the method I have now indicated, by giving due precedence in the teaching of history to the present over the past."

The most noteworthy outcome of this effort was the two courses of lectures which were published under the title of the *Expansion of England* (1883), the one series dealing with the Colonies, the other with India. The book is historical in character, and occupied chiefly with the rivalry of the French and English in the eighteenth century. But its object was to put the relation between England and her colonies in a new and true light, and to show that those relations were mutually beneficial and might be permanent. It would not be true to say that this was the beginning of the modern " imperialistic " movement, for Froude and Carlyle had both of them already protested against Turgot's view, that colonies were like fruit and necessarily fell from the parent tree as soon as they were ripe. It would be rather true to say that the book gave precision to ideas widely but vaguely held, and an appearance of scientific and historical support to a general aspiration. The book linked itself to much that was vulgar and violent (with which Seeley would have no sympathy at all), and soon became a watchword with certain journalists and politicians. It does not fall within the province of this book to consider the value of the movement with which the book was connected; enough that the wishes of its author were thoroughly realized. The Cambridge historical school co-operated in a striking manner with modern statesmanship, in giving to the policy of England the trend that has characterized the last twenty years. Yet Seeley has found no successors among the foremost exponents of history. On the one side, the school of philosophical historians would maintain that it is wholly illogical to confine the conclusions of history to politics, and that not political but sociological science must be its goal. On the other side, the scientific historians will point austerely to the vast array of documents and " origines " still unstudied, and will say (with MM. Langlois and Seignobos) that " it is an obsolete illusion to suppose that history supplies information of practical utility in the conduct of life, lessons directly profitable to individuals and peoples ".[1]

The names contained in our second list must be

[1] *Introduction to the Study of History*, by Langlois & Seignobos (Duckworth & Co.), p. 319.

far more summarily dealt with. Their work is of
a more ordinary character, and a few words of
appreciation will alone be necessary. We will
glance at them in the order of the publication of
their most important works. James Anthony
Froude (1818–1894) published the first volume of
his *History of England from the Fall of Wolsey to
the Defeat of the Spanish Armada* in 1856, and
the work was continued down to 1870. It was
written under the influence of Carlyle's methods
and ideas. " I fancied myself writing it to him,"
says Froude, " reflecting at each word what he
would think of it, as a check on affectation."
And this mixture of the delicacy and scholarship
of Oxford with the fire and smoke of Carlyle's
philosophy makes sometimes rather a strange
blend. We find in Froude the same praise of
the strong man that characterized Carlyle's later
years; the same distrust of democracy and of
the Celtic Irish; the same unhistoric attitude
towards the mediæval church and the Reformation. The book has been severely handled by
critics, and there is no doubt that Froude has
made serious and damaging mistakes in great
matters and in small. It is more to the purpose
here to note that the book lacks historical perspective; that the narrative does not attain to the
even flow and sustained interest of Gibbon, and
has none of the robust reasoning of Macaulay, and
that the purple passages seem thrust in rather than
woven into the texture of the narrative. Yet
Froude can describe a dramatic scene with striking
vividness. If any one doubts it, let him turn to

the account of Drake's voyage round the world, of the execution of Mary Queen of Scots, or of the Spanish Armada.

In the next year after the appearance of Froude's first volume, Freeman's *History of the Norman Conquest* began to be published, and in Edward Augustus Freeman (1823–1892) Froude found a life-long critic and rival. Freeman was a thorough-going champion of liberty, and Froude seemed to him an apologist for despotism: but it was on the score of accuracy that Freeman brought against him the most damaging charges. His own work was founded on a thorough study of all the authorities for his period that had been printed. It was, he thought, no part of the historian's task to dig among manuscripts, and he ridiculed those who thought that it was necessary for him to spend his days at the British Museum. He has in his turn been severely criticised for this neglect of unprinted material. But no historian before Freeman's day, not Gibbon himself, had such a vivid sense of the unity of history, such a feeling of the continuity of the whole human record. His most-read and best-remembered work is his elaborate (perhaps too elaborate) *History of the Norman Conquest*; but he wrote of Greek and Roman and of mediæval history; and, though he composed no historical narrative of quite modern times, his interest in contemporary politics was intense and passionate. Indeed, the dominant characteristic of Freeman's work is his sense of the indivisibility of history. Each period, and the history of each nation, was not only known but felt by him to be indissolubly

connected with all others.   Every epoch in history,
even the most important, was to him a scene " in
one unbroken drama which takes in the political
history of European man".   No catalogue of his
works need be given here.   In addition to his great
work on the Norman Conquest, he planned a comprehensive history of federal government, which
was to have stretched from the fourth century B.C.
to the construction of the American Republic; but
he only actually carried out that part which concerned the history of Greece and Rome.   He published courses of lectures (delivered by him as
Professor of History at Oxford, to which office he
was appointed in 1884) on *Periods of European
History and Methods of Historical Study*.   He
compressed the history of Europe, moreover, into
a volume of some 400 pages, and even into a
" primer" of 100 pages.   The protest that his
whole work implied against the treatment of history
in periods, and his affirmation of the " unity and
indivisibility of history", are the greatest services
he rendered to the study and composition of the
subject in England.   It is not possible to give
high praise to Freeman's work from the point of
view of literary style, which is often harsh and
occasionally pompous.   He has a way, too, weari-
some and at times ludicrous, of iterating certain
points where he thought mistakes were commonly
made, as that Charlemagne was not a Frenchman,
that Austria represents neither a nationality nor a
language, that the modern use of the word " empire "
is unhistorical.   But Freeman may be regarded as
one of the men who most contributed to put the

study of history in England on sound and fruitful lines.

With Freeman, John Richard Green (1837–1883), and William Stubbs, Bishop of Oxford (1825–1901), were closely associated. They were both of them friends and allies in study, and were in harmony with at least some part of Freeman's spirit. Green's life-work was interrupted by ill health, and he died at the age of forty-six. His academic career at Oxford was not one of distinction, but the university, by its spirit and associations, did much to mould his work. He had Freeman's intense interest in historical geography and archæology; but his chief attention was given to the history of his own country. He wrote, at the end of his life, volumes on early English history (*The Making of England* and *The Conquest of England*), but the real importance of his work is summed up in his *Short History of the English People*. No historical narrative had had such a success in England since the publication of Macaulay's *England*. The book owed its success in the first place to the grace and brightness of its style; but it also embodied ideas which were new, at any rate to the public which the *Short History* reached. The narrative began with the coming of the English invaders, and thus Roman and Celtic Britain were dismissed as not belonging to the story of the English people. Such a procedure was in harmony with Freeman's ideas, but would find little support at the present day. Further, the *Short History* neglected the usual divisions into reigns and dynasties: it was a history of the people, not of the kings. This treatment of the subject reflected Green's own popular sympathies, and marked a real advance in the understanding of the nation's development. Further, its survey extended far beyond the mere government of the people. " History is past politics " was a favourite motto of Freeman's; but to Green history was religion and social life, art and literature, as well as politics. He fell in here with one of the dominant currents of historical thought in the nineteenth century— the tendency to a synthetic treatment of human development, which had been powerfully championed by Carlyle.

The name of Bishop Stubbs must be closely linked with those of Freeman and Green. He was first a distinguished student of Oxford, and in 1867 the reputation of his historical work secured for him the Professorship of History at the university. But he was appointed Bishop of Chester (1884) and then Bishop of Oxford (1888), and during the latter part of his life his official duties prevented him from devoting sufficient attention to historical study to allow him to publish much. Professor Maitland, in his striking and eloquent obituary notice of Stubbs,[1] claims that the verdict of the recognized historians of the time would un- doubtedly acclaim Stubbs as the greatest of all. " No other Englishman has so completely dis- played to the world the whole business of the historian, from the mincing of the raw material to the narrating and generalizing. We are taken behind the scenes and shown the ropes and pulleys. . . . This ' practical demonstration ', if we

[1] *English Historical Review*, July, 1901.

may so call it, of the historian's art and science—
from the preliminary hunt for manuscripts, through
the work of collation and filiation and minute
criticism, onward to the perfected tale, the eloquence and the reflexions — has been of incal-
culable benefit to the cause of history in England,
and far more effective than any abstract discourse
on methodology could be."

His works make a long list; but as most important and most characteristic, we may take his work
in connection with the "Rolls Series" and his
Constitutional History of England. He edited for
the "Rolls Series" *The Chronicles and Memorials
of Richard I, The Chronicles of Henry II, The
Chronicles of Hoveden,* and several others, and each
volume was introduced by a full preface. It was
in these works that he first showed of what he
was capable, and in the prefaces some of his most
brilliant writing is to be found. The *Constitutional
History* began to be published in 1874, and it so far
outstripped anything that had been done on the
subject before, that for many years the study of
constitutional history in the universities merely
meant the study of Stubbs' three volumes. The
book describes the course of the development of
the English constitution down to the coming of
the Tudors. The conclusions of his first volume
are not now universally accepted; he was dealing
there with a period where the preliminary studies
had not advanced far enough to allow any book
written on it to approach finality. "Many an investigator", says Professor Maitland, "will leave his
bones to bleach on that desert before it is accu-

rately mapped"; and he doubts whether Stubbs was "fully aware of the treachery of the ground that he traversed". But the second and third volumes, that take us from the twelfth century to the fifteenth, will need rivals of almost superhuman qualities to displace them.

In his Inaugural Lecture of 1867 Stubbs spoke of the objects of historical study in a way that makes it necessary to quote a few sentences. " I should not like to be thought to be advocating any study on the mere grounds of utility, although I believe that utility, both as regards the training of the study and the information attained in it, to be the highest, humanly speaking, of all utilities; it helps to qualify a man to act in his character of a politician as a Christian man should. But this is not all: beyond the educational purpose, beyond the political purpose, beyond the philosophical use of history and its training, it has something of the preciousness of everything that is clearly true. In common with natural philosophy it has its value, I will not say as a science, for that would be to use a term which has now become equivocal, but it has a value analogous to the value of science; a value as something that is worth knowing and retaining in the knowledge for its own and for the truth's sake. . . . But even this is not all. There is, I speak humbly, in common with natural science, in the study of living history, a gradual approximation to a consciousness that we are growing into a perception of the workings of the Almighty Ruler of the world; . . . that we are coming to see not only in his ruling of his Church in her spiritual character, but in his overruling of the world, . . . a hand of justice and mercy, a hand of progress and order, a kind and wise disposition, ever leading the world on to the better, but never forcing, and out of the evil of man's working bringing continually that which is good."

The names of Gardiner, Lecky, Creighton, and Hodgkin remain. Samuel Rawson Gardiner (1829–1902) gave an example, unsurpassed among English historians, of a life devoted to the accomplishment of a single purpose. He was drawn to the period of the Stuarts and the Commonwealth by an interest in the issues involved, and a belief that prejudice had played too large a part in the narratives that the world already possessed of that period. To discover the truth and to state it with unflinching honesty and impartiality was the task to which he devoted his life. The view that he took of history may be found in the preface to the tenth volume of his *History of England from the Accession of James I to the Outbreak of the Civil War*. A portion of this will be found quoted in our first set of quotations. It will be seen that he dismisses Seeley's contention that history should be made the school of politics, and maintains that such a course is neither good for politics nor history: " He who studies the society of the past will be of the greater service to the society of the present in proportion as he leaves it out of account ". The whole passage deserves careful study; it is a most interesting revelation of the spirit of patience and sympathy in which Gardiner worked at his great task.

In the aim that he set before him Gardiner gained a complete success. No one has ventured to charge him with prejudice or with insufficient effort in investigating the facts. Lord Acton singled out Gardiner's volumes (or a "few" of them) as being among the very few in the literature of Europe "where the resources have been so employed that we can be content with the work done for us, and never wish it to be done over again". Of the style in which this hardly-won truth is presented there is no need to say much. It is as clear, as sound, as unpretentious as the man himself. He did not cultivate any repellent austerity of manner, and thought it an advantage that a true tale should be told intelligibly and attractively. His power of vivid presentation increased as his work advanced, and certain pages from his later volumes are here given as proof of how historical narrative seeking only to be true may acquire a high quality of literary beauty.

W. E. H. Lecky (1838–1903) surveyed, in a sense, a wider field than Freeman, Stubbs, or Gardiner, inasmuch as he wrote definitely on ethical and current political questions. Like many of the great English historians—like Gibbon and Macaulay and Grote and Carlyle and Gardiner— he never held any post at the universities, and did his work aloof from the academical atmosphere. His first book, *Leaders of Public Opinion in Ireland*, was published when he was only twenty-three years of age, and contained opinions favourable to the Nationalist movement in Ireland, which he afterwards recanted. His next works, *The*

History of Rationalism in Europe (1860) and *The Development of European Morals from Augustus to Charlemagne* (1869), were written under the influence, though not in harmony with the opinions of, Buckle's work on *Civilization in England.* Nine years later (in 1878) he published the first two volumes of his *History of England in the Eighteenth Century*, but he was working at the subject until 1890, though the subject cannot be said to have been brought to an end even with the publication of the last volume. His later books, *Democracy and Liberty* and the *Map of Life*, are interesting criticisms of politics and society only possible to a life-long student of history, but not in themselves historical works.

Lecky's great work, *The History of England*, showed decided originality in its form and in the treatment of the subject. He who turns to it for a straightforward narrative of the events of the eighteenth century will be disappointed. Famous military incidents are dismissed in a line; the goings out and comings in of ministries are given, if at all, in the baldest manner. The book consists of two parts. There is, firstly, a series of essays, in loose chronological order, on the different social, political, and religious aspects of English life from the accession of the Hanoverian dynasty to the outbreak of the war with France in 1793; and there is, secondly, an account of Irish history from 1714 to 1801, full in detail and annalistic in form. Some want of constructive power seems implied by so confused an arrangement; and the matter of the book (that part of it that concerns English history) has been adversely criticised as not taking into account the vast unpublished material available. The book offends also directly against the canons of those who regard all ethical judgments as a mere otiose appendage to the historian's work. Lecky sits in judgment everywhere: on Wesley, on Burke, on Chatham, on C. J. Fox, on George III, on all the great characters and forces that pass under his wide survey. And yet withal there is a great reserve in his work, too great a reserve sometimes: the reader has the feeling, both in political and religious topics, that Lecky is not speaking out his full mind, sometimes even that he has not got the full courage of his opinions. But his *History of the Eighteenth Century* is, in spite of all, a work of the first class, full of knowledge carefully acquired by the labour of half a lifetime; its verdicts are impartial, and, coming from a mind so stored with wide and varied learning, in the highest degree valuable. His treatment of Methodism, Chatham, Burke, and George III may be specially noted. In his *Irish History* it is admitted on all hands that he has vastly widened and deepened our knowledge of an extremely obscure and difficult time.

Among the great historians of the latter part of the nineteenth century it would be absurd to omit the name of Mandell Creighton (1843–1901), for not only did he write one of the most important works of his time, but his work shows some well-marked characteristics of the historiography of the age. He was educated at Oxford, but in 1884 was appointed to the Dixie Professorship of Ecclesiastical History at Cambridge. In 1886 he became the first editor of the *English Historical Review*, which had been one of the aspirations of J. R. Green. In 1891 he became Bishop of Peterborough, and in 1897 Bishop of London. He was the author of numerous historical works, but his reputation will rest on the *History of the Papacy during the Reformation*, the five volumes of which appeared between 1882 and 1894. In this work, though an official member of the Anglican Church, he did not hesitate to claim that he treated the greatest of ecclesiastical crises with absolute impartiality, and his claim has been allowed. A passage from a letter to Mr. R. L. Poole, quoted by him in the *English Historical Review* of April, 1901, gives his attitude to historical study.

" My view of history is not to approach things with any preconceived ideas, but with the natural *pietas* and sympathy which I try to feel toward all men who do or try to do great things. *Mentem mortalia tangunt* is my motto. I try to put myself in their place; to see their limitations, and leave the course of events to pronounce the verdict upon systems and men alike."

His history perfectly reflects this temper. He passes through a period laden with vice and crime in high places—for, be it noted, he wisely extends the meaning of the Period of the Reformation so as to cover the fourteenth and fifteenth centuries— and abstains from the moral censures so usually lavished on this particular period. The politician, though not the party-politician, was always near the surface in Bishop Creighton, and he clearly feels an intense interest in the problems of ad-

ministration and statesmanship that confronted
the Popes. It is in this preoccupation with the
politics of his period, to the exclusion or subordination of the movement of thought, which has
been charged against him as a fault. Lord Acton
wrote: The readers of Creighton's volumes "will
know by what means the Papacy, borne on the
stormy tide of absolutism, established an independent state on the subjugation of Italy. But
the marrow of things does not lie in the making
of a distinct principality; other causes changed the
axis of the world." Considering his effectiveness
as a speaker and pamphleteer, the style of the
book is sometimes dry; but the whole history is
a justification of the claim of the modern school
of history, that impartiality is possible even in the
periods where controversy has been hottest.[1] He
had designed to prolong his work far into the
sixteenth century; but the pressure of official
duties was too great, and the fifth volume ends
with the Sack of Rome in 1527.

The work of Dr. Thomas Hodgkin comes last
upon our list of historical works. The first volume
of his *Italy and her Invaders* appeared in 1880, and
the work was completed in 1899 by the publication
of two volumes on the Frankish invasions of Italy
and the imperial establishment of Charlemagne.
The book claims notice here, not only on its own
merits, but because it belongs to a class of books

[1] Lord Acton said of Creighton's methods: "He is not striving to
prove a case, or burrowing towards a conclusion, but wishes to pass
through scenes of raging controversy and passion with a serene curiosity,
a suspended judgment, a divided jury, and a pair of white gloves".

peculiarly characteristic of English historical literature. Foreign critics, and especially German critics,
have always noticed with wonder how many of our
prominent writers of history have been unconnected
with the universities, how many have been actively
engaged in business or politics. Grote, the great
historian of Greece, was, as we have seen, a banker
and a politician; and in the person of Dr. Hodgkin
a banker again comes forward to tell the story of
Rome's decay and of the barbarian invasions, and
tells it in a way that does not indeed threaten the
narrative of Gibbon with eclipse, but gives him an
invaluable supplement. The plan of the book is
perfectly indicated by its name. Dr. Hodgkin
proposed to tell the fate of Italy from the time
when its frontiers ceased to be an adequate defence, down to a date which was at first somewhat
indefinite, but came in the end to be the death of
Charlemagne. He has told us in the preface to
his first volume that he has written both for a
learned and a popular audience, and he has ad-
mirably succeeded. It may indeed be urged that
after 476, when even the shadow of the imperial
sceptre passed from the soil of Italy, the thread of
the story is frequently and inevitably broken, and
the barbarian invasions no longer form a satisfactory connecting cord for a continuous narrative.
Moreover, the obscurity of the Lombard and Caro-
lingian period has prevented the later volumes from
becoming so generally popular as the early ones.
But there are few finer pieces of narrative than
Dr. Hodgkin's descriptions of the careers of Alaric,
Theodoric, and Belisarius, and the book is a most

welcome proof that it is still possible to combine (with mutual advantage) a knowledge of practical affairs, scholarly research, and a sense of literary style.

VII. We have thus brought down this sketch of English historiography as far as the very end of the nineteenth century: it will be of interest now to consider what forces are at present acting upon those who concern themselves with the study and writing of history, and what directions their labours seem likely to take. The two tendencies that have been noticed as operative in England, especially since the death of Macaulay, are growing stronger rather than weaker. On the one hand, the study of documents grows more intense, the record offices are diligently explored, and the end, if it is ever to come, is not yet in sight. The method of dealing with these documents has been developed into a separate science. The *Introduction to the Study of History* by MM. Langlois and Seignobos gives an outline of the processes that are to be employed. Some of them may seem to the reader to be labelled with a needlessly repellent phraseology; such words as " heuristic" for the discovery of documents bearing on a period, or " hermeneutic " for the interpretation of them, are not likely to become naturalized in the English language, and some of the processes elaborately defined and labelled seem merely the operations of common sense. But the study of documents has gone far past the point at which it stood even in the days of Ranke. On the other hand, the scope of history grows continually wider. It is clear that Freeman's fine phrase about "the one unbroken drama which takes in the political history of European man" is no longer sufficient. Professor Bury, in his Inaugural Lecture at Cambridge (1903), noted that the principle "must be carried beyond the limits within which he [Freeman] enforced it". It must be extended to social and religious as well as to political questions; it can no longer stop at the boundaries of Europe, even though by Europe we mean all the races that draw their blood or their language from Europe; it can stop nowhere short of the record of humanity upon the planet. It becomes a pressing question to determine by what methods so vast a survey can be made, and through what medium the results can be presented to that wide general public which it is necessary that it should reach. The "world-history" has not, up to the present, been a popular or literary success. There is no reason to doubt that in the right hands, and handled in the right spirit, it may be made so.

An external influence that has been very potent on men's thoughts about history during the last twenty years has been the influence of physical science. Not only have its practical achievements been the commonplace topic of admiration, but, as generalized by Darwin and Spencer, it has profoundly modified every department of thought and reached the popular imagination. Students and teachers of history, impressed by its victories and prestige, and convinced of the reality and utility of their own studies, have adopted some of its methods and occasionally its terminology. They have claimed that they too are concerned with science. "History is simply a science, no less and no more", are the concluding words of Professor Bury's inaugural address, in which he repudiates any but the most occasional alliance between history and literature. And now the question "Is history a science?" is one to which every professional exponent of the subject seems bound to give an answer, though certain historians regard such a question as "puerile". And the question is indeed puerile unless it is preceded or accompanied by a definition of "science"; for the word is now so loosely used that it is in danger of losing all its meaning. Similarly, a definition of the word "literature" is a necessary preliminary to any fruitful discussion of the relations between literature and history. In much of the controversy as it has proceeded hitherto "science" seems to be applied to any branch of study that has the discovery of objective truth for its aim, while literature is taken to mean writings in which the affording of artistic pleasure is an indispensable, if not the only, object. But these definitions are not satisfactory in either case. It seems best to restrict the term "science" to studies which include both experiment and generalization; and such a restriction would exclude most, if not all, of the works which are usually called "historical". Little is gained and much is lost by confusing processes that are essentially distinct. Historians have paid needless flattery to science in thus claiming its title and terminology: the study of history has been defended as being the highest development of biology, when the truth is, that the parallel with animal biology has been a real bar to the true appreciation of social evolution. The development of the human race has proceeded according to laws of its own, not yet wholly discovered, but not identical with those formulated by Darwin for the animal kingdom.

Historians are now universally or generally agreed on certain points, as, for instance, the need for a thorough study of documents, and the impossibility of isolating the history of an epoch or of a state from the general course of human development. But there are in every direction questions relating to the study of history on which there is not as yet any consensus of opinion. What is the relation of the historian to politics? what to ethics? what to sociology? In what style, and after what plan, can the results of historical research best be presented to the public? These are questions on which the most prominent exponents of history have come to widely different conclusions.

We have seen how Seeley laid it down that "history should be the school of statesmanship", and how his life through he laboured to make it so. But when Lord Acton succeeded to the chair of history in Cambridge he found it impossible fully to accept the doctrine. He found, indeed, that there was a "sense in which this is true. For the science of politics is the one science that is deposited by the streams of history like the grains of gold in the sands of a river." But he went on, "Politics and history are interwoven but are not commensurate. Ours is a domain that reaches farther than affairs

of state, and is not subject to the jurisdiction of
governments. It is our function to keep in view and
to command the movement of ideas which are not
the effect but the cause of public events, and even
to allow some priority to ecclesiastical history over
civil." But in this inaugural lecture, in which Lord
Acton thus repudiated the limitations of Seeley's
theory, he went on himself to urge that the historian should sit in austere moral judgment on the
characters and events that he contemplates. " Our
historical judgments ", he said in his striking way,
" have as much to do with hopes of heaven as
public or private conduct." He urged that in
forming these judgments it is better " to risk excess
in vigour than in indulgence ", and the closing
words of his address were that " if we lower our
standard in history we cannot uphold it in church
or state ". When in 1903 Professor Bury filled the
chair vacated by Lord Acton's death, he would
only go so far in Seeley's direction as to admit
" that history supplies the material for political and
social science ". He did not notice Lord Acton's
claim that history should sit in judgment on men
and movements; and ended by declaring his conviction that history, " though she may supply
material for literary art or philosophical speculation, is herself simply a science, no less and no
more ". He did not deny the practical utility of history; but held that it was for the present and many
succeeding generations to accumulate materials;
and that it would only be possible for far-distant
centuries to enjoy the results.

Further, some have maintained that history as

a department of literature has come to an end. It was a product, they say, of the Renaissance, with its copying of the classical models and of the Romantic movement of the early nineteenth century. But, they urge, the scientific period has come, and with it history, so written as to form a part of literature, will be known no more. Gibbon and Macaulay and Carlyle will have no successors. If that is so it is for the world at large a somewhat serious outlook. Even those who most insist on the purely "scientific" character of historical study have recognized its value for purposes of general culture, though they have denied its practical value for politics and scorned ,its supposed connection with ethics. But if history severs for ever its long-established connection with literature, the number of the readers of history will indefinitely diminish; the contention of the historians that their work is of no immediate practical use will be readily granted; and the world at large will concern itself with history hardly more than it does with petrology or psychology.

The purpose of this preface is historical, not prophetic. But it may be allowable to say, in conclusion, that there is no probability and no sign that this divorce between history and literature will really take place. The subject-matter of history is too important, and too immediately concerns the whole being of man, to allow it to be written without feeling; and if history is written with clearness and with feeling, literature issues at once. History itself may teach us that the writing of history cannot become purely "scientific" and objective. The long roll of historians, who deal with a great subject in a style and manner corresponding, has not come to an end, and is not likely to do so.

It seems that the study and the writing of history is likely to proceed along three main lines. On the one side there is the work of erudition, compilation, interpretation of documents; on the other side there is political and social science, or sociology, to give it a now widely accepted title, based partly, but by no means wholly, upon the record of the past, which it is the task of the historian to produce and to verify. Between these two, different from both but sharing in the character of each, there will be in the future, as there has been in the past, the historical narrative, in the production of which literary taste and skill will play an important part. It may be that for the near future no one man will be able to do what Gibbon did, and write with the confidence of a master the story of a thousand years: and that the co-operative history, of which the *Cambridge Modern History*, now in process of publication, is the most prominent example, may be the form which will be usually adopted in the near future. But as the whole story of man's development becomes clearly unrolled, and the relation between the present and the past is in its main features established, it cannot be doubted that a topic which touches so intimately all the deepest feelings and the highest hopes of man will still claim to be treated with the highest literary art. It may even be that as the dependence of the present and future upon the past becomes more intensely felt the world may see again the historical poem, a form well known to the ancient literature, but almost completely neglected by the moderns.

Part I

Passages to illustrate the view taken by
Historians at different periods of the
Objects and Methods of History.

1. FRANCIS BACON, LORD VERULAM

[From the *Advancement of Learning*, Book II, published in 1605. For comment on Bacon's view of history and the means whereby he desired to see its study advanced, see Introduction, p. viii.]

HISTORY is natural, civil, ecclesiastical, and literary; whereof the three first I allow as extant, the fourth I note as deficient. For no man hath propounded to himself the general state of learning to be described and represented from age to age, as many have done the works of nature, and the state civil and ecclesiastical; without which the history of the world seemeth to me to be as the statua of Polyphemus with his eye out; that part being wanting which doth most show the spirit and life of the person. And yet I am not ignorant that in divers particular sciences, as of the jurisconsults, the mathematicians, the rhetoricians, the philosophers, there are set down some small memorials of the schools, authors, and books; and so likewise some barren relations touching the invention of arts or usages. But a just story of learning, containing the antiquities and originals of knowledges and their sects, their inventions, their traditions, their diverse administrations and managings, their flourishings, their oppositions, decays, depressions, oblivions, removes, with the causes and occasions of them, and all other events concerning learning, throughout the ages of the world, I may truly affirm to be wanting. The use and end of which work I do not so much design for curiosity or satisfaction of those that are the lovers of learning, but chiefly for a more serious and grave purpose, which is this in few words, that it will make learned men wise in the use and administration of learning. For it is not Saint Augustine's nor Saint Ambrose's works that will make so wise a divine, as ecclesiastical history, thoroughly read and observed; and the same reason is of learning. . . . _____

For civil history, it is of three kinds; not unfitly to be compared with the three kinds of pictures or images. For of pictures or images, we see some are unfinished, some are perfect, and some are defaced. So of histories we may find three kinds, memorials, perfect histories, and antiquities; for memorials are history unfinished, or the first or rough draughts of history; and antiquities are history defaced, or some remnants of history which have casually escaped the shipwreck of time.

Memorials, or preparatory history, are of two sorts; whereof the one may be termed commentaries, and the other registers. Commentaries are they which set down a continuance of the naked events and actions, without the motives or designs, the counsels, the speeches, the pretexts, the occasions and other passages of action: for this is the true nature of a commentary (though Cæsar, in modesty mixed with greatness, did for his pleasure apply the name of a commentary to the best history of the world). Registers are collections of public acts, as decrees of council, judicial proceedings, declarations and letters of estates, orations, and the like, without a perfect continuance or contexture of the thread of the narration.

Antiquities, or remnants of history, are, as was said, *tanquam tabula naufragii*: when industrious persons, by an exact and scrupulous diligence and observation, out of monuments, names, words, proverbs, traditions, private records and evidences, fragments of stories, passages of books that concern not story, and the like, do save and recover somewhat from the deluge of time.

In these kinds of unperfect histories I do assign no deficience, for they are *tanquam imperfecte mista*; and therefore any deficience in them is but their nature. As for the corruptions and moths of history, which are epitomes, the use of them deserveth to be banished, as all men of sound judgment have confessed, as those that have fretted and corroded the sound bodies of many excellent histories, and wrought them into base and unprofitable dregs.

History, which may be called just and perfect history, is of three kinds, according to the object which it propoundeth, or pretendeth to represent: for it either representeth a time, or a person, or an action. The first we call chronicles, the second lives, and the third narrations or relations. Of these, although the first be the most complete and absolute kind of history, and hath most estimation and glory, yet the second excelleth it in profit and use, and the third in verity and sincerity. For history of times representeth the magnitude of actions and the public faces and deportments of persons, and passeth over in silence the smaller passages and motions of men and matters. But such being the workmanship of God, as he doth hang the greatest weight upon the smallest wires, *maxima è minimis suspendens*, it comes therefore to pass, that such histories do rather set forth the pomp of business than the true and inward resorts thereof. But lives, if they be well written, propounding to themselves a person to represent, in whom actions both greater and smaller, public and private, have a commixture, must of necessity contain a more true, native, and lively representation. So again narrations and relations of actions, as the war of Peloponnesus, the expedition of Cyrus Minor, the conspiracy of Catiline, cannot but be more purely and exactly true than histories of times, because they may choose an argument comprehensible within the notice and instructions of the writer: whereas he that undertaketh the story of a time, specially of any length, cannot but meet with many blanks and spaces which he must be forced to fill up out of his own wit and conjecture.

For the history of times (I mean of civil history), the providence of God hath made the distribution. For it hath pleased God to ordain and illustrate two exemplar states of the world for arms, learning, moral virtue, policy, and laws—the state of Grecia and the state of Rome— the histories whereof, occupying the middle part of time, have more ancient to them histories which may by one common name be termed the antiquities of the world: and after them, histories which may be likewise called by the name of modern history.

Now to speak of the deficiences. As to the heathen antiquities of the world, it is in vain to note them for deficient. Deficient they are, no doubt, consisting most of fables and fragments; but the deficience cannot be holpen; for antiquity is like fame, *caput inter nubila condit*, her head is muffled from our sight. For the history of the exemplar states it is extant in good perfection. Not but I could wish there were a perfect course of history for Grecia from Theseus to Philopœmen (what time the affairs of Grecia were drowned and extinguished in the affairs of Rome), and for Rome from Romulus to Justinianus, who may be truly said to be *ultimus Romanorum*. In which sequences of story the text of Thucydides and Xenophon in the one, and the texts of Livius, Polybius, Sallustius, Cæsar, Appianus, Tacitus, Herodianus in the other, to be kept entire without any diminution at all, and only to be supplied and continued. But this is matter of magnificence, rather to be commended than required: and we speak now of parts of learning supplemental and not of supererogation.

But for modern histories, whereof there are some few very worthy, but the greater part beneath mediocrity, leaving the care of foreign stories to foreign states, because I will not be *curiosus in aliena republica*, I cannot fail to represent to your Majesty the unworthiness of the history of England in the main continuance thereof, and the partiality and obliquity of that of Scotland in the latest and largest author that I have seen: supposing that it would be honour for your Majesty, and a work very memorable, if this island of Great Brittany, as it is now joined in monarchy for the ages to come, so were joined in one history for the times past; after the manner of the sacred history, which draweth down the story of the ten tribes and of the two tribes as twins together. And if it shall seem that the greatness of this work may make it less exactly performed, there is an excellent period of a much smaller compass of time, as to the story of England; that is to say, from the uniting of the Roses to the uniting of the kingdoms; a portion of time wherein, to my understanding, there hath been the rarest varieties that in like number of successions of any hereditary monarchy hath been known. For it beginneth with the mixed adoption of a crown by arms and title; an entry by battle, an establishment by marriage; and therefore times answerable, like water after a tempest, full of working and swelling, though without extremity of storm; but well passed through by the wisdom of the pilot, being one of the most sufficient kings of all the number. Then followeth the reign of a king, whose actions, howsoever conducted, had much intermixture with the affairs of Europe, balancing and inclining them variably; in whose time also began that great alteration in the state ecclesiastical, an action which seldom cometh upon the stage. Then the reign of a minor: then an offer of an usurpation (though it was but as *febris ephemera*). Then the reign of a queen matched with a foreigner: then of a queen that lived solitary and unmarried, and yet her government so masculine, as it had greater impression and operation upon the states abroad than in any ways received from thence. And now last, this most happy and glorious event, that this island of Brittany, divided from all the world, should be united in itself: and that oracle of rest given to Æneas, *antiquam exquirite matrem*, should now be performed and fulfilled upon the nations of England and Scotland, being now reunited in the ancient mother name of Brittany, as a full period of all instability and peregrinations. So that as it cometh to pass in massive bodies, that they have certain trepidations and waverings before they fix and settle, so it seemeth that by the providence of God this monarchy, before it was to settle in your Majesty and your generations (in which I hope it is now established for ever), it had these prelusive changes and varieties.

2. EDMUND BOLTON

(From the *Hypercritica*, Addresses II and III. The author lived from 1575 to 1633. He was an antiquary and a diligent accumulator of books, and is best known for his proposal to found a Royal Academy for the promotion and glorification of science and letters. The following passages are taken from a small volume entitled "*Hypercritica*, or a rule of judgement for writing and reading our histories; delivered in four supercensorian addresses, by occasion of a censorian epistle prefixed by Sir Henry Savile, Knight, to his edition of some of our oldest historians in Latin, dedicated to the late Queen Elizabeth". The Addresses were written about the year 1618.)

THIS admirable justice and integrity of Historians, as necessary as it is, yet is nothing in these days farther off from hope. For all late authors that ever yet I could read among us, convey with them to narrations of things done fifteen or sixteen hundred years past the jealousies, passions, and affections of their own time. Our Historian must therefore avoid this dangerous syren alluring us to follow our own prejudices, unless he mean only to serve a side and not to serve truth and honesty, and so to remain but in price while his party is able to bear him out with all his faults for quarrel's sake. He is therefore simply to set forth, without prejudices, depravations, or sinister items things as they are. They who do otherwise *ob id ipsum quia non rogati sententiam ferunt valde suspecti sunt.* . . .

This strict rule whosoever honestly follows, may perhaps write uncommodiously for some momentany purposes, but shall thereby, both in present and to posterity, live with honour through the justice of his monuments. And if for them he should suffer death, as brave Cremutius

Cordus did, yet other historians shall eternise his sufferings, and that prince's great disgrace under whom that
tragedy was committed.   Nor in so sacred a business as
the putting into books, for immortal remembrance, the
acts of famous men need I fear to call it a canonical
aphorism of historiography, because it is observed in the
historical volume of holy scripture; whose majesty no
Attick nor Tullian eloquence can express, nor to whose
entireness of verity any human wit or diligence can come
near.   For in those divine records facts, whether good
or bad, and their circumstances are simply and clearly
related without (for the more part) any manner of censure, or judgements upon the facts, as in the writer's
person.   On the contrary let those other writings, which
abound in the different humour, be stript by readers,
who have discretion, into the bare matter which they
profess to handle, so that all their authors, commenta-
tions, conjectures, notes, passions, and censures which
they utter as in their proper persons be diligently marked,
abstracted, and laid apart; and then the things which
they write may be reviewed without danger or certainly
with little.   For the judgements of interested authors are
commonly not judgements so much as prejudices and
preventions, *ne quid suae partes detrimenti capiant.*   In-
iquities practised in this point are not more ordinary
than odious, and are sometimes laid on so impudently
thick that with less than half an eye the paintings are
discernable; others, while the more cunningly, yet so as
that with a little attention they may readily be discovered.
Nor have the translators of history any more privilege
than their authors.   Whether therefore they corrupt the
original by the familiar courses of corruption, as addition,
mutation, mutilation, subtraction, distraction, or otherwise, as they generally do, who in the phrase of their
own education, sect, faction, or affection utter anti-

quities and truths of another tenour, it is like worthy of blame.

And why should any of these devices or dealings be at all? For who compelleth to write? And, if we write, why should we deceive? Or if we would not deceive why do we not use proper and received terms? Even lying Lucian gives it for a precept to his historian that he should call a *fig* a *fig*. What other effect can the ignobility of all the formerly taxed courses produce, than in a short time (as they already have for the most part) to bring the dignity of writing unto nothing? And who is he that rightly weighs an historian's duty and can dare to profane or embase the same without remorse or confusion? Every man is free to hold his hand off from paper; but if one will needs write, then the nobility of the office commands him rather to die than with the injury of truth to humour times and readers and content himself. *Quid enim fortius desideret anima* (saith Saint Augustine) *quam veritatem?*

An historiographer's office therefore abhorreth all sorts of abuse and deceit, as impiety or sacrilege; and so our writer must, if he will live indeed, and live with love and glory.

History in general hath as many praises as any muse among the nine. One tells us, as from out of ancient authors, that history is nothing else but a kind of philosophy using examples; another that history is the metropolis of philosophy. Plainlier and more to our purpose, Tully among other titles calls her the Light of Truth and Mistress of Life. St. Gregory Nazianzen (that excellent Greek Father) styleth her a World of Wisdom, for so his *quaedam conglobata sapientia* (as his translator calls it) may be Englished. Our Malmesbury saith well and worthily that it is *jucunda quaedam gestorum notitia mores condiens quae ad bona sequenda vel mala cavenda legentes exemplis irritat.* To like purpose writes Venerable Beda to King Ceolulph. Excellent is that of Sir Thomas North, in his preface to his *Plutarch's Lives.* "Histories" (saith he there) "are fit for every place, serve for all times, reach to all persons, teach the living, revive the dead, so excelling all other books, as it is better to see Learning in noble men's lives than to read it in philosophers' writings."

3. HENRY ST. JOHN, LORD VISCOUNT BOLINGBROKE

(From his *Letters on the Study and Use of History*, dated 1735. See Introduction, p. xxvii.)

THE motives that carry men to the study of history are different. Some intend, if such as they may be said to study, nothing more than amusement, and read the life of Aristides or Phocion, of Epaminondas or Scipio, Alexander or Cæsar, just as they play a game at cards, or as they would read the story of the seven champions.

Others there are, whose motive to this study is nothing better, and who have the further disadvantage of becoming a nuisance very often to society, in proportion to the progress they make. The former do not improve their reading to any good purpose: the latter pervert it to a very bad one, and grow in impertinence as they increase in learning. I think I have known most of the first kind in England, and most of the last in France. The persons I mean are those who read to talk, to shine in conversation, and to impose in company: who having few ideas to vend of their own growth, store their minds with crude unruminated facts and sentences; and hope to supply, by bare memory, the want of imagination and judgment.

But these are in the two lowest forms. The next I shall mention are in one a little higher; in the form of those who grow neither wiser nor better by study themselves, but who enable others to study with greater ease, and to purposes more useful; who make fair copies of foul manuscripts, give the signification of hard words, and take a great deal of other grammatical pains. The obligation to these men would be great indeed, if they were in general able to do anything better, and submitted to this drudgery for the sake of the public: as some of them, it must be owned with gratitude, have done, but not later, I think, than about the time of the resurrection of letters. When works of importance are pressing, generals themselves may take up the pick-axe and the spade; but in the ordinary course of things, when that pressing necessity is over, such tools are left in the hands destined to use them, the hands of common soldiers and peasants. I approve therefore very much the devotion of a studious man at Christ Church, who was overheard in his oratory entering into a detail with God, as devout persons are apt to do, and, amongst other particular thanksgivings, acknowledging the divine goodness in furnishing the world with makers of dictionaries! These men court fame, as well as their betters, by such means as God has given them to acquire it; and Littleton exerted all the genius he had, when he made a dictionary, though Stephens did not. They deserve encouragement, however, whilst they continue to compile, and neither affect wit, nor presume to reason.

There is a fourth class, of much less use than these, but of much greater name. Men of the first rank in learning, and to whom the whole tribe of scholars bow with reverence. A man must be as indifferent as I am to common censure or approbation, to avow a thorough contempt for the whole business of these learned lives; for all the researches into antiquity, for all the systems of chronology and history, that we owe to the immense labours of a Scaliger, a Bochart, a Petavius, an Usher, and even a Marsham. The same materials are common to them all; but these materials are few, and there is a moral impossibility that they should ever have more.

They have combined these into every form that can be given to them; they have supposed, they have guessed, they have joined disjointed passages of different authors, and broken traditions of uncertain originals, of various people, and of centuries remote from one another as well as from ours. In short, that they might leave no liberty untaken, even a wild fantastical similitude of sounds has served to prop up a system. As the materials they have are few, so are the very best, and such as pass for authentic, extremely precarious; as some of these learned persons themselves confess.

In short, my lord, all these systems are so many enchanted castles; they appear to be something, they are nothing but appearances ; like them too, dissolve the charm, and they vanish from the sight. To dissolve the charm, we must begin at the beginning of them: the expression may be odd, but it is significant. We must examine scrupulously and indifferently the foundations on which they lean: and when we find these either faintly probable, or grossly improbable, it would be foolish to expect anything better in the superstructure. This science is one of those that are *a limine salutandae*. To do thus much may be necessary, that grave authority may not impose on our ignorance: to do more, would be to assist this very authority in imposing false science upon us. I had rather take the Darius whom Alexander conquered, for the son of Hystaspes, and make as many anachronisms as a Jewish chronologer, than sacrifice half my life to collect all the learned lumber that fills the head of an antiquary.

Let me say something of history in general, before I descend into the consideration of particular parts of it, or of the various methods of study, or of the different views of those that apply themselves to it, as I had begun to do in my former letter.

The love of history seems inseparable from human nature, because it seems inseparable from self-love. The same principle in this instance carries us forward and backward, to future and to past ages. We imagine that the things, which affect us, must affect posterity: this sentiment runs through mankind, from Cæsar down to the parish clerk in Pope's miscellany. We are fond of preserving, as far as it is in our frail power, the memory of our own adventures, of those of our own time, and of those that preceded it. Rude heaps of stones have been raised, and ruder hymns have been composed, for this purpose, by nations who had not yet the use of arts and letters. To go no farther back, the triumphs of Odin were celebrated in runic songs, and the feats of our British ancestors were recorded in those of their bards. The savages of America have the same custom at this day: and long historical ballads of their huntings and their wars are sung at all their festivals. There is no need of saying how this passion grows, among civilized nations, in proportion to the means of gratifying it: but let us observe that the same principle of nature directs us as strongly, and more generally as well as more early, to indulge our own curiosity, instead of preparing to gratify that of others. The child hearkens with delight to the tales of his nurse: he learns to read, and he devours with eagerness fabulous legends and novels: in riper years he applies himself to history, or to that which he takes for history, to authorized romance: and, even in age, the desire of knowing what has happened to other men, yields to the desire alone of relating what has happened to ourselves. Thus history, true or false, speaks to our passions always. What pity is it, my lord, that even the best should speak to our understandings so seldom?

That it does so, we have none to blame but ourselves. Nature has done her part. She has opened this study to every man who can read and think: and what she has made the most agreeable, reason can make the most useful, application of our minds. But if we consult our reason, we shall be far from following the examples of our fellow-creatures, in this as in most other cases, who are so proud of being rational. We shall neither read to soothe our indolence, nor to gratify our vanity: as little shall we content ourselves to drudge like grammarians and critics, that others may be able to study with greater ease and profit, like philosophers and statesmen; as little shall we affect the slender merit of becoming great scholars at the expense of groping all our lives in the dark mazes of antiquity. All these mistake the true drift of study, and the true use of history. Nature gave us curiosity to excite the industry of our minds; but she never intended it should be made the principal, much less the sole object of their application. The true and proper object of this application is a constant improvement in private and in public virtue. An application to any study that tends neither directly nor indirectly to make us better men and better citizens, is at best but a specious and ingenious sort of idleness, to use an expression of Tillotson: and the knowledge we acquire by it is a creditable kind of ignorance, nothing more. This creditable kind of ignorance is, in my opinion, the whole benefit which the generality of men, even of the most learned, reap from the study of history: and yet the study of history seems to me, of all other, the most proper to train us up to private and public virtue.

Your lordship may very well be ready by this time, and after so much bold censure on my part, to ask me, what then is the true use of history? in what respects it may serve to make us better and wiser? and what method is to be pursued in the study of it, for attaining these great ends? I will answer you by quoting what I have read somewhere or other, in Dionysius of Halicarnassus. I think that history is philosophy teaching by examples. We need but to cast our eyes on the world, and we shall see the daily force of example; we need but to turn them inward, and we shall soon discover why example has this force. "Pauci prudentia", says Tacitus, "honesta ab deterioribus, utilia ab noxiis discernunt: plures aliorum eventis docentur." [1] Such is the imperfection of human understanding, such the frail temper of our minds, that abstract or general propositions, though ever so true, appear obscure or doubtful to us very often, till they are explained by examples; and that the wisest lessons in favour of virtue go but a little way to convince the judgment, and determine the will, unless they are enforced by the same means; and we are obliged to apply to ourselves what we see happen to other men. Instructions by precept have the further disadvantage of coming on the authority of others, and frequently require a long deduction of reasoning. "Homines amplius oculis, quam auribus, credunt: longum iter est per praecepta, breve et efficax per exempla." [2]

The school of example, my lord, is the world: and the masters of this school are history and experience. I am far from contending that the former is preferable to the latter. I think upon the whole otherwise: but this I say, that the former is absolutely necessary to prepare us for the latter, and to accompany us whilst we are under the

[1] Few men have the sagacity to distinguish what is virtuous from what is vicious, what is expedient from what is harmful. The majority are taught by the experience of others.

[2] Men trust their eyes more than they do their ears: long is the path of precept, that of example short and effective.

discipline of the latter, that is, through the whole course of our lives. No doubt some few men may be quoted, to whom nature gave what art and industry can give to no man. But such examples will prove nothing against me, because I admit that the study of history, without experience, is insufficient; but assert that experience itself is so without genius. Genius is preferable to the other two; but I would wish to find the three together: for how great soever a genius may be, and how much soever he may acquire new light and heat, as he proceeds in his rapid course, certain it is that he will never shine with the full lustre, nor shed the full influence he is capable of, unless to his own experience he adds the experience of other men and other ages. Genius, without the improvement, at least of experience, is what comets once were thought to be, a blazing meteor, irregular in his course, and dangerous in his approach; of no use to any system, and able to destroy any. Mere sons of earth, if they have experience without any knowledge of the history of the world, are but half scholars in the science of mankind. And if they are conversant in history without experience, they are worse than ignorant; they are pedants, always incapable, sometimes meddling and presuming. The man, who has all three, is an honour to his country, and a public blessing.

———————

Besides the advantage of beginning our acquaintance with mankind sooner, and of bringing with us into the world, and the business of it, such a cast of thought and such a temper of mind, as will enable us to make a better use of our experience, there is this further advantage in the study of history, that the improvement we make by it extends to more objects, and is made at the expense of other men: whereas that improvement, which is the effect of our own experience, is confined to fewer objects, and is made at our own expense. To state the account fairly, therefore, between these two improvements; though the latter be the more valuable, yet allowance being made on one side for the much greater number of examples that history presents to us, and deduction being made on the other of the price we often pay for our experience, the value of the former will rise in proportion. " I have recorded these things," says Polybius, after giving an account of the defeat of Regulus, "that they who read these commentaries may be rendered better by them; for all men have two ways of improvement, one arising from their own experience, and one from the experience of others." Polybius goes on, and concludes, "that since the first of these ways exposes us to great labour and peril, whilst the second works the same good effect, and is attended by no evil circumstance, every one ought to take for granted that the study of history is the best school where he can learn how to conduct himself in all the situations of life ".

Thus again, as to events that stand recorded in history; we see them all, we see them as they followed one another, or as they produced one another, causes or effects, immediate or remote. We are cast back, as it were, into former ages: we live with the men who lived before us, and we inhabit countries that we never saw. Place is enlarged, and time prolonged, in this manner; so that the man who applies himself early to the study of history, may acquire in a few years, and before he sets his foot abroad in the world, not only a more extended knowledge of mankind, but the experience of more centuries than any of the patriarchs saw. The events we are witnesses of, in the course of the longest life, appear to us very often original, unprepared, single, and unrelative, if I may use such an expression for want of a better in English; in French I would say *isolés*: they appear such very often, are called accidents, and looked on as the effects of chance; a word, by the way, which is in constant use, and has frequently no determinate meaning. We get over the present difficulty, we improve the momentary advantage, as well as we can, and we look no farther. Experience can carry us no farther; for experience can go a very little way back in discovering causes : and effects are not the objects of experience till they happen. From hence many errors in judgment, and by consequence in conduct, necessarily arise. And here too lies the difference we are speaking of between history and experience. The advantage on the side of the former is double. In ancient history, as we have said already, the examples are complete, which are incomplete in the course of experience. The beginning, the progression, and the end appear, not of particular reigns, much less of particular enterprises, or systems of policy alone, but of governments, of nations, of empires, and of all the various systems that have succeeded one another in the course of their duration. In modern history, the examples may be, and sometimes are, incomplete; but they have this advantage when they are so, that they serve to render complete the examples of our own time. Experience is doubly defective; we are born too late to see the beginning, and we die too soon to see the end of many things. History supplies both these defects.

That the study of history, far from making us wiser and more useful citizens, as well as better men, may be of no advantage whatsoever; that it may serve to render us mere antiquaries and scholars; or that it may help to make us forward coxcombs and prating pedants, I have already allowed. But this is not the fault of history: and to convince us that it is not, we need only contrast the true use of history with the use that is made of it by such men as these. We ought always to keep in mind that history is philosophy teaching by examples how to conduct ourselves in all the situations of private and public life; that, therefore, we must apply ourselves to it in a philosophical spirit and manner; that we must rise from particular to general knowledge, and that we must fit ourselves for the society and business of mankind by accustoming our minds to reflect and meditate on the characters we find described, and the course of events we find related there.

There are certain general principles, and rules of life and conduct, which always must be true, because they are conformable to the invariable nature of things. He who studies history as he would study philosophy, will soon distinguish and collect them, and by doing so will soon form to himself a general system of ethics and politics on the surest foundations, on the trial of these principles and rules in all ages, and on the confirmation of them by universal experience. I said he will distinguish them; for once more I must say, that as to particular modes of actions and measures of conduct which the customs of different countries, the manners of different ages, and the circumstances of different conjunctures, have appropriated, as it were, it is always ridiculous, or imprudent and dangerous, to employ them. But this is not all. By contemplating the vast variety of particular characters and events; by examining the strange combinations of causes — different, remote, and seemingly opposite — that often concur in producing one effect, and the surprising fertility of one single and uniform cause in the producing of a multitude of effects as different, as remote, and

seemingly as opposite; by tracing carefully, as carefully
as if the subject he considers were of personal and immediate concern to him, all the minute and sometimes
scarce perceivable circumstances, either in the character
of actors, or in the course of actions, that history enables
him to trace, and according to which the success of
affairs, even the greatest, is mostly determined; by these,
and such methods as these, for I might descend into a
much greater detail, a man of parts may improve the
study of history to its proper and principal use; he
may sharpen the penetration, fix the attention of his
mind, and strengthen his judgment; he may acquire
the faculty and the habit of discerning quicker, and
looking farther; and of exerting that flexibility and
steadiness, which are necessary to be joined in the
conduct of all affairs that depend on the concurrence
or opposition of other men.

As men are apt to carry their judgments into extremes,
there are some that will be ready to insist that all history
is fabulous, and that the very best is nothing better than
a probable tale, artfully contrived, and plausibly told,
wherein truth and falsehood are indistinguishably blended
together.   All the instances, and all the commonplace
arguments, that Bayle and others have employed to
establish this sort of Pyrrhonism, will be quoted: and
from thence it will be concluded, that if the pretended
histories of the first ages, and of the originals of nations,
be too improbable and too ill-vouched to procure any
degree of belief, those histories that have been writ later,
that carry a greater air of probability, and that boast even
contemporary authority, are at least insufficient to gain
that degree of firm belief, which is necessary to render
the study of them useful to mankind.   But here that
happens which often happens: the premises are true, and

the conclusion is false; because a general axiom is established precariously on a certain number of partial observations. This matter is of consequence; for it tends to ascertain the degrees of assent that we may give to history.

I agree, then, that history has been purposely and systematically falsified in all ages, and that partiality and prejudice have occasioned both voluntary and involuntary errors even in the best. Let me say without offence, my lord, since I may say it with truth and am able to prove it, that ecclesiastical authority has led the way to this corruption in all ages, and all religions. How monstrous were the absurdities that the priesthood imposed on the ignorance and superstition of mankind in the pagan world, concerning the originals of religions and governments, their institutions and rites, their laws and customs! What opportunities had they for such impositions, whilst the keeping the records and collecting the traditions was in so many nations the peculiar office of this order of men! A custom highly extolled by Josephus, but plainly liable to the grossest frauds, and even a temptation to them. If the foundations of Judaism and Christianity have been laid in truth, yet what numberless fables have been invented to raise, to embellish, and to support these structures, according to the interest and taste of the several architects! That the Jews have been guilty of this will be allowed: and, to the shame of Christians, if not of Christianity, the fathers of one Church have no right to throw the first stone at the fathers of the other.

I might fill many pages with instances of extravagant fables that have been invented in several nations, to celebrate their antiquity, to ennoble their originals, and to make them appear illustrious in the arts of peace and the triumphs of war. When the brain is well heated,

and devotion or vanity, the semblance of virtue or real
vice, and, above all, disputes and contests, have inspired
that complication of passions we term zeal, the effects
are much the same, and history becomes very often a
lying panegyric or a lying satire; for different nations,
or different parties in the same nation, belie one another
without any respect for truth, as they murder one another without any regard to right or sense of humanity.
Religious zeal may boast this horrid advantage over civil
zeal, that the effects of it have been more sanguinary, and
the malice more unrelenting. In another respect they
are more alike, and keep a nearer proportion: different
religions have not been quite so barbarous to one another
as sects of the same religion; and, in like manner, nation
has had better quarter from nation, than party from party.
But, in all these controversies, men have pushed their
rage beyond their own and their adversaries' lives: they
have endeavoured to interest posterity in their quarrels,
and by rendering history subservient to this wicked purpose, they have done their utmost to perpetuate scandal,
and to immortalize their animosity. The Heathen taxed
the Jews even with idolatry; the Jews joined with the
Heathen to render Christianity odious: but the Church,
who beat them at their own weapons during these contests,
has had this further triumph over them, as well as over
the several sects that have arisen within her own pale:
the works of those who have writ against her have been
destroyed; and whatever she advanced, to justify herself
and to defame her adversaries, is preserved in her annals,
and the writings of her doctors.

A reasonable man will not establish the truth of history
on single, but on concurrent testimony. If there be
none such, he will doubt absolutely: if there be a little
such, he will proportion his assent or dissent accordingly.

A small gleam of light, borrowed from foreign anecdotes, serves often to discover a whole system of falsehood: and even they who corrupt history frequently betray themselves by their ignorance or inadvertency. Examples whereof I could easily produce. Upon the whole matter, in all these cases we cannot be deceived essentially, unless we please; and therefore there is no reason to establish Pyrrhonism, that we may avoid the ridicule of credulity.

In all other cases, there is less reason still to do so; for when histories and historical memorials abound, even those that are false serve to the discovery of the truth. Inspired by different passions, and contrived for opposite purposes, they contradict; and, contradicting, they convict one another. Criticism separates the ore from the dross, and extracts from various authors a series of true history, which could not have been found entire in any one of them, and will command our assent, when it is formed with judgment, and represented with candour. If this may be done, as it has been done sometimes, with the help of authors who writ òn purpose to deceive; how much more easily, and more effectually may it be done, with the help of those who paid a greater regard to truth? In a multitude of writers there will be always some, either incapable of gross prevarication from the fear of being discovered, and of acquiring infamy whilst they seek for fame; or else attached to truth upon a nobler and surer principle.

4. DAVID HUME

(From the *Essays: Moral, Political, and Literary,* published in 1741. This extract is far from doing justice to this great historian and philosopher; but it is characteristic of one side of his genius and of the tone often adopted by the writers of the eighteenth century. They were apt to underrate the seriousness of their work, to speak of their speculations, even when they touched the most profound subjects, as "entertaining and amusing", never forgetting that it was the general public and not merely the learned world that they desired to reach. Hume is quite in harmony with the tone of the writers of the time, whether in England or France, in specially commending the study of history to his "female readers".)

THERE is nothing which I would recommend more earnestly to my female readers than the study of history as an occupation, of all others, the best suited both to their sex and education, much more instructive than their ordinary books of amusement, and more entertaining than those serious compositions, which are usually to be found in their closets. Among other important truths, which they may learn from history, they may be informed of two particulars, the knowledge of which may contribute very much to their quiet and repose. That our sex, as well as theirs, are far from being such perfect creatures as they are apt to imagine, and that love is not the only passion which governs the male world, but is often overcome by avarice, ambition, vanity, and a thousand other passions. Whether they be the false representations of mankind in those two particulars, which endear novels and romances so much to the fair sex, I know not; but must confess, that I am sorry to see them have such an aversion to matter of fact, and such an appetite for falsehood. I remember I was once desired by a young beauty, for whom I had some passion, to send her some novels and romances for her amusement to the country; but was not so ungenerous as to take the advantage, which such a course of reading might have given me, being resolved not to make use of poisoned arms against her. I therefore sent her Plutarch's *Lives*, assuring her, at the same time, that there was not a word of truth in them from beginning to end. She perused them very attentively, till she came to the lives of Alexander and Cæsar, whose names she had heard of by accident, and then returned me the book, with many reproaches for deceiving her.

I may, indeed, be told, that the fair sex have no such aversion to history as I have represented, provided it be *secret* history, and contain some memorable transaction proper to excite their curiosity. But as I do not find that truth, which is the basis of history, is at all regarded in these anecdotes, I cannot admit of this as a proof of their passion for that study. However this may be, I see not why the same curiosity might not receive a more proper direction, and lead them to desire accounts of those who lived in past ages, as well as of their contemporaries. What is it to Cleora whether Fulvia entertains a secret commerce of love with Philander or not? Has she not equal reason to be pleased, when she is informed (what is whispered about amongst historians) that Cato's sister had an intrigue with Cæsar, and palmed her son, Marcus Brutus, upon her husband for his own, though in reality he was her gallant's? And are not the loves of Messalina or Julia as proper subjects of discourse as any intrigue that this city has produced of late years?

But I know not whence it comes that I have been thus seduced into a kind of raillery against the ladies; unless, perhaps, it proceed from the same cause, which makes the person, who is the favourite of the company, be often the object of their good-natured jests and pleasantries. We are pleased to address ourselves after any manner to one who is agreeable to us, and at the same time presume, that nothing will be taken amiss by a person who is secure of the good opinion and affections of everyone present. I shall now proceed to handle my subject more seriously, and shall point out the many advantages which flow from the study of history, and show how well suited it is to everyone, but particularly to those who are debarred the severer studies, by the tenderness of their complexion, and the weakness of their education. The advantages found in history seem to be of three kinds, as it amuses the fancy, as it improves the understanding, and as it strengthens virtue.

In reality, what more agreeable entertainment to the mind than to be transported into the remotest ages of the world, and to observe human society, in its infancy, making the first faint essays towards the arts and sciences; to see the policy of government and the civility of conversation refining by degrees, and everything which is ornamental to human life advancing towards its perfection? To remark the rise, progress, declension, and final extinction of the most flourishing empires; the virtues which contributed to their greatness, and the vices which drew on their ruin? In short, to see all the human race, from the beginning of time, pass, as it were, in review before us, appearing in their true colours without any of those disguises which, during their lifetime, so much perplexed the judgment of the beholders. What spectacle can be imagined so magnificent, so various, so interesting? What amusement, either of the senses or imagination, can be compared with it? Shall those trifling pastimes, which engross so much of our time, be preferred as more satisfactory, and more fit to engage our attention? How perverse must that taste be which is capable of so wrong a choice of pleasures!

But history is a most improving part of knowledge, as well as an agreeable amusement; and a great part of what we commonly call erudition, and value so highly, is nothing but an acquaintance with historical facts. An extensive knowledge of this kind belongs to men of letters; but I must think it an unpardonable ignorance in persons, of whatever sex or condition, not to be acquainted with the history of their own country, together with the histories of ancient Greece and Rome. A woman may behave herself with good manners, and have even some vivacity in her turn of wit; but where her mind is so unfurnished, it is impossible her conversation can afford any entertainment to men of sense and reflection.

I must add, that history is not only a valuable part of knowledge, but opens the door to many other parts, and affords materials to most of the sciences. And, indeed, if we consider the shortness of human life, and our limited knowledge, even of what passes in our own time, we must be sensible that we should be for ever children in understanding, were it not for this invention, which extends our experience to all past ages, and to the most distant nations, making them contribute as much to our improvement in wisdom as if they had actually lain under our observation. A man acquainted with history may, in some respect, be said to have lived from the beginning of the world, and to have been making continual additions to his stock of knowledge in every century.

There is also an advantage in that experience, which is acquired by history, above what is learned by the practice of the world, that it brings us acquainted with human affairs, without diminishing in the least from the most delicate sentiments of virtue. And to tell the truth, I know not any study or occupation so unexceptionable as history in this particular. Poets can paint virtue in the most charming colours; but as they address themselves entirely to the passions, they often become advocates for vice. Even philosophers are apt to bewilder themselves in the subtlety of their speculations; and we have seen some go so far as to deny the reality of all moral distinctions. But I think it a remark worthy the attention of the speculative, that the historians have been, almost without exception, the true friends of virtue, and have always represented it in its proper colours, however they may have erred in their judgments of particular persons. Machiavel himself discovers a true sentiment of virtue in his history of Florence. When he talks as a politician, in his general reasonings, he considers poisoning, assassination, and perjury as lawful arts of power; but when he speaks as an historian, in his particular narrations, he shows so keen an indignation against vice, and so warm an approbation of virtue in many passages, that I could not forbear applying to him that remark of Horace, that if you chase away Nature, though with ever so great indignity, she will always return upon you. Nor is this combination of historians in favour of virtue at all difficult to be accounted for. When a man of business enters into life and action, he is more apt to consider the characters of men, as they have relation to his interest, than as they stand in themselves; and has his judgment warped on every occasion by the violence of his passion. When a philosopher contemplates characters and manners in his closet, the general abstract view of the objects leaves the mind so cold and unmoved, that the sentiments of nature have no room to play, and he scarce feels the difference between vice and virtue. History keeps in a just medium between these extremes, and places the objects in their true point of view. The writers of history, as well as the readers, are sufficiently interested in the characters and events to have a lively sentiment of blame or praise, and, at the same time, have no particular interest or concern to pervert their judgment.

> " Verae voces tum demum pectore ab imo
> Eliciuntur." —*Lucret.*

5. EDWARD GIBBON

(From the Autobiography. It is difficult to find in Gibbon any statement of the objects which, in his opinion, the historian should set before him; or of the advantages which flow from the study of history. But the following extracts give, as he would have said, an "entertaining" account of the genesis of his great work, and of the studies that he pursued in preparation for it. Gibbon rewrote his autobiography again and again. These extracts are taken from Memoir D in Murray's edition of the *Autobiographies*.)

BUT alas! we were soon summoned, my father from his farm, and myself from my books, by the sound of the militia drum.

We had rashly given our names to that popular service, and when the order came down for embodying the South Battalion of the Hampshire, it was too soon to repent, and too late to retreat. In this corps, which consisted of four hundred and seventy-six officers and men, my proper station was that of first captain; but as the major was my father, and the lieutenant-colonel commandant (Sir Thomas Worsley) was my friend, as they were often absent and always inattentive, I exercised the effective government of the battalion, to the titular command of which I was promoted after the resignation of the one and the death of the other. The history of our bloodless campaigns may be despatched in a few words: we moved our quarters from Dover to the Devizes; we guarded some thousands of French prisoners in Porchester and Sissinghurst castles; we formed a part of a summer camp near Winchester; and had the war continued another year, we might have vied in appearance and discipline with the best of our brethren. A youth of any spirit is fired even by the play of arms, and my enthusiasm aspired to the character of a *real* soldier; but the martial fever was cooled by the enjoyment of our mimic Bellona, who soon revealed to my eyes her naked deformity, and I seriously panted for a life of liberty and letters. A larger introduction into the English world was a poor compensation for such company and such employment—for the loss of time and health in the daily and nocturnal exercises of the field and of the bottle.

> " Of seeming arms they make a short essay;
> Then hasten to get drunk—the business of the day."

From a service without danger I might have fled without disgrace; but my father's authority and the entreaties of the colonel kept me chained to the oar, till at the end of two years and seven months, I was released by the final dissolution of the militia. Yet even in the tumult of an inn, a barrack, or a camp, I had stolen some moments of literary amusement: I had read Homer in my tent; and in our more settled quarters, I forced my rude companions to respect those studies of which they were ignorant. My accidental profession invited me to examine the best authors on military tactics: I compared the theory of the ancients with the practice of the moderns; and the captain of the Hampshire Grenadiers (the reader may smile) has not been useless to the historian of the Roman empire. A rare and short leave of absence I sometimes snatched; and in my excursions to Buriton each precious hour was diligently occupied.

A tour of Italy had long been the object of my hopes and wishes; but I shall not expatiate on a country which has been seen by thousands and described by hundreds of our modern travellers. From the regular streets of

Turin, the Gothic cathedral of Milan, and the marble
palaces of Genoa, I proceeded by the ordinary road to
the beauties of Florence, the wonders of Rome, and the
curiosities of Naples.   After a winter of enchantment in
the Eternal City, I again ascended along the Adriatic
coast to the galleries of Bologna and the canals of
Venice, bestowed a rapid glance on the Palladian archi-
tecture of Vicenza and the amphitheatre of Verona, and
again repassing Mount Cenis I returned home by way of
Lyons and Paris.   During my stay at Florence I read
the classics of the country with a Tuscan master; but as
I never could acquire a liberty of speech, my intercourse
with the natives was rare and formal, and my leisure was
idly wasted with the English colony, the pilgrims of the
year.   For the harmony of music I had no ear, and I
beheld the capital works of painting and sculpture with
the eyes of nature rather than of art.   But I was not
ignorant of the science of medals and manuscripts, I had
accurately surveyed the geography of Italy, and the topo-
graphy of ancient Rome; her heroes and her writers
were present to my mind, and the flame of enthusiasm
was blended with the light of critical enquiry.   I must
not forget the day, the hour, the most interesting in my
literary life.   It was on the fifteenth of October, in the
gloom of evening, as I sat musing in the Capitol, while
the barefooted friars were chanting their litanies in the
temple of Jupiter, that I conceived the first thought ot
my history.   My original plan was confined to the decay
of the city, my reading and reflection pointed to that
aim; but several years elapsed, and several avocations
intervened, before I grappled with the decline and fall ot
the Roman empire.

Between my Essay and the first volume of the decline
and fall, fifteen years (1761–1776) of strength and free-

dom elapsed, without any other publications than my criticism on Warburton and some articles in the *Mémoires Littéraires*. The four first years may be deducted for the militia and foreign travel, the three last for the actual composition of my first volume; but in the intermediate period (1765–1772) I gradually advanced from the wish to the hope, from the hope to the design, from the design to the execution, of my historical work, of whose nature and limits I had yet a very inadequate notion. The classics, as low as Tacitus, the younger Pliny, and Juvenal, were my old and familiar companions; and from this era I insensibly plunged into the ocean of the Augustan history. The subsidiary rays of laws, of medals, and of inscriptions were cast on their proper objects; and in the descending series I investigated, with my pen almost always in my hand, the original records, both Greek and Latin, from Dion Cassius to Ammianus Marcellinus, from the reign of Trajan to the last age of the Western Cæsars. Through the darkness of the Middle Ages I explored my way, in the annals and antiquities of Italy of Muratori, and compared them with the parallel or transverse lines of Sigonius and Maffei, of Baronius and Pagi, till I almost grasped the ruins of Rome in the fourteenth century, without suspecting that this final chapter must be attained by the labour of six quartos and twenty years. The connection of the church and state compelled me to assume the character of a theologian; I read my Greek Bible, with the notes of the best interpreters; and the ecclesiastical history of Eusebius was accompanied by the apologies of the primitive Christians. I am not ashamed to acknowledge a debt of gratitude to the inimitable accuracy of Tillemont, the learned paradoxes of Dodwell, the sagacity of Mosheim, the candour of Beausobre, the free spirit of Middleton, the good sense of Le Clere, the just morality of Barbeyrac, and the honest diligence of Lardner; but the labours of the moderns have served to guide, not to supersede, my enquiries; and as I have presumed to think with my own reason, so I have endeavoured to see with my own eyes. These various studies were productive of many remarks and memorials, and in this supplement I may perhaps introduce a critical dissertation on the miraculous darkness of the Passion.

6. MACAULAY

(The following extracts are from an Essay on History in Macaulay's Miscellaneous Works. It does not form a part of his Collected Essays; but the same views on history may be found expressed there in the Essay on Sir William Temple. This essay appeared in the *Edinburgh Review* of May, 1828.)

TO write history respectably—that is, to abbreviate despatches, and make extracts from speeches, to intersperse in due proportion epithets of praise and abhorrence, to draw up antithetical characters of great men, setting forth how many contradictory virtues and vices they united, and abounding in *withs* and *withouts* —all this is very easy. But to be a really great historian is perhaps the rarest of intellectual distinctions. Many scientific works are, in their kind, absolutely perfect. There are poems which we should be inclined to designate as faultless, or as disfigured only by blemishes which pass unnoticed in the general blaze of excellence. There are speeches, some speeches of Demosthenes particularly, in which it would be impossible to alter a word without altering it for the worse. But we are acquainted with no history which approaches to our notion of what a history ought to be—with no history which does not widely depart, either on the right hand or on the left, from the exact line.

The cause may easily be assigned. This province of literature is a debatable land. It lies on the confines of two distinct territories. It is under the jurisdiction of two hostile powers; and, like other districts similarly situated, it is ill defined, ill cultivated, and ill regulated. Instead of being equally shared between its two rulers, the Reason and the Imagination, it falls alternately under the sole and absolute dominion of each. It is sometimes fiction. It is sometimes theory.

History, it has been said, is philosophy teaching by examples. Unhappily, what the philosophy gains in soundness and depth, the examples generally lose in vividness. A perfect historian must possess an imagination sufficiently powerful to make his narrative affecting and picturesque. Yet he must control it so absolutely as to content himself with the materials which he finds, and to refrain from supplying deficiences by additions of his own. He must be a profound and ingenious reasoner. Yet he must possess sufficient self-command to abstain from casting his facts in the mould of his hypothesis. Those who can justly estimate these almost insuperable difficulties will not think it strange that every writer should have failed, either in the narrative or in the speculative department of history.

Narration, though an important part of the business of a historian, is not the whole. To append a moral to a work of fiction is either useless or superfluous. A fiction may give a more impressive effect to what is already known; but it can teach nothing new. If it presents to us characters and trains of events to which our experience furnishes us with nothing similar, instead of deriving instruction from it, we pronounce it unnatural. We do not form our opinions from it; but we try it by our pre-conceived opinions. Fiction, therefore, is essentially imitative. Its merit consists in its resemblance to a model with which we are already familiar, or to which at least we can instantly refer. Hence it is that the anecdotes which interest us most strongly in authentic narrative are offensive when introduced into novels; that what is called the romantic part of history is in fact the

least romantic. It is delightful as history, because it
contradicts our previous notions of human nature, and
of the connection of causes and effects. It is, on that
very account, shocking and incongruous in fiction. In
fiction, the principles are given, to find the facts: in
history, the facts are given, to find the principles; and
the writer who does not explain the phenomena as well
as state them performs only one-half of his office. Facts
are the mere dross of history. It is from the abstract
truth which interpenetrates them, and lies latent among
them like gold in the ore, that the mass derives its whole
value: and the precious particles are generally combined
with the baser in such a manner that the separation is a
task of the utmost difficulty.

The writers of history seem to entertain an aristo-
cratical contempt for the writers of memoirs. They think
it beneath the dignity of men who describe the revolutions of nations to dwell on the details which constitute
the charm of biography. They have imposed on themselves a code of conventional decencies as absurd as that
which has been the bane of the French drama. The
most characteristic and interesting circumstances are
omitted or softened down, because, as we are told, they
are too trivial for the majesty of history. The majesty
of history seems to resemble the majesty of the poor
King of Spain, who died a martyr to ceremony because
the proper dignitaries were not at hand to render him
assistance.

That history would be more amusing if this etiquette
were relaxed will, we suppose, be acknowledged. But
would it be less dignified or less useful? What do we
mean when we say that one past event is important and
another insignificant? No past event has any intrinsic
importance. The knowledge of it is valuable only as it

leads us to form just calculations with respect to the future. A history which does not serve this purpose, though it may be filled with battles, treaties, and commotions, is as useless as the series of turnpike tickets collected by Sir Matthew Mite.

Let us suppose that Lord Clarendon, instead of filling hundreds of folio pages with copies of state papers, in which the same assertions and contradictions are repeated till the reader is overpowered with weariness, had condescended to be the Boswell of the Long Parliament. Let us suppose that he had exhibited to us the wise and lofty self-government of Hampden, leading while he seemed to follow, and propounding unanswerable arguments in the strongest forms with the modest air of an inquirer anxious for information; the delusions which misled the noble spirit of Vane; the coarse fanaticism which concealed the yet loftier genius of Cromwell, destined to control a mutinous army and a factious people, to abase the flag of Holland, to arrest the victorious arms of Sweden, and to hold the balance firm between the rival monarchies of France and Spain. Let us suppose that he had made his Cavaliers and Roundheads talk in their own style; that he had reported some of the ribaldry of Rupert's pages, and some of the cant of Harrison and Fleetwood. Would not his work in that case have been more interesting? Would it not have been more accurate?

A history in which every particular incident may be true may on the whole be false. The circumstances which have most influence on the happiness of mankind, the changes of manners and morals, the transition of communities from poverty to wealth, from knowledge to ignorance, from ferocity to humanity—these are, for the most part, noiseless revolutions. Their progress is rarely indicated by what historians are pleased to call important events. They are not achieved by armies, or enacted by senates. They are sanctioned by no treaties, and recorded in no archives. They are carried on in every school, in every church, behind ten thousand counters, at ten thousand firesides. The upper current of society presents no certain criterion by which we can judge of the direction in which the under current flows. We read of defeats and victories. But we know that nations may be miserable amidst victories and prosperous amidst defeats. We read of the fall of wise ministers and of the rise of profligate favourites. But we must remember how small a proportion the good or evil effected by a single statesman can bear to the good or evil of a great social system.

Bishop Watson compares a geologist to a gnat mounted on an elephant, and laying down theories as to the whole internal structure of the vast animal, from the phenomena of the hide. The comparison is unjust to the geologists; but it is very applicable to those historians who write as if the body politic were homogeneous, who look only on the surface of affairs, and never think of the mighty and various organization which lies deep below.

In the works of such writers as these, England, at the close of the Seven Years' war, is in the highest state of prosperity: at the close of the American war she is in a miserable and degraded condition; as if the people were not on the whole as rich, as well governed, and as well educated at the latter period as at the former. We have read books called Histories of England, under the reign of George the Second, in which the rise of Methodism is not even mentioned. A hundred years hence this breed of authors will, we hope, be extinct. If it should still exist, the late ministerial interregnum will be described in terms which will seem to imply that all government was at an end; that the social contract was annulled; and that the hand of every man was against his neighbour, until the wisdom and virtue of the new cabinet educed order out of the chaos of anarchy. We are quite certain that misconceptions as gross prevail at this moment respecting many important parts of our annals.

The effect of historical reading is analogous, in many respects, to that produced by foreign travel. The student, like the tourist, is transported into a new state of society. He sees new fashions. He hears new modes of expression. His mind is enlarged by contemplating the wide diversities of laws, of morals, and of manners. But men may travel far, and return with minds as contracted as if they had never stirred from their own market-town. In the same manner, men may know the dates of many battles and the genealogies of many royal houses, and yet be no wiser. Most people look at past times as princes look at foreign countries. More than one illustrious stranger has landed on our island amidst the shouts of a mob, has dined with the king, has hunted with the master of the staghounds, has seen the guards reviewed, and a knight of the garter installed, has cantered along Regent Street, has visited St. Paul's, and noted down its dimensions; and has then departed, thinking that he has seen England. He has, in fact, seen a few public buildings, public men, and public ceremonies. But of the vast and complex system of society, of the fine shades of national character, of the practical operation of government and laws, he knows nothing. He who would understand these things rightly must not confine his observations to palaces and solemn days. He must see ordinary men as they appear in their ordinary business and in their ordinary pleasures. He must mingle in the crowds of the exchange and the coffee-house. He must obtain admittance to the convivial table and the domestic hearth. He must bear with vulgar expressions. He must not shrink from exploring even the retreats of misery. He who wishes to understand the condition of mankind in former ages must proceed on the same principle. If he attends only to public transactions, to wars, congresses, and debates, his studies will be as unprofitable as the travels of those imperial, royal, and serene sovereigns who form their judgment of our island from having gone in state to a few fine sights, and from having held formal conferences with a few great officers.

The perfect historian is he in whose work the character and spirit of an age is exhibited in miniature. He relates no fact, he attributes no expression to his characters, which is not authenticated by sufficient testimony. But, by judicious selection, rejection, and arrangement, he gives to truth those attractions which have been usurped by fiction. In his narrative a due subordination is observed: some transactions are prominent, others retire. But the scale on which he represents them is increased or diminished, not according to the dignity of the persons concerned in them, but according to the degree in which they elucidate the condition of society and the nature of man. He shows us the court, the camp, and the senate. But he shows us also the nation. He considers no anecdote, no peculiarity of manner, no familiar saying, as too insignificant for his notice which is not too insignificant to illustrate the operation of laws, of religion, and of education, and to mark the progress of the human mind. Men will not merely be described, but will be made intimately known to us. The changes of manners will be indicated, not merely by a few general phrases or a few extracts from statistical documents, but by appropriate images presented in every line.

If a man, such as we are supposing, should write the history of England, he would assuredly not omit the

battles, the sieges, the negotiations, the seditions, the
ministerial changes. But with these he would intersperse
the details which are the charm of historical romances.
At Lincoln Cathedral there is a beautiful painted window,
which was made by an apprentice out of the pieces of
glass which had been rejected by his master. It is so
far superior to every other in the church, that, according
to the tradition, the vanquished artist killed himself from
mortification. Sir Walter Scott, in the same manner, has
used those fragments of truth which historians have
scornfully thrown behind them in a manner which may
well excite their envy. He has constructed out of their
gleanings works which, even considered as histories, are
scarcely less valuable than theirs. But a truly great
historian would reclaim those materials which the novelist
has appropriated. The history of the government, and
the history of the people, would be exhibited in that
mode in which alone they can be exhibited justly, in
inseparable conjunction and intermixture. We should
not then have to look for the wars and votes of the
Puritans in Clarendon, and for their phraseology in *Old
Mortality*; for one half of King James in Hume, and for
the other half in the *Fortunes of Nigel.*

The early part of our imaginary history would be rich
with colouring from romance, ballad, and chronicle. We
should find ourselves in the company of knights such as
those of Froissart, and of pilgrims such as those who
rode with Chaucer from the Tabard. Society would be
shown from the highest to the lowest—from the royal
cloth of state to the den of the outlaw; from the throne
of the legate, to the chimney-corner where the begging
friar regaled himself. Palmers, minstrels, crusaders—the
stately monastery, with the good cheer in its refectory
and the high-mass in its chapel—the manor-house, with
its hunting and hawking — the tournament, with the

heralds and ladies, the trumpets and the cloth of gold—
would give truth and life to the representation. We
should perceive, in a thousand slight touches, the importance of the privileged burgher, and the fierce and haughty
spirit which swelled under the collar of the degraded
villain. The revival of letters would not merely be described in a few magnificent periods. We should discern,
in innumerable particulars, the fermentation of mind, the
eager appetite for knowledge, which distinguished the
sixteenth from the fifteenth century. In the Reformation
we should see, not merely a schism which changed the
ecclesiastical constitution of England and the mutual
relations of the European powers, but a moral war which
raged in every family, which set the father against the son,
and the son against the father, the mother against the
daughter, and the daughter against the mother. Henry
would be painted with the skill of Tacitus. We should
have the change of his character from his profuse and
joyous youth to his savage and imperious old age. We
should perceive the gradual progress of selfish and tyrannical passions in a mind not naturally insensible or
ungenerous; and to the last we should detect some
remains of that open and noble temper which endeared
him to a people whom he oppressed, struggling with the
hardness of despotism and the irritability of disease. We
should see Élizabeth in all her weakness and in all her
strength, surrounded by the handsome favourites whom
she never trusted, and the wise old statesmen whom she
never dismissed, uniting in herself the most contradictory
qualities of both her parents—the coquetry, the caprice,
the petty malice of Anne—the haughty and resolute spirit
of Henry. We have no hesitation in saying that a great
artist might produce a portrait of this remarkable woman
at least as striking as that in the novel of *Kenilworth*,
without employing a single trait not authenticated by

ample testimony. In the meantime, we should see arts cultivated, wealth accumulated, the conveniences of life improved. We should see the keeps, where nobles, insecure themselves, spread insecurity around them, gradually giving place to the halls of peaceful opulence, to the oriels of Longleat, and the stately pinnacles of Burleigh. We should see towns extended, deserts cultivated, the hamlets of fishermen turned into wealthy havens, the meal of the peasant improved, and his hut more commodiously furnished. We should see those opinions and feelings which produced the great struggle against the house of Stuart slowly growing up in the bosom of private families, before they manifested themselves in parliamentary debates. Then would come the civil war. Those skirmishes on which Clarendon dwells so minutely would be told, as Thucydides would have told them, with perspicuous conciseness. They are merely connecting links. But the great characteristics of the age, the loyal enthusiasm of the brave English gentry, the fierce licentiousness of the swearing, dicing, drunken reprobates, whose excesses disgraced the royal cause, the austerity of the Presbyterian Sabbaths in the city, the extravagance of the independent preachers in the camp, the precise garb, the severe countenance, the petty scruples, the affected accent, the absurd names and phrases which marked the Puritans — the valour, the policy, the public spirit, which lurked beneath these ungraceful disguises — the dreams of the raving Fifth-monarchy-man, the dreams, scarcely less wild, of the philosophic republican—all those would enter into the representation, and render it at once more exact and more striking.

The instruction derived from history thus written would be of a vivid and practical character. It would be received by the imagination as well as by the reason. It would be not merely traced by the mind, but branded into it. Many truths, too, would be learned, which can be learned in no other manner. As the history of states is generally written, the greatest and most momentous revolutions seem to come upon them like supernatural inflictions, without warning or cause. But the fact is, that such revolutions are almost always the consequences of moral changes, which have gradually passed on the mass of the community, and which originally proceed far before the progress is indicated by any public measure. An intimate knowledge of the domestic history of nations is therefore absolutely necessary to the prognosis of political events. A narrative, defective in this respect, is as useless as a medical treatise which should pass by all the symptoms attendant on the early stage of disease and mention only what occurs when the patient is beyond the reach of remedies.

A historian, such as we have been attempting to describe, would indeed be an intellectual prodigy. In his mind, powers scarcely compatible with each other must be tempered into an exquisite harmony. We shall sooner see another Shakspeare or another Homer. The highest excellence to which any single faculty can be brought would be less surprising than such a happy and delicate combination of qualities. Yet the contemplation of imaginary models is not an unpleasant or useless employment of the mind. It cannot, indeed, produce perfection; but it produces improvement, and nourishes that generous and liberal fastidiousness which is not inconsistent with the strongest sensibility to merit, and which, while it exalts our conceptions of the art, does not render us unjust to the artist.

7. THOMAS ARNOLD

(From the Inaugural Lecture delivered by Doctor Arnold as Regius Professor of History in December, 1841.)

THE general idea of history seems to be that it is the biography of a society. It does not appear to me to be history at all, but simple biography, unless it finds in the persons who are its subject something of a common purpose, the accomplishment of which is the object of their common life. History is to this common life of many what biography is to the life of an individual. Take, for instance, any common family, and its members are soon so scattered from one another, and are engaged in such different pursuits, that though it is possible to write the biography of each individual, yet there can be no such thing, properly speaking, as the history of the family. But suppose all the members to be thrown together in one place, amidst strangers or savages, and there immediately becomes a common life—an unity of action, interest, and purpose, distinct from others around them, which renders them at once a fit subject of history. Perhaps I ought not to press the word "purpose"; because purpose implies consciousness in the purposer, and a society may exist without being fully conscious of its own business as a society. But whether consciously or not, every society—so much is implied in the very word —must have in it something of community; and so far as the members of it are members, so far as they are each incomplete parts, but taken together form a whole, so far, it appears to me, their joint life is the proper subject of history.

Accordingly we find the term history often applied to small and subordinate societies. We speak of the history of literary or scientific societies; we have histories of commercial bodies; histories of religious orders; histories of universities. In all these cases history has to do with that which the several members of each of these societies have in common: it is, as I said, the biography of their common life. And it seems to me that it could not perform its office, if it had no distinct notion in what this common life consisted.

But if the life of every society belongs to history, much more does the life of that highest and sovereign society which we call a state or a nation. And this, in fact, is considered the proper subject of history; insomuch that if we speak of it simply, without any qualifying epithet, we understand by it not the biography of any subordinate society, but of some one or more of the great national societies of the human race, whatever political form their bond of connection may assume. And thus we get a somewhat stricter definition of history properly so-called; we may describe it not simply as the biography of a society, but as the biography of a political society or commonwealth.

Now in a commonwealth or state, that common life which I have ventured to call the proper subject of history, finds its natural expression in those who are invested with the state's government. Here we have the varied elements which exist in the body of a nation, reduced as it were to an intelligible unity; the state appears to have a personal existence in its government. And where that government is lodged in the hands of a single individual, then biography and history seem to melt into one another, inasmuch as one and the same person combines in himself his life as an individual, and the common life of his nation.

That common life, then, which we could not find represented by any private members of the state, is brought to a head, as it were, and exhibited intelligibly and visibly in the government. And thus history has generally taken governments as the proper representatives of nations; it has recorded the actions and fortunes of kings or national councils, and has so appeared to fulfil its appointed duty, that of recording the life of a commonwealth. Nor is this theoretically other than true; the idea of government is no doubt that it should represent the person of the state, desiring those ends, and contriving those means to compass them, which the state itself, if it could act for itself, ought to desire and to contrive. But practically and really this has not been so; governments have less represented the state than themselves; the individual life has so predominated in them over the common life, that what in theory is history, because it is recording the actions of a government, and the government represents the nation, becomes, in fact, no more than biography; it does but record the passions and actions of an individual who is abusing the state's name for the purposes of selfish rather than public good.

We see, then, in practice how history has been beguiled, so to speak, from its proper business, and has ceased to describe the life of a commonwealth. For taking governments as the representatives of commonwealths, which in idea they are, history has watched their features, as if from them might be drawn the portrait of their respective nations. But as in this she has been deceived, so her portraits were necessarily unlike what they were intended to represent; they were not portraits of the commonwealth, but of individuals.

Again, the life of a commonwealth, like that of an individual, has two parts; it is partly external, and partly internal. Its external life is seen in its dealings with other commonwealths; its internal life, in its dealings with itself. Now in the former of these, government must ever be in a certain degree the representative of the nation: there must here be a community of interest, at least up to a certain point, and something also of a community of feeling. If a government be overthrown by a foreign enemy, the nation shares in the evils of the conquest and in the shame of the defeat; if it be victorious, the nation, even if not enriched with the spoils, is yet proud to claim its portion of the glory. And thus in describing a government's external life, that is, its dealings with other governments, history has remained, and could not but remain, true to its proper subject; for in foreign war the government must represent more than its individual self; here it really must act and suffer, not altogether but yet to a considerable degree, for and with the nation.

I have assumed that the external life of a state is seen in little else than its wars; and this, I fear, is true, with scarcely any qualification. A state acting out of itself is mostly either repelling violence, or exercising it upon others; the friendly intercourse between nation and nation is for the most part negative. A nation's external life, then, is displayed in its wars, and here history has been sufficiently busy. The wars of the human race have been recorded when the memory of everything else has perished. Nor is this to be wondered at; for the external life of nations, as of individuals, is at once the most easily known and the most generally interesting. Action, in the common sense of the word, is intelligible to everyone; its effects are visible and sensible; in itself, from its necessary connection with outward nature, it is often highly picturesque, while the qualities displayed in it are some of those which by an irresistible instinct we are most led to admire. Ability in the adaptation of means to ends, courage, endurance, and perseverance, the complete conquest over some of the most universal weaknesses of our nature, the victory over some of its most powerful temptations, these are qualities displayed in action, and particularly in war. And it is our deep sympathy with these qualities, much more than any fondness for scenes of horror and blood, which has made descriptions of battles, whether in poetry or history, so generally attractive. He who can read these without interest, differs, I am inclined to think, from the mass of mankind rather for the worse than for the better; he rather wants some noble qualities which other men have, than possesses some which other men want.

But still we have another life besides that of outward action; and it is this inward life after all which determines the character of the actions and of the man. And how eagerly do we desire in those great men whose actions fill so large a space in history, to know not only what they did but what they were: how much do we prize their letters or their recorded words, and, not least, such words as are uttered in their most private moments, which enable us to look, as it were, into the very nature of that mind, whose distant effects we know to be so marvellous. But a nation has its inward life no less than an individual, and from this its outward life also is characterized. For what does a nation effect by war, but either the securing of its existence or the increasing of its power? We honour the heroism shown in accomplishing these objects; but power, nay even existence, are not ultimate ends. The question may be asked of every created being why he should live at all, and no satisfactory answer can be given, if his life does not, by doing God's will consciously or unconsciously, tend to God's glory and to the good of his brethren. And if a nation's annals contain the records of deeds ever so heroic, done in defence of the national freedom or existence, still we may require that the freedom or the life so bravely maintained shouid be also employed for worthy purposes; or else even the names of Thermopylæ and of Morgarten become in after-years a reproach rather than a glory.

8. HENRY THOMAS BUCKLE

(From Chapter I of the *History of Civilisation in England.* The first volume was published in 1857. It is interesting to compare its strong, scientific tone with the more literary quality of Macaulay, even when their views are in superficial agreement.)

OF all the great branches of human knowledge, history is that upon which most has been written, and which has always been most popular. And it seems to be the general opinion that the success of historians has, on the whole, been equal to their industry; and that if on this subject much has been studied, much also is understood.

This confidence in the value of history is very widely diffused, as we see in the extent to which it is read, and in the share it occupies in all plans of education. Nor can it be denied that, in a certain point of view, such confidence is perfectly justifiable. It cannot be denied that materials have been collected which, when looked at in the aggregate, have a rich and imposing appearance. The political and military annals of all the great countries in Europe, and of most of those out of Europe, have been carefully compiled, put together in a convenient form, and the evidence on which they rest has been tolerably well sifted. Great attention has been paid to the history of legislation, also to that of religion: while considerable, though inferior, labour has been employed in tracing the progress of science, of literature, of the fine arts, of useful inventions, and, latterly, of the manners and comforts of the people. In order to increase our knowledge of the past, antiquities of every kind have been examined; the sites of ancient cities have been laid bare, coins dug up and deciphered, inscriptions copied, alphabets restored, hieroglyphics interpreted, and, in some instances, long-forgotten languages reconstructed and rearranged. Several of the laws which regulate the changes of human speech have been discovered, and, in the hands of philologists, have been made to elucidate even the most obscure periods in the early migration of nations. Political economy has been raised to a science, and by it much light has been thrown on the causes of that unequal distribution of wealth which is the most fertile source of social disturbance. Statistics have been so sedulously cultivated, that we have the most extensive information, not only respecting the material interests of men, but also respecting their moral peculiarities; such as, the amount of different crimes, the proportion they bear to each other, and the influence exercised over them by age, sex, education, and the like. With this great movement physical geography has kept pace: the phenomena of climate have been registered, mountains measured, rivers surveyed and tracked to their source, natural productions of all kinds carefully studied, and their hidden properties unfolded; while every food which sustains life has been chemically analysed, its constituents numbered and weighed, and the nature of the connection between them and the human frame has, in many cases, been satisfactorily ascertained. At the same time, and that nothing should be left undone which might enlarge our knowledge of the events by which man is affected, there have been instituted circumstantial researches in many other departments; so that in regard to the most civilized peoples, we are now acquainted with the rate of their mortality, of their marriages, the proportion of their births, the character of their employments, and the fluctuations both in their wages and in the prices of the commodities necessary to their existence. These and similar facts have been collected, methodized, and are ripe for use. Such results, which form, as it were, the anatomy of a nation, are remarkable for their minuteness; and to them there have been joined other results less minute, but more extensive. Not only have the actions and characteristics of the great nations been recorded, but a prodigious number of different tribes in all parts of the known world have been visited and described by travellers, thus enabling us to compare the condition of mankind in every stage of civilization, and under every variety of circumstance. When we, moreover, add that this curiosity respecting our fellow-creatures is apparently insatiable; that it is constantly increasing; that the means of gratifying it are also increasing; and that most of the observations which have been made are still preserved; —when we put all these things together, we may form a faint idea of the immense value of that vast body of facts which we now possess, and by the aid of which the progress of mankind is to be investigated.

But if, on the other hand, we are to describe the use that has been made of these materials, we must draw a very different picture. The unfortunate peculiarity of the history of man is, that although its separate parts have been examined with considerable ability, hardly anyone has attempted to combine them into a whole, and ascertain the way in which they are connected with each other. In all the other great fields of enquiry the necessity of generalization is universally admitted, and noble efforts are being made to rise from particular facts in order to discover the laws by which those facts are governed. So far, however, is this from being the usual course of historians, that among them a strange idea prevails that their business is merely to relate events, which they may occasionally enliven by such moral and political reflections as seem likely to be useful. According to this scheme, any author who, from indolence of thought or from natural incapacity, is unfit to deal with the highest branches of knowledge, has only to pass some years in reading a certain number of books, and then he is qualified to be an historian: he is able to write the history of a great people, and his work becomes an authority on the subject which it professes to treat.

The establishment of this narrow standard has led to results very prejudicial to the progress of our knowledge. Owing to it, historians, taken as a body, have never recognized the necessity of such a wide and preliminary study as would enable them to grasp their subject in the whole of its natural relations. Hence the singular spectacle of one historian being ignorant of political economy; another knowing nothing of law; another nothing of ecclesiastical affairs and changes of opinion; another neglecting the philosophy of statistics, and another physical science; although these topics are the most essential of all, inasmuch as they comprise the principal circumstances by which the temper and character of mankind have been affected, and in which they are displayed. These important pursuits being, however, cultivated, some by one man and some by another, have been isolated rather than united: the aid which might be derived from analogy and from mutual illustration has been lost; and no disposition has been shown to concentrate them upon history, of which they are, properly speaking, the neces sary components.

Since the early part of the eighteenth century, a few great thinkers have indeed arisen who have deplored the backwardness of history, and have done everything in their power to remedy it. But these instances have been extremely rare: so rare, that in the whole literature of Europe there are not more than three or four really original works which contain a systematic attempt to investigate the history of man according to those exhaustive methods which in other branches of knowledge have proved successful, and by which alone empirical observations can be raised to scientific truths.

Among historians in general, we find, after the sixteenth century, and especially during the last hundred years, several indications of an increasing comprehensiveness of view, and of a willingness to incorporate into their works subjects which they would formerly have excluded. By this means their assemblage of topics has become more diversified, and the mere collection and relative position of parallel facts has occasionally suggested generalizations no traces of which can be found in the earlier literature of Europe. This has been a great gain, in so far as it has familiarized historians with a wider range of thought, and encouraged those habits of speculation which, though liable to abuse, are the essential condition of all real knowledge, because without them no science can be constructed.

But, notwithstanding that the prospects of historical literature are certainly more cheering now than in any former age, it must be allowed that, with extremely few exceptions, they are only prospects, and that as yet scarcely anything has been done towards discovering the principles which govern the character and destiny of nations. What has been actually effected I shall endeavour to estimate in another part of this Introduction: at present it is enough to say, that for all the higher purposes of human thought history is still miserably deficient, and presents that confused and anarchical appearance natural to a subject of which the laws are unknown, and even the foundation unsettled.

Our acquaintance with history being so imperfect, while our materials are so numerous, it seems desirable that something should be done on a scale far larger than has hitherto been attempted, and that a strenuous effort should be made to bring up this great department of enquiry to a level with other departments, in order that we may maintain the balance and harmony of our knowledge.   It is in this spirit that the present work has been conceived.   To make the execution of it fully equal to the conception is impossible; still I hope to accomplish for the history of man something equivalent, or at all events analogous, to what has been effected by other inquirers for the different branches of natural science. In regard to nature, events apparently the most irregular and capricious have been explained, and have been shown to be in accordance with certain fixed and universal laws.   This has been done because men of ability, and, above all, men of patient, untiring thought, have studied natural events with the view of discovering their regularity: and if human events were subjected to a similar treatment, we have every right to expect similar results.   For it is clear that they who affirm that the facts of history are incapable of being generalized, take for granted the very question at issue.   Indeed they do more than this.   They not only assume what they cannot prove, but they assume what in the present state of knowledge is highly improbable.   Whoever is at all acquainted with what has been done during the last two centuries must be aware that every generation demonstrates some events to be regular and predictable, which the preceding generation had declared to be irregular and unpredictable; so that the marked tendency of advancing civilization is to strengthen our belief in the universality of order, of method, and of law.   This being the case, it follows that if any facts, or class of facts, have not yet been reduced to order, we, so far from pronouncing them to be irreducible, should rather be guided by our experience of the past, and should admit the probability that what we now call inexplicable will at some future time be explained. This expectation of discovering regularity in the midst of confusion is so familiar to scientific men, that among the most eminent of them it becomes an article of faith: and if the same expectation is not generally found among historians, it must be ascribed partly to their being of inferior ability to the investigators of nature, and partly to the greater complexity of those social phenomena with which their studies are concerned.

Both these causes have retarded the creation of the science of history. The most celebrated historians are manifestly inferior to the most successful cultivators of physical science: no one having devoted himself to history who in point of intellect is at all to be compared with Kepler, Newton, or many others that might be named. And as to the greater complexity of the phenomena, the philosophic historian is opposed by difficulties far more formidable than those which meet the student of nature; since, while on the one hand, his observations are more liable to those causes of error which arise from prejudice and passion, he, on the other hand, is unable to employ the great physical resource of experiment, by which we can often simplify even the most intricate problems in the external world.

It is not, therefore, surprising that the study of the movements of Man should be still in its infancy, as compared with the advanced state of the study of the movements of Nature. Indeed the difference between the progress of the two pursuits is so great, that while in physics the regularity of events, and the power of predicting them, are often taken for granted, even in cases still unproved, a similar regularity is in history not only not taken for granted, but is actually denied. Hence it is that whoever wishes to raise history to a level with other branches of knowledge is met by a preliminary obstacle; since he is told that in the affairs of men there is something mysterious and providential, which makes them impervious to our investigations, and which will always hide from us their future course.   To this it might be sufficient to reply, that such an assertion is gratuitous; that it is by its nature incapable of proof; and that it is, moreover, opposed by the notorious fact that everywhere else increasing knowledge is accompanied by increasing confidence in the uniformity with which under the same circumstances, the same events must succeed each other.   It will, however, be more satisfactory to probe the difficulty deeper, and enquire at once into the foundation of the common opinion that history must always remain in its present empirical state, and can never be raised to the rank of a science.   We shall thus be led to one vast question, which indeed lies at the root of the whole subject, and is simply this: Are the actions of men, and therefore of societies, governed by fixed laws, or are they the result either of chance or of supernatural interference?   The discussion of these alternatives will suggest some speculations of considerable interest . . .

It will be observed, that the preceding proofs of our actions being regulated by law, have been derived from statistics; a branch of knowledge which, though still in its infancy, has already thrown more light on the study of human nature than all the sciences put together.   But although the statisticians have been the first to investigate this great subject by treating it according to those methods of reasoning which in other fields have been found successful; and although they have, by the application of numbers, brought to bear upon it a very powerful engine for eliciting truth, we must not, on that account, suppose that there are no other resources remaining by which it may likewise be cultivated: nor should we infer that because the physical sciences have not yet been applied to history, they are therefore inapplicable to it. Indeed, when we consider the incessant contact between man and the external world, it is certain that there must be an intimate connection between human actions and physical laws; so that if physical science has not hitherto been brought to bear upon history, the reason is, either that historians have not perceived the connection, or else that, having perceived it, they have been destitute of the knowledge by which its workings can be traced. Hence there has arisen an unnatural separation of the two great departments of enquiry, the study of the internal and that of the external: and although, in the present state of European literature, there are some unmistakable symptoms of a desire to break down this artificial barrier, still it must be admitted that as yet nothing has been actually accomplished towards effecting so great an end. The moralists, the theologians, and the metaphysicians continue to prosecute their studies without much respect for what they deem the inferior labours of scientific men; whose enquiries, indeed, they frequently attack as dangerous to the interests of religion, and as inspiring us with an undue confidence in the resources of the human understanding. On the other hand, the cultivators of physical science, conscious that they are an advancing body, are naturally proud of their own success; and, contrasting their discoveries with the more stationary position of their opponents, are led to despise pursuits the barrenness of which has now become notorious.

It is the business of the historian to mediate between these two parties, and reconcile their hostile pretensions by showing the point at which their respective studies ought to coalesce. To settle the terms of this coalition will be to fix the basis of all history. For since history deals with the actions of men, and since their actions are merely the product of a collision between internal and external phenomena, it becomes necessary to examine the relative importance of those phenomena, to enquire into the extent to which their laws are known, and to ascertain the resources for future discovery possessed by these two great classes, the students of the mind and the students of nature. This task I shall endeavour to accomplish in the next two chapters; and if I do so with anything approaching to success, the present work will at least have the merit of contributing something towards filling up that wide and dreary chasm which, to the hindrance of our knowledge, separates subjects that are intimately related, and should never be disunited.

9. THOMAS CARLYLE

(From the essay on "History", written in 1830; but, though so early a piece of work, it represents fairly the spirit that animated Carlyle's historical writing to the end. See preface, pp. lviii–lxi.)

UNDER a limited, and the only practicable shape, history proper, that part of history which treats of remarkable action, has, in all modern as well as ancient times, ranked among the highest arts, and perhaps never stood higher than in these times of ours. For whereas, of old, the charm of history lay chiefly in gratifying our common appetite for the wonderful, for the unknown, and her office was but as that of a minstrel and story-teller, she has now farther become a schoolmistress, and professes to instruct in gratifying. Whether, with the stateliness of that venerable character, she may not have taken up something of its austerity and frigidity; whether, in the logical terseness of a Hume or Robertson, the graceful ease and gay pictorial heartiness of a Herodotus or Froissart may not be wanting, is not the question for us here. Enough that all learners, all enquiring minds of every order, are gathered round her footstool, and reverently pondering her lessons, as the true basis of wisdom. Poetry, divinity, politics, physics have each their adherents and adversaries; each little guild supporting a defensive and offensive war for its own special domain; while the domain of history is as a free emporium, where all these belligerents peaceably meet and furnish themselves; and sentimentalist and utilitarian, sceptic and theologian, with one voice advise us: Examine history, for it is "philosophy teaching by experience".

Far be it from us to disparage such teaching, the very attempt at which must be precious. Neither shall we too rigidly enquire: how much it has hitherto profited? Whether most of what little practical wisdom men have has come from study of professed history, or from other less boasted sources, whereby, as matters now stand, a Marlborough may become great in the world's business, with no history save what he derives from Shakespeare's plays? Nay, whether in that same teaching by experience, historical philosophy has yet properly deciphered the first element of all science in this kind: what the aim and significance of that wondrous changeful life it investigates and paints may be? Whence the course of man's destinies in this earth originated, and whither they are tending? Or, indeed, if they have any course and tendency, are really guided forward by an unseen mysterious wisdom, or only circle in blind mazes without recognizable guidance? Which questions, altogether fundamental, one might think, in any philosophy of history, have, since the era when monkish annalists were wont to answer them by the long-ago extinguished light of their missal and breviary, been by most philosophical historians only glanced at dubiously and from afar; by many, not so much as glanced at.

The truth is, two difficulties, never wholly surmountable, lie in the way. Before philosophy can teach by experience, the philosophy has to be in readiness, the experience must be gathered and intelligibly recorded. Now, overlooking the former consideration, and with regard only to the latter, let anyone who has examined the current of human affairs, and how intricate, perplexed, unfathomable, even when seen into with our own eyes, are their thousandfold blending movements, say whether the true representing of it is easy or impossible. Social life is the aggregate of all the individual men's lives who constitute society; history is the essence of innumerable biographies. But if one biography, nay our own biography, study and recapitulate it as we may, remains in so many points unintelligible to us, how much more must these million, the very facts of which, to say nothing of the purport of them, we know not, and cannot know!

Neither will it adequately avail us to assert that the general inward condition of life is the same in all ages; and that only the remarkable deviations from the common endowment and common lot, and the more important variations which the outward figure of life has from time to time undergone, deserve memory and record. The inward condition of life, it may rather be affirmed, the conscious or half-conscious aim of mankind, so far as men are not mere digesting machines, is the same in no two ages; neither are the more important outward variations easy to fix on, or always well capable of representation. Which was the greatest innovator, which was the more important personage in man's history, he who first led armies over the Alps, and gained the victories of Cannæ and Thrasymene, or the nameless boor who first hammered out for himself an iron spade? When the oak-tree is felled, the whole forest echoes with it; but a hundred acorns are planted silently by some unnoticed breeze. Battles and war-tumults, which for the time din every ear, and with joy or terror intoxicate every heart, pass away like tavern-brawls; and, except some few Marathons and Morgartens, are remembered by accident, not by desert. Laws themselves, political constitutions, are not our life, but only the house wherein our life is led; nay, they are but the bare walls of the house; all whose essential furniture, the inventions and traditions, and daily habits that regulate and support our existence, are the work not of Dracos and Hampdens, but of Phœnician mariners, of Italian masons and Saxon metallurgists, of philosophers, alchymists, prophets, and all the long-forgotten train of artists and artisans, who from the first have been jointly teaching us how to think and how to act, how to rule over spiritual and over physical nature. Well may we say that of our history the more important part is lost without recovery; and, as thanksgivings were once wont to be offered " for un-recognized mercies ", look with reverence into the dark untenanted places of the past, where, in formless obli-vion, our chief benefactors, with all their sedulous endea-vours, but not with the fruit of these, lie entombed.

But the artist in history may be distinguished from the artisan in history; for here, as in all other provinces, there are artists and artisans; men who labour mechanic-ally in a department, without eye for the whole, not feel-ing that there is a whole; and men who inform and ennoble the humblest department with an idea of the whole, and habitually know that only in the whole is the partial to be truly discerned. The proceedings and the duties of these two, in regard to history, must be altogether different. Not, indeed, that each has not a real worth in his several degree. The simple husbandman can till his field, and, by knowledge he has gained of its soil, sow it with the fit grain, though the deep rocks and central fires are unknown to him: his little crop hangs under and over the firmament of stars, and sails through whole untracked celestial spaces, between Aries and Libra; nevertheless it ripens for him in due season, and he gathers it safe into his barn. As a husbandman he is blameless in disregarding those higher wonders; but as a thinker, and a careful inquirer into nature, he were wrong. So likewise is it with the historian, who ex-amines some special aspect of history; and from this or that combination of circumstances, political, moral, economical, and the issues it has led to, infers that such and such properties belong to human society, and that the like circumstances will produce the like issue; which inference, if other trials confirm it, must be held true and practically valuable. He is wrong only, and an artisan, when he fancies that these properties, discovered or discoverable, exhaust the matter; and sees not, at every step, that it is inexhaustible.

However, that class of cause-and-effect speculators, with whom no wonder would remain wonderful, but all things in heaven and earth must be computed and "accounted for"; and even the unknown, the infinite in man's life, had under the words *enthusiasm, superstition, spirit of the age*, and so forth, obtained, as it were, an algebraical symbol and given value,—have now well-nigh played their part in European culture; and may be considered, as in most countries, even in England itself where they linger the latest, verging towards extinction. He who reads the inscrutable book of nature as if it were a merchant's ledger, is justly suspected of having never seen that book, but only some school synopsis thereof; from which, if taken for the real book, more error than insight is to be derived.

Doubtless, also, it is with a growing feeling of the infinite nature of history, that in these times, the old principle, division of labour, has been so widely applied to it. The political historian, once almost the sole cultivator of history, has now found various associates, who strive to elucidate other phases of human life; of which, as hinted above, the political conditions it is passed under are but one, and though the primary, perhaps not the most important, of the many outward arrangements. Of this historian himself, moreover, in his own special department, new and higher things are beginning to be expected. From of old, it was too often to be reproachfully observed of him, that he dwelt with disproportionate fondness in senate-houses, in battle-fields, nay, even in kings' antechambers; forgetting, that far away from such scenes, the mighty tide of thought and action was still rolling on its wondrous course, in gloom and brightness; and in its thousand remote valleys, a whole world of existence, with or without an earthly sun of happiness to warm it, with or without a heavenly sun of holiness to purify and sanctify it, was blossoming and fading, whether the " famous victory " were won or lost. The time seems coming when much of this must be amended; and he who sees no world but that of courts or camps, and writes only how soldiers were drilled and shot, and how this ministerial conjuror out-conjured that other, and then guided, or at least held, something which he called the rudder of government, but which was rather the spigot of taxation, where-with, in place of steering, he could tap, and the more cunningly the nearer the lees,—will pass for a more or less instructive gazetteer, but will no longer be called a historian.

However, the political historian, were his work per-formed with all conceivable perfection, can accomplish but a part, and still leaves room for numerous fellow-labourers. Foremost among these comes the ecclesiastical historian; endeavouring, with catholic or sectarian view, to trace the progress of the church; of that portion of the social establishments, which respects our religious condition; as the other portion does our civil, or rather, in the long run, our economical condition. Rightly conducted, this department were undoubtedly the more important of the two; inasmuch as it concerns us more to understand how man's moral well-being had been and might be promoted, than to understand in the like sort his physical well-being; which latter is ultimately the aim of all political arrangements. For the physically happiest is simply the safest, the strongest; and, in all conditions of government, power (whether of wealth as in these days, or of arms and adherents as in old days) is the only outward emblem and purchase-money of good. True good, however, unless we reckon pleasure synonymous with it, is said to be rarely, or rather never, offered for sale in the market where that coin passes current. So that, for man's true advantage, not the outward condition of his life, but the inward and spiritual, is of prime influence; not the form of government he lives under, and the power he can accumulate there, but the church he is a member of, and the degree of moral elevation he can acquire by means of its instruction. Church history, then, did it speak wisely, would have momentous secrets to teach us: nay, in its highest degree, it were a sort of holy writ; our sacred books being, indeed, only a history of the primeval church, as it first arose in man's soul, and symbolically embodied itself in his external life. How far our actual church historians fall below such unattainable standards, nay, below quite attainable approximations thereto, we need not point out. Of the ecclesiastical historian we have to complain, as we did of his political fellow-craftsman, that his inquiries turn rather on the outward mechanism, the mere hulls and superficial accidents of the object, than on the object itself: as if the church lay in bishops' chapter-houses, and ecumenic council-halls, and cardinals' conclaves, and not far more in the hearts of believing men; in whose walk and conversation, as influenced thereby, its chief manifestations were to be looked for, and its progress or decline ascertained. The history of the church is a history of the invisible as well as of the visible church; which latter, if disjoined from the former, is but a vacant edifice; gilded, it may be, and overhung with old votive gifts, yet useless, nay pestilentially unclean; to write whose history is less important than to forward its downfall.

Of a less ambitious character are the histories that relate to special separate provinces of human action; to sciences, practical arts, institutions, and the like; matters which do not imply an epitome of man's whole interest and form of life; but wherein, though each is still connected with all, the spirit of each, at least its material results, may be in some degree evolved without so strict a reference to that of the others. Highest in dignity and difficulty, under this head, would be our histories of philosophy, of man's opinions and theories respecting the nature of his being, and relations to the universe visible and invisible: which history, indeed, were it fitly treated, or fit for right treatment, would be a province of church history; the logical or dogmatical province thereof; for philosophy, in its true sense, is or should be the soul, of which religion, worship is the body; in the healthy state of things the philosopher and priest were one and the same. But philosophy itself is far enough from wearing this character; neither have its historians been men, generally speaking, that could in the smallest degree approximate it thereto. Scarcely since the rude era of the Magi and Druids has that same healthy identification of priest and philosopher had place in any country: but rather the worship of divine things, and the scientific investigation of divine things, have been in quite different hands, their relations not friendly but hostile. Neither have the Brückers and Bühles, to say nothing of the many unhappy Enfields who have treated of that latter department, been more than barren reporters, often unintelligent and unintelligible reporters, of the doctrine uttered; without force to discover how the doctrine originated, or what reference it bore to its time and country, to the spiritual position of mankind there and then. Nay, such a task did not perhaps lie before them, as a thing to be attempted.

Art also and literature are intimately blended with religion; as it were, outworks and abutments, by which that highest pinnacle in our inward world gradually connects itself with the general level, and becomes accessible therefrom. He who should write a proper history of poetry, would depict for us the successive revelations which man had obtained of the spirit of nature; under what aspects he had caught and endeavoured to body forth some glimpse of that unspeakable beauty, which in its highest clearness is religion, is the inspiration of a prophet, yet in one or the other degree must inspire every true singer, were his theme never so humble. We should see by what steps men had ascended to the temple; how near they had approached; by what ill hap they had, for long periods, turned away from it, and grovelled on the plain with no music in the air, or blindly struggled towards other heights. That among all our Eichhorns and Wartons there is no such historian, must be too clear to everyone. Nevertheless let us not despair of far nearer approaches to that excellence. Above all, let us keep the ideal of it ever in our eye; for thereby alone have we even a chance to reach it.

Our histories of laws and constitutions, wherein many a Montesquieu and Hallam has laboured with acceptance, are of a much simpler nature; yet deep enough if thoroughly investigated; and useful, when authentic, even with little depth. Then we have histories of medicine, of mathematics, of astronomy, commerce, chivalry, monkery; and Goguets and Beckmanns have come forward with what might be the most bountiful contribution of all, a history of inventions. Of all which sorts, and many more not here enumerated, not yet devised, and put in practice, the merit and the proper scheme may, in our present limits, require no exposition.

In this manner, though, as above remarked, all action is extended three ways, and the general sum of human action is a whole universe, with all limits of it unknown, does history strive by running path after path, through the impassable, in manifold directions and intersections, to secure for us some oversight of the whole; in which endeavour, if each historian look well around him from his path, tracking it out with the *eye*, not, as is more common, with the *nose*, she may at last prove not altogether unsuccessful. Praying only that increased division of labour do not here, as elsewhere, aggravate our already strong mechanical tendencies, so that in the manual dexterity for parts we lose all command over the whole, and the hope of any philosophy of history be farther off than ever,—let us all wish her great and greater success.

10. J. R. SEELEY

(From *The Teaching of Politics*, an inaugural lecture delivered at Cambridge in 1869. See Introduction, p. lxiii, where another extract is given from the same discourse.)

I TURN now to the question of the place of history in education. Why should history be studied? Mathematics may teach us precision in our thoughts, consecutiveness in our reasonings, and help us to raise general views into propositions accurately qualified and quantified. Classics may train in us the gift of speech, and at the same time elevate our minds with the thoughts of great men, and accustom us to exalted pleasures. Physical science may make us at home in nature, may educate the eye to observe, and reveal to us the excellent order of the universe we live in. Philosophy may make us acquainted with ourselves, may teach us to wonder in the difficult contemplation of that "dark fluxion, all unfixable by thought", the personal subject, and to watch its varied activities of apprehending, doubting, believing, knowing, desiring, loving, praising, blaming. Such are the manifest claims of these great subjects. Does history recommend itself by less obvious uses? Are its claims upon our attention less urgent? Are they obscure, difficult to state, or make good?

On the contrary, in discussing them I should feel embarrassed by the very easiness of my task, by the too glaring obviousness of the thesis I have to maintain, if I did not remember that after all the claims of history are practically very little admitted, not only in this university, but in English education generally. Let me say, then, that history is the school of statesmanship. If I were not addressing the students of Cambridge, I might take lower ground. I should choose rather to say, that as in a free country every citizen must be at least remotely interested in public affairs, it is desirable both for the public good and for the self-respect of each individual that great events and large interests should make part of the studies which are to prepare the future citizen for his duties, in order that he may follow with some intelligence the march of contemporary history, and may at least take an interest in the great concerns of his generation, even though he may not be called to take any considerable part in them, or to exert any great influence upon them. This more modest view is well worthy of consideration even here. The mass of those that are educated here will work in after-life in some very limited sphere. They will be compelled to concentrate themselves upon some humble task, to tread diligently some obscure routine. In these circumstances, their views are likely to become narrow, their thoughts paltry and sordid, if their education received here have not given them eyes to see whatever is largest and most elevating in life. Who has not met with some hard-working country curate, living remote from all intellectual society, and clinging with fondness to the remembrance of some college study which seems still to connect him with the world in which thinkers live? Who has not wished that he had some stouter rope to cling to than such reminiscences as college studies generally furnish—that he could remember something better, something more fruitful and suggestive, than scraps of Virgil or rules of gender and prosody? The most secluded man is living in the midst of momentous social changes, whether he can interpret them or not; the most humble task upon which any man is engaged makes part, even though he forgets it, of a total of human work by which a new age is evolved out of the old; the smallest individual life belongs to a national life which is great, to a universal life of the race which is illimitably great. There are studies which show a man the whole of which he is a part, and which throw light upon the great process of which his own life is a moment; the course along which the human race travels can be partially traced, and still more satisfactorily can the evolution of particular nations during limited periods be followed. Studies like this leave something more behind them than a refinement imparted to the mind, or even than faculties trained for future use; they furnish a theory of human affairs, a theory which is applicable to the phenomena with which life has to deal, and which serves the purpose of a chart or a compass. The man that has even a glimpse of such a theory, if the theory be itself a hopeful one, cannot but feel tranquillized and reassured; his life, from being a wandering or a drifting, becomes a journey or a voyage to a definite port; the changes that go on around him cease to appear capricious, and he is more often able to refer them to laws; hence his hopes become more measurable, and his plans more reasonable, and it may be that where his own efforts fail he is supported by faith in a law of good, of which he has traced the workings. Such a study— teaching each man his place in the republic of man, the post at which he is stationed, the function with which he is invested, the work that is required of him—such a study is history when comprehensively pursued.

History, then, I might well urge, is the school of public feeling and patriotism. Without at least a little knowledge of history no man can take a rational interest in politics, and no man can form a rational judgment about them without a good deal. There is no one here, however humble his prospects, who does not hope to do as

much as this.   There are, it is true, men who, without
any knowledge of history, are hot politicians, but it
would be better for them not to meddle with politics at
all: there are men who, knowing something of history,
are indifferentists in politics; it is because they do not
know history enough.   But what I choose rather to say
here, is not that history is the school of public feeling,
but that it is the school of statesmanship.   If it is an
important study to every citizen, it is the one important
study to the legislator and ruler.   There are many things,
doubtless, which it is desirable for the politician to know.
It is so much the better if he acquires the cultivation that
characterized the older race of our statesmen, the literary
and classical taste of Fox and Canning.   In the same way
a lawyer or a clergyman will be the better for being a
man of letters and scholarship.   But as the indispensable
thing for a lawyer is a knowledge of law, and for a clergyman the indispensable thing is a knowledge of divinity,
so I will venture to say that the indispensable thing for
a politician is a knowledge of political economy and of
history.   And, though perhaps we seldom think of it,
our university is, and must be, a great seminary of politicians.   Here are assembled to prepare themselves for
life the young men from whom the legislators and statesmen of the next age must be taken.   In this place they
will begin to form the views and opinions which will
determine their political career.   During the years they
spend here, and through influences that operate here,
perhaps not in the lecture-room, but at any rate in the
meetings of friends, or in the Union—their preparation
for political life is made.   It may seem a somewhat
exaggerated view of my function, but I cannot help
regarding myself as called to join with the professor of
political economy in presiding over this preparation.
What will at any rate be learnt *at* the university it should

be possible, I hold, to learn *from* the university, and I shall consider it to be in great part my own fault if this does not prove to be the case.

But when I say that a knowledge of history is indispensable to the statesman, there will rise up in the minds of many a doubt which it is desirable to lay. Political economy is indispensable; yes, but is history so necessary? After all, how easy for a profound historian to be a very shallow politician! The light which is shed upon contemporary affairs by the experience of remote ages and quite different states of society is surely faint enough. How utterly inapplicable seem inferences drawn from ancient Rome or Athens to the disputed political questions of the present day! Even less connection is there between mediæval barbarism and the complicated civilization we live in the midst of. Cannot high authorities be quoted to prove the uselessness of history in politics! No statesman ever towered above his contemporaries, not only in power, but in statesmanlike qualities, more decidedly than Sir Robert Walpole, who was a contemner of every kind of learning. On the other hand, Carteret, full of historical knowledge, makes but a poor figure. The most influential politician of the last age, Cobden, was never tired of sneering at the pedants who busied themselves with the affairs of other ages. Can we avoid suspecting him to have been in the right when we remark the evident superiority as a statesman of a man so unlearned and so moderately gifted as Cobden, to such a prodigy both of ability and historical acquirement as Macaulay? Outmatched in eloquence, in acuteness, in cultivation, and most of all in knowledge of history, how did Cobden succeed in winning the race at last? Was it not evidently by occupying himself exclusively with the questions of the time and the place, by encumbering himself with no useless knowledge, by not obscuring plain matters with ambitious illustrations, curious parallels, and obsolete authorities?

There is a very simple answer to all this. It is an argument that presupposes that history refers only to what is long past. Now it is not unnatural to give this meaning to the word history. We often in common parlance use the word so. We say that a thing belongs to history when it is past and gone. The title of history is given to books which contain narratives of occurrences that are past, and in most instances long past; it would not be given to a simple account of existing institutions or communities. We must remember, however, that the language of common life is one thing, and scientific language another. I do not intend on this occasion to give an exact definition of history as I understand it. The attempt to do so would lead me too far. But, however we determine the province of history, it must be under stood that I use the word, and shall throughout use it, without any thought of time past or present. There are multitudes of past occurrences which do not belong, in my view, to history, and there are multitudes of phe- nomena belonging to the present time which do. Phe- nomena are classed together in science according to resemblances in kind, not according to date. If history were taken to have for its subject-matter all that has happened in the world, it would not be a single science, but the inductive basis of all sciences whatever. Evi- dently it must be taken scientifically to deal only with occurrences and phenomena of a certain kind, and this being so, it is evident that *vice versâ* phenomena of that particular kind must be reckoned as historical, to what- ever period they belong. Now, whatever phenomena we exclude, it is evident that we must include political insti- tutions within the limits of historical phenomena. Every one, therefore, who studies political institutions, whether in the past or in the present, studies history.

It is therefore a misconception to think that a politician disregards history because he disregards the remote past. It is misleading to call Macaulay a student of history and Cobden a contemner of history. Both men evidently were occupied with phenomena of the same kind; they laboured at perfectly similar problems. The power and weakness of states, their advance and decline, their chances of success in war, their political and social institutions, the stability or transience of their order, the state of civilization, the influences promoting it and the influences retarding it, the character and qualifications of public men — these and similar questions occupied both. However you describe the studies of the one, you must give the same name to the studies of the other. It cannot be just to rank them among the students of different sciences because the one examined the power of Louis XIV, and the other that of the Emperor Nicholas; because the one studied the struggle of political freedom with despotism, and the other the struggle of commercial freedom with monopoly; or because the one was rather too much disposed to measure a country by its eminence in literature, and the other by its activity in manufactures and trade.

11. SAMUEL RAWSON GARDINER

(From the preface to the tenth volume of Gardiner's *History of England* from 1603 to 1642. This volume was published in 1884.)

IT is impossible to publish ten volumes of history without being led to face the question whether the knowledge acquired by the historian has any practical bearing on the problems of existing society—whether, in short, if, as has been said, history is the politics of the past, the historian is likely to be able to give better advice than other people on the politics of the present.

It does not indeed follow that if the reply to this question were in the negative, the labour of the historian would be wholly thrown away. All intellectual conception of nature is a good in itself, as enlarging and fortifying the mind, which is thereby rendered more capable of dealing with problems of life and conduct, though there may be no evident connection between them and the subject of study. Still, it must be acknowledged that there would be cause for disappointment if it could be shown that the study of the social and political life of men of a past age had no bearing whatever on the social and political life of the present.

At first sight it might seem as if this were the case. Certainly the politics of the seventeenth century, when studied for the mere sake of understanding them, assume a very different appearance from that which they had in the eyes of men who, like Macaulay and Forster, regarded them through the medium of their own political struggles. Eliot and Strafford were neither Whigs nor Tories, Liberals nor Conservatives. As Professor Seeley was, I believe, the first to teach directly, though the lesson is indirectly involved in every line written by Ranke, the father of modern historical research, the way in which Macaulay and Forster regarded the development of the past—that is to say, the constant avowed or unavowed comparison of it with the present—is altogether destructive of real historical knowledge. Yet those who take the truer view, and seek to trace the growth of political principles, may perhaps find themselves cut off from the present, and may regret that they are launched on questions so unfamiliar to themselves and their contemporaries. Hence may easily arise a dissatisfaction with the study of distant epochs, and a resolution to attend mainly to the most recent periods—to neglect, that is to say, the scientific study of history as a whole, through over-eagerness to make a practical application of its teaching.

Great, however, as the temptation may be, it would be most unwise to yield to it. It would be invidious to ask whether the counsel given by historians to statesmen has always been peculiarly wise, or their predictions peculiarly felicitous. It is enough to say that their mode of approaching facts is different from that of a statesman, and that they will always therefore be at a disadvantage in meddling with current politics. The statesman uses his imagination to predict the result of changes to be produced in the actually existing state of society, either by the natural forces which govern it, or by his own action. The historian uses his imagination in tracing out the causes which produced that existing state of society. As is always the case, habit gives to the intelligence of the two classes of men a peculiar ply which renders each comparatively inefficient for the purposes of the other. Where they meet is in the effort to reach a full comprehension of existing facts. So far as the understanding of existing facts is increased by a knowledge of the causes of their existence, or so far as the misunderstanding of them is diminished by clearing away false analogies supposed to be found in the past, the historian can be directly serviceable to the statesman.   He cannot expect to do more.   "Nur ein Theil der Kunst kann gelehrt werden, der Künstler braucht sie ganz."   The more of a student he is—and no one can be a historian without being a very devoted student—the more he is removed from that intimate contact with men of all classes and of all modes of thought, from which the statesman derives by far the greater part of that knowledge of mankind which enables him to give useful play to his imaginative power for their benefit.

If, however, the direct service to be rendered by the historian to the statesman is but slight, it is, I believe, impossible to over-estimate the indirect assistance which he can offer.   If the aims and objects of men at different periods are different, the laws inherent in human society are the same.   In the nineteenth, as well as the seventeenth century, existing evils are slowly felt, and still more slowly remedied.   In the nineteenth, as well as in the seventeenth century, efforts to discover the true remedy end for a long time in failure, or at least in very partial success, till at last the true remedy appears almost by accident and takes root, because it alone will give relief.

He, therefore, who studies the society of the past will be of the greater service to the society of the present in proportion as he leaves it out of account.   If the exceptional statesman can get on without much help from the historian, the historian can contribute much to the arousing of a statesmanlike temper in the happily increasing mass of educated persons without whose support the statesman is powerless.   He can teach them to regard society as ever evolving new wants and new diseases, and therefore requiring new remedies. He can teach them that true tolerance of mistakes and follies which is perfectly consistent with an ardent love of truth and wisdom. He can teach them to be hopeful of the future, because the evil of the present evolves a demand for a remedy which sooner or later is discovered by the intelligence of mankind, though it may sometimes happen that the whole existing organization of society is overthrown in the process. He can teach them also not to be too sanguine of the future, because each remedy brings with it fresh evils which have in their turn to be faced. These, it may be said, are old and commonplace lessons enough. It may be so, but the world has not yet become so wise as to be able to dispense with them.

A further question may arise as to the mode in which this teaching shall be conveyed. Shall a writer lay down the results at which he has arrived, and sketch out the laws which he conceives to have governed the course of society; or shall he, without forgetting these, make himself familiar, and strive to make his readers familiar, with the men and women in whose lives these laws are to be discerned? Either course is profitable, but it is the latter that I have chosen. As there is a danger of converting our knowledge either of past or present society into a collection of anecdotes, there is also a danger of regarding society as governed by eternal forces, and not by forces evolved out of itself. The statesman of the present wants perpetually to be reminded that he has to deal with actual men and women. Unless he sympathizes with them and with their ideas, he will never be able to help them, and in like manner a historian who regards the laws of human progress in the same way that he would regard the laws of mechanics, misses, in my opinion, the highest inspiration for his work. Unless the historian can feel an affectionate as well as an intelligent interest in the personages with whom he deals, he will hardly discover the key to the movements of the society of which they formed a part. The statesman, too, will be none the worse if, in studying the past, he is reminded that his predecessors had to deal with actual men and women in their complex nature, and if thereby he learns that pity for the human race which was the inspiring thought of the *New Atlantis*, and which is the source of all true and noble effort.

12. LORD ACTON

(From his Inaugural Lecture, delivered at Cambridge, June 11, 1895.)

IN the second quarter of this century a new era began
for historians.

I would point to three things in particular, out of many,
which constitute the amended order. Of the incessant
deluge of new and unsuspected matter I need say little.
For some years the secret archives of the papacy were
accessible at Paris; but the time was not ripe, and almost
the only man whom they availed was the archivist himself.
Towards 1830 the documentary studies began on a large
scale, Austria leading the way. Michelet, who claims,
towards 1836, to have been the pioneer, was preceded by
such rivals as Mackintosh, Bucholtz, and Mignet. A
new and more productive period began thirty years later,
when the war of 1859 laid open the spoils of Italy.
Every country in succession has now allowed the ex
ploration of its records, and there is more fear of drown-
ing than of drought. The result has been that a lifetime
spent in the largest collection of printed books would not
suffice to train a real master of modern history. After he
had turned from literature to sources, from Burnet to
Pocock, from Macaulay to Madame Campana, from
Thiers to the interminable correspondence of the Bona-
partes, he would still feel instant need of inquiry at
Venice or Naples, in the Ossuna Library or at the
Hermitage.

These matters do not now concern us. For our purpose, the main thing to learn is not the art of accumulating
material, but the sublimer art of investigating it, of

discerning truth from falsehood, and certainty from doubt. It is by solidity of criticism more than by the plenitude of erudition that the study of history strengthens, and straightens, and extends the mind. And the accession of the critic in the place of the indefatigable compiler, of the artist in coloured narrative, the skilled limner of character, the persuasive advocate of good, or other, causes, amounts to a transfer of government, to a change of dynasty, in the historic realm. For the critic is one who, when he lights on an interesting statement, begins by suspecting it. He remains in suspense until he has subjected his authority to three operations. First, he asks whether he has read the passage as the author wrote it. For the transcriber, and the editor, and the official or officious censor on the top of the editor, have played strange tricks, and have much to answer for. And if they are not to blame, it may turn out that the author wrote his book twice over, that you can discover the first jet, the progressive variations, things added, and things struck out. Next is the question where the writer got his information. If from a previous writer, it can be ascertained, and the enquiry has to be repeated. If from unpublished papers, they must be traced, and when the fountain-head is reached, or the track disappears, the question of veracity arises. The responsible writer's character, his position, antecedents, and probable motives have to be examined into; and this is what, in a different and adapted sense of the word, may be called the higher criticism, in comparison with the servile and often mechanical work of pursuing statements to their root. For a historian has to be treated as a witness, and not believed unless his sincerity is established. The maxim that a man must be presumed to be innocent until his guilt is proved, was not made for him.

The third distinctive note of the generation of writers who dug so deep a trench between history as known to our grandfathers and as it appears to us, is their dogma of impartiality. To an ordinary man the word means no more than justice. He considers that he may proclaim the merits of his own religion, of his prosperous and enlightened country, of his political persuasion, whether democracy, or liberal monarchy, or historic conservatism, without transgression or offence, so long as he is fair to the relative, though inferior merits of others, and never treats men as saints or as rogues for the side they take. There is no impartiality, he would say, like that of a hanging judge. The men who, with the compass of criticism in their hands, sailed the uncharted sea of original research, proposed a different view. History, to be above evasion or dispute, must stand on documents, not on opinions. They had their own notion of truthfulness, based on the exceeding difficulty of finding truth, and the still greater difficulty of impressing it when found. They thought it possible to write, with so much scruple, and simplicity, and insight, as to carry along with them every man of good will, and, whatever his feelings, to compel his assent. Ideas which, in religion and in politics, are truths, in history are forces. They must be respected; they must not be affirmed. By dint of a supreme reserve, by much self-control, by a timely and discreet indifference, by secrecy in the matter of the black cap, history might be lifted above contention, and made an accepted tribunal, and the same for all. If men were truly sincere, and delivered judgment by no canons but those of evident morality, then Julian would be described in the same terms by Christian and pagan, Luther by Catholic and Protestant, Washington by Whig and Tory, Napoleon by patriotic Frenchman and patriotic German.

I shall never again enjoy the opportunity of speaking my thoughts to such an audience as this, and on so privileged an occasion a lecturer may well be tempted to bethink himself whether he knows of any neglected truth, any cardinal proposition, that might serve as his selected epigraph, as a last signal, perhaps even as a target. I am not thinking of those shining precepts which are the registered property of every school; that is to say— Learn as much by writing as by reading; be not content with the best book; seek side-lights from the others; have no favourites; keep men and things apart; guard against the prestige of great names; see that your judgments are your own, and do not shrink from disagreement; no trusting without testing; be more severe to ideas than to actions; do not overlook the strength of the bad cause or the weakness of the good; never be surprised by the crumbling of an idol or the disclosure of a skeleton; judge talent at its best and character at its worst; suspect power more than vice, and study problems in preference to periods; for instance: the derivation of Luther, the scientific influence of Bacon, the predecessors of Adam Smith, the mediæval masters of Rousseau, the consistency of Burke, the identity of the first Whig. Most of this, I suppose, is undisputed, and calls for no enlargement. But the weight of opinion is against me when I exhort you never to debase the moral currency or to lower the standard of rectitude, but to try others by the final maxim that governs your own lives, and to suffer no man and no cause to escape the undying penalty which history has the power to inflict on wrong.

13. J. B. BURY

(From the Inaugural Lecture delivered at Cambridge, January, 1903.)

THE dark imminence of this unknown future in front of us, like a vague wall of mist, every instant receding, with all its indiscernible contents of world-wide change, soundless revolutions, silent reformations, undreamed ideas, new religions, must not be neglected, if we would grasp the unity of history in its highest sense. For though we are unable to divine what things indefinite time may evolve, though we cannot look forward with the eyes of

" the prophetic soul
Of the wide world brooding on things to come ",

yet the unapparent future has a claim to make itself felt as an idea controlling our perspective. It commands us not to regard the series of what *we* call ancient and mediæval history as leading up to the modern age and the twentieth century; it bids us consider the whole sequence up to the present moment as probably no more than the beginning of a social and psychical development, whereof the end is withdrawn from our view by countless millenniums to come. All the epochs of the past are only a few of the front carriages, and probably the least wonderful, in the van of an interminable procession.

This, I submit, is a controlling idea for determining objectively our historical perspective. We must see our petty periods *sub specie perennitatis*. Under this aspect the modern age falls into line with its predecessors and loses its obtrusive prominence. Do not say that this view sets us on too dizzy a height. On the contrary, it is a supreme confession of the limitations of our knowledge. It is simply a limiting and controlling conception; but it makes all the difference in the adjustment of our mental balance for the appreciation of values,—like the symbol of an unknown quantity in the denominator of a fraction. It teaches us that history ceases to be scientific, and passes from the objective to the subjective point of view, if she does not distribute her attention, so far as the sources allow, to all periods of history. It cannot perhaps be too often reiterated that a university, in the exercise and administration of learning, has always to consider that more comprehensive and general utility which consists in the training of men to contemplate life and the world from the highest, that is the scientifically truest point of view, in the justest perspective that can be attained. If one were asked to define in a word the end of higher education, I do not know whether one could find a much better definition than this: the training of the mind to look at experience objectively, without immediate relation to one's own time and place. And so, if we recognize the relative importance of the modern period for our own contemporary needs, we must hold that the best preparation for interpreting it truly, for investigating its movements, for deducing its practical lessons, is to be brought up in a school where its place is estimated in scales in which the weight of contemporary interest is not thrown.

Beyond its value as a limiting controlling conception, the idea of the future development of man has also a positive importance. It furnishes, in fact, the justification of much of the laborious historical work that has been done and is being done to-day. The gathering of materials bearing upon minute local events, the collation of MSS. and the registry of their small variations, the patient drudgery in archives of states and municipalities, all the microscopic research that is carried on by armies of toiling students—it may seem like the bearing of mortar and bricks to the site of a building which has hardly been begun, of whose plan the labourers know but little. This work, the hewing of wood and the drawing of water, has to be done in faith—in the faith that a complete assemblage of the smallest facts of human history will tell in the end. The labour is performed for posterity—for remote posterity; and when, with intelligible scepticism, someone asks the use of the accumulation of statistics, the publication of trivial records, the labour expended on minute criticism, the true answer is: "That is not so much our business as the business of future generations. We are heaping up material and arranging it, according to the best methods we know; if we draw what conclusions we can for the satisfaction of our own generation, we never forget that our work is to be used by future ages. It is intended for those who follow us rather than for ourselves, and much less for our grandchildren than for generations very remote." For a long time to come one of the chief services that research can perform is to help to build, firm and solid, some of the countless stairs by which men of distant ages may mount to a height unattainable by us, and have a vision of history which we cannot win, standing on our lower slope.

One of the features of the renovation of the study of history has been the growth of a larger view of its dominion. Hitherto I have been dwelling upon its longitudinal aspect as a sequence in time, but a word may be said about its latitude. The exclusive idea of political history, *Staatengeschichte*, to which Ranke held so firmly, has been gradually yielding to a more comprehensive definition which embraces as its material all records, whatever their nature may be, of the material and spiritual development, of the culture and the works, of man in society, from the stone age onwards. It may be said that the wider view descends from Herodotus, the narrower from Thucydides. The growth of the larger conception was favoured by the national movements which vindicated the idea of the people as distinct from the idea of the state; but its final victory is assured by the application of the principle of development and the "historical method" to all the manifestations of human activity—social institutions, law, trade, the industrial and the fine arts, religion, philosophy, folk-lore, literature. Thus history has acquired a much ampler and more comprehensive meaning, along with a deeper insight into the constant interaction and reciprocity among all the various manifestations of human brain-power and human emotion. Of course in actual practice labour is divided; political history and the histories of the various parts of civilization can and must be separately treated; but it makes a vital difference that we should be alive to the interconnection, that no department should be isolated, that we should maintain an intimate association among the historical sciences, that we should frame an ideal—an ideal not the less useful because it is impracticable—of a true history of a nation or a true history of the world in which every form of social life and every manifestation of intellectual development should be set forth in its relation to the rest, in its significance for growth or decline.

I may conclude by repeating that, just as he will have the best prospect of being a successful investigator of any group of nature's secrets who has had his mental attitude determined by a large grasp of cosmic problems, even so the historical student should learn to realize the human story *sub specie perennitatis*; and that, if, year by year, history is to become a more and more powerful force for stripping the bandages of error from the eyes of men, for shaping public opinion and advancing the cause of intellectual and political liberty, she will best prepare her disciples for the performance of that task, not by considering the immediate utility of next week or next year or next century, not by accommodating her ideal or limiting her range, but by remembering always that, though she may supply material for literary art or philosophical speculation, she is herself simply a science, no less and no more.

Part II

Passages illustrating the Method and Style adopted by Historians at different periods.

1. ANGLO-SAXON CHRONICLE

(The following passages, modernized from the *Anglo-Saxon Chronicle*,
illustrate the earliest stage of historiography in the English language.
The chronicle contains an annalistic account of events in England
from the invasion of Julius Cæsar down to the accession of Henry II
in 1154. It presents many problems, some probably insoluble, with
regard to its authorship, methods of composition, &c. The earliest
entries are meagre in the extreme; and it is not until the year 853 A.D.
that the narrative acquires any fulness. This fact lends colour to the
supposition, which is, however, only a supposition, that King Alfred
and the ecclesiastics of his time were the authors of the first part of the
chronicle. The two extracts that follow are both drawn from this
earliest part of the chronicle, though the narrative is even fuller for
the last days of the Saxon monarchy and the reigns of the early Nor-
mans. The first series of extracts deal with the reign of King Alfred,
and is representative of the chronicle at its best. These extracts at
least (whatever may be true of some others) seem to be written down
soon after the events which are narrated, and are based upon the personal knowledge of the writers. The second extract consists of the
fine Early English poem of the Battle of Brunanburgh (937 A.D.). Here
the poem is given in its entirety as a poem: there are other parts of the
chronicle where a poem seems to form the basis of the narrative, though
it is not verbally quoted.)

AN. DCCC.LXXXVIII. In this year the aldorman
Becca conveyed the alms of the West Saxons and
of King Aelfred to Rome. And Queen Aelswith, who
was King Aelfred's sister, died on the way to Rome, and
her body lies at Pavia. And in the same year Arch-
bishop Aethelred of Canterbury and the aldorman Aethel-
wold died in one month.

An. DCCC.LXXXIX. In this year there was no
journey to Rome, except that King Aelfred sent two
couriers with letters.

An. DCCC.XC. In this year the abbot Beornhelm
conveyed the alms of the West Saxons and of King

Aelfred to Rome. And Guthorm, the northern king, died, whose baptismal name was Aethelstân; he was King Aelfred's godson, and he abode in East Anglia, and first occupied that land. And in the same year the army went from the Seine to St. Lô, which is between the Bretons and the Franks, and the Bretons fought against them, and had the victory, and drove them out into a river, and drowned many of them. In this year Plegemund was chosen of God and of all the people to the archbishopric of Canterbury.

An. DCCC.XCI. In this year the army went east, and King Armulf, with the East Franks, and Saxons, and Bavarians, fought against the mounted force before the ships came and put it to flight. And three Scots came to King Aelfred in a boat without any oars, from Ireland, whence they had stolen away because they desired, for love of God, to be in a state of pilgrimage, they recked not where. The boat in which they came was wrought of two hides and a half, and they took with them food sufficient for seven nights; and on the seventh night they came to land in Cornwall, and then went straightways to King Aelfred. Thus they were named: Dubslane, and Maccbethu, and Maclinmum. And Swifneh, the best teacher that was among the Scots, died.

An. DCCC.XCII. And in the same year after Easter, about the Rogations, or earlier, appeared the star which in Book-Latin is called "cometa". Some men say in English, that it is a long-haired (feaxed) star, because there stands a long ray from it, sometimes on one side, sometimes on each side.

An DCCC.XCIII. In this year the great army, of which we long before spoke, came again from the east kingdom westward to Boulogne, and was there shipped, so that they in one voyage made the transit, with horses and all; and they came up to the mouth of the Limen with two hundred and fifty ships. The mouth is in the East of Kent, at the east end of the great wood which we call Andred. The wood is in length, from east to west, one hundred and twenty miles long, or longer, and thirty miles broad. The river, of which we before spoke, flows out from the weald. On the river they towed up their ships as far as the weald, four miles from the outward mouth, and there stormed a work; within the fastness a few country-men were stationed, and it was only half-constructed. Then soon after that came Haesten with eighty ships into the Thames mouth, and wrought him a work at Middleton (Milton), and the other army one at Appledore.

An. DCCC.XCIV. In this year, that was a twelvemonth after they had wrought a work in the east kingdom, Northumbria and East Anglia had given oaths to King Aelfred, and East Anglia six hostages; and yet against the compact, as often as the other armies with all their force went out, then they went out, either with them or on their side. And then King Aelfred gathered his force, and went until he encamped between the two armies, the nearest where he had room, for wood-fastness and for water-fastness, so that he might reach either, if they would seek any field. Then after that, they went through the weald in bands and troops, on whichever side was then without a force. And they also were sought by other bands, almost every day, or by night, both from the (king's) force and also from the burghs. The king had divided his force into two, so that they were constantly half at home, half abroad, besides those men that held the burghs. The whole army did not come out of their quarters, oftener than twice; one time, when they first came to land, before the (king's) force was assembled, the other time when they would go from their quarters. They had then taken a great booty, and would convey it

northwards over the Thames into Essex towards the
ships.   The (king's) force then rode before them, and
fought against them at Farnham, and put the army to
flight, and rescued the booty, and they fled over the
Thames without any ford; then up by the Colne to an
island.   The (royal) army then beset them there from
without, for the longest time that they had provisions;
but they had then stayed their appointed time and consumed their provisions; and the king was then on his
march thitherwards with the division which was advancing
with himself.   Then he was thitherward, and the other
force was homeward, and the Danish remained there
behind, because their king had been wounded in the
fight, so that he could not be conveyed.   Then those
who dwell with the Northumbrians and with the East
Angles, gathered some hundred ships, and went south
about, and besieged a work in Devonshire by the North
Sea; and those who went south about, besieged Exeter.
When the king heard that, he turned west towards Exeter
with all the force, save a very powerful body of the people,
eastwards.   These went on until they came to London,
and then, with the townsmen, and with the aid which
came to them from the west, marched east to Benfleet.
Haesten was then come there with his army, which had
previously sat at Middleton; and the great army also
was come thereto, which had before sat at the mouth of
the Limen, at Appledore.   Haesten had before wrought
the work at Benfleet, and was then gone out harrying,
and the great army was at home.   They then marched
up and put the army to flight, and stormed the work,
and took all that there was within, as well money, as
women and children, and brought all to London; and
all the ships they either broke in pieces, or burned, or
brought to London, or to Rochester; and Haesten's wife
and his two sons were brought to the king, and he re-

stored them to him, because one of them was his godson, the other the aldorman Aethered's. They had been their sponsors, before Haesten came to Benfleet, and he had given him oaths and hostages; and the king had also given him much money, and so likewise, when he gave up the boy and the woman. But as soon as they came to Benfleet, and had wrought the work, he harried on that end of his realm, which Aethered his gossip had to defend; and again a second time, he had arrived on a plundering expedition on that same kingdom, when his work was taken by storm. When the king turned west with his force towards Exeter, as I before said, and the army had beset the burgh, when he had arrived there, they went to their ships. While he was busied in the west against the army there, and both the armies had formed a junction at Shoebury, in Essex, and there wrought a work, they then went both together up along the Thames, and a great increase came to them both from the East Angles and the Northumbrians. They then went up along the Thames, until they reached the Severn, then up along the Severn. Then the aldorman Aethered, and the ¡aldorman Aethelm, and the aldorman Aethelnoth, and the king's thanes, who were then at home in the works, gathered together from every town east of the Parret, as well west as east of Selwood, as also north of the Thames and west of the Severn, and also some part of the North Welsh race. When they were all gathered together, they followed after the army to Buttington on the bank of the Severn, and there beset them on every side in a fastness. When they had sat there many weeks on the two sides of the river, and the king was west in Devon, against the naval force, they were distressed for want of food, and had eaten a great part of their horses, and the others had died of hunger; they then went out to the men who were encamped on the east side of the river, and fought against them, and the Christians had the victory.   And there was Ordheh, a king's thane, slain, and also many other king's thanes were slain; and of the Danish there was a very great slaughter made; and the part that came away thence was saved by flight.   When they came into Essex, to their work and to their ships, the remnant gathered again a great army from the East Angles and from the Northumbrians, before winter, and committed their wives and their ships and their chattels to the East Angles, and went at one stretch, by day and by night, until they arrived at a desolated city in Wirrall, which is called Legaceaster (Chester).   Then could the force not overtake them before they were within the work; they, however, beset the work from without for two days, and took all the cattle which was there without, and slew the men that they might intercept outside of the work, and burned all the corn, and with their horses consumed it on every plain, and that was a twelvemonth after they had come over sea hither.

An. D.CCCCXXXVII.

This year King Aethelstân,
lord of earls,
ring-giver of warriors,
and his brother eke,
Eadmund Aetheling,
life-long glory
in battle won,
with edges of swords,
at Brunanburh.
The board-wall clave,
hew'd the war linden,
with hammers' leavings,
Eadward's offspring,

as was to them congenial
from their ancestors,
that they in conflict oft,
'gainst every foe,
should the land defend,
treasure and homes.
The foes lay low,
the Scots people,
and the shipmen
death-doom'd fell.
The field stream'd
with warriors' blood,
what time the sun up,
at morning tide,
the glorious star,
glided o'er grounds,
God's candle bright,
the eternal Lord's,
until the noble creature
sank to its setting.
There many a warrior lay,
by javelins scattered,
northern men,
o'er the shield shot,
so the Scots eke,
weary, war-sated.
The West Saxons forth,
the live-long day,
in martial bands,
follow'd the footsteps
of the hostile nations.
They hew'd the fugitives
from behind amain,
with falchions mill-sharp.
The Mercians refus'd not

the hard hand-play
to any of the warriors,
who with Olaf,
o'er the waves mingling,
in the ship's bosom,
the land had sought,
death-doom'd in fight.
Five lay
on that battle-stead,
young kings,
by swords laid to sleep;
so seven eke
of Olaf's jarls,
of the army countless,
shipmen and Scots.
There was put to flight
the Northmen's prince,
by need constrain'd,
to the vessel's prow
with a little band.
The bark drove afloat,
the king departed
on the fallow flood,
his life preserved.
So there eke the aged
came by flight
to his country north,
Constantine,
hoary warrior;
he needed not exult
in the falchions' intercourse;
he of his kinsmen was bereft,
of his friends depriv'd,
on the trysting-place,
in conflict slain;

and his son he left
on the slaughter-place,
mangled with wounds,
young in warfare.
Needed not boast
the grizzly-lock'd warrior
of the bill-clashing,
the old deceiver,
nor Olaf the more,
with their armies' relics;
they needed not to laugh
that they in works of war
the better were
on the battle-stead,
at the rush of banners,
the meeting of javelins,
the tryst of men,
the clash of weapons,
that on the field of slaughter they
with Eadweard's
offspring play'd.
Departed then the Northmen
in their nail'd barks,
the darts' gory leaving,
on the roaring sea,
o'er the deep water,
Dublin to seek,
Ireland once more,
in mind abash'd.
Likewise the brothers,
both together
king and Aetheling,
their country sought,
the West Saxon's land,
in war exulting.

They left behind them,
the carcases to share
with pallid coat
the swart raven,
with horned neb,
and him of goodly coat,
the eagle white behind,
the carrion to devour,
the greedy war-hawk,
and that grey beast,
the wolf in the weald.
No slaughter has been greater
in this island
ever yet,
of folk laid low,
before this,
by the sword's edges,
from what books tell us,
old chroniclers,
since hither from the east
Angles and Saxons
came to land,
o'er the broad seas.
Britain sought,
proud war-smiths
the Welsh o'ercame,
men for glory eager,
the country gain'd.

2. CAPGRAVE'S CHRONICLE OF ENGLAND

(An extract from this chronicle has already been given in the Introduction (p. xi). But the passage there quoted was rather intended to show what fabulous and legendary matter found its way into the mediæval chronicles. The passage that here follows shows Capgrave at his best. He is dealing with contemporary events, and his narrative of the siege of Harfleur and the battle of Agincourt contribute materially to our knowledge of those events. But it will be observed that Capgrave's chronicle makes no advance either in style or conception of the subject, if it is compared with the Anglo-Saxon Chronicle already quoted.)

THE kyng, with his nave, took the se, and londid at Kidkaus, with a thousand schippis and five hundred. He entered the lond on a Wednesday, whech was the vigil of Assumpcioune of oure Lady; and on the Satirday aftir he leyde sege to the town of Hareflw, he be lond, the schippis be the watir. And this sege lested til the Sundy befor Myhilmesse. In the Tewisday befor that Sunday, the lordes that were keperes of the town sent oute a man onto the duke of Clarense, praying him enterly that thei myte trete with the Kyng, and that he schuld make his gunneres to sese, for it was to hem intollerabil. The names of hem were these:—the lord Gauncort, the lord Stutevyle, the lord Botevyle, and the lord Clare. The duke of Clarens spake for hem to the Kyng; and the Kyng sent to hem the erle of Dorset and Ser Thomas Erpingham, to knowe her desire. Thei prayed the Kyng mekely that he schuld ses of his schot onto Sunday; and if the Kyng of Frauns cam not be that tyme, thei schuld delyver him the town. Thei profered him eke that if he

wold gyve hem leve and save conduct to ride to the
Kyng of Frauns, thei schuld ley pleggis xxii knytes with
the best of the town. So the lord Hakevile and xii
persones had leve to ride thorw the host. And on the
Wednesday erly, cam oute of the town the lordes, xxii
knytes, swires, and burgeys of the town. And ageyn
hem the Kyng sent a solempne procession of prelatis and
prestis, and the Sacrament; and after folowand lordis,
knytes, and the puple. Whan thei had mad a solempne
oth, thei went to mete into the Kyngis tent, but thei sey
not the Kyng. Aftir mete thei were comaunded for to
go with certeyn lordes that schuld kepe hem. On the
Sunday com the messageres ageyn withoute ony help of
Kyng or of Daufyn. Therfor thei that were in the town
submitted hem onto the Kyng; and thei that were with
the Kyng, sent be the Frensch Kyng to keping of the
town, remayned as prisoneres.

The Kyng mad capteyn of the town his uncle Ser
Thomas, erle of Dorset. In this sege many men deied
of cold in nytes, and frute etyng; eke of stynk of careynes.
He deied there, Maister Richard Courtney, bischop of
Norwich; in whos place the monkes chosen Jon Waker-
yng. Ther deyed Mychael at the Pool. The duke of
Clarensis, the erle of March, the erle Arundel, and the
erle Marchale, took gret seknes there.

The Kyng, aftir this conquest, purposed to go to
Caleys, with foot-men for the most part. For al his
hoost was not accoundid passing viii thousand; so many
were left seck at Harflew. Merveile it was that he with
so fewe durst go thorw alle the thik wodis in that cuntre.
For the Frensch parti in al this tyme had mad an hoost
of an hundred thousand and forty thousand. Vitailes
were kept fro hem, that xviii dayes thei had walnotes for
bred; and flech had thei sum: but her drynk was watir.

So in the xxiii day of Octobir the hostis met not a

myle asundir.   The Kyng coumforted gretly his men, that thei schuld trost in God, for her cause was rithful. The Frensch part stod on the hille, and we in the vale. Betwix hem was a lond new heried, where was evel fotyng.   Schort for to sey, the feld fel onto the Kyng, and the Frensch party lost it, for al her noumbyr and her pride.   Ther were ded the duke of Lauson, the duke of Braban, the duke of Bavers, Verles, the Constable eke of Frauns, and a hundred lordes; knytes and swires, iiii thousand, sexti, and ix: the comon puple was not noumbered.   These were take—the duke of Aurelianensis, the duke of Burbon, the erles of Ew and Vendone, Arthure, the duke's brothir of Bretayne, whech cleymeth to be erl of Richemund, and a knyte thei cleped Brucegald, Marchale of Frauns, and othir were take there, of cote armoure, into a vii hundred.   On oure side were ded Edward, duke of York, the erle of Suthfolk, iiii knytes, a swiere, Davy Gamme; of the comones xxviii.   In the tyme of the bataile the brigauntis of the Frensch side took the Kyngis cariage, and led it awey, in whech thei fonde the Kyngis crowne.   Thei mad the bellis to rynge and men for to sing—"Te Deum laudamus", telling verily that the Kyng was ded.   But within a fewe houres aftir her ioye was chaunged.   The Kyng rood to Caleis, and ovir the se to Dover, and in the xxiii day of Novembir cam to London, and there was receyved in the best maner

3. THE EARL OF CLARENDON

(There is no need here to consider the exact value that is to be placed
upon Clarendon's account of the great Civil War. The circumstances
of its composition, and the personal record and character of the author,
make it certain that the whole story is presented from a strongly Royalist
and Anglican point of view. But worse charges than mere partiality
have been brought against Clarendon: he stands accused of deliberate
falsification of his evidence. None will, however, deny that his work
marks a very decided advance in historical composition: there is nothing
in English literature of an earlier date at all comparable to it: nothing,
at least, on anything like so large a scale.

The writing is at its best vigorous and clear; the reflections, whether
we agree with them or not, show that the author has a real understanding
of affairs of state; and the character-sketches are from a literary point
of view the most admirable part of the work.

It will be interesting to compare these extracts from Clarendon with
those given from Hume and Gardiner. All three deal with the period
of the Civil War, and touch from very different points of view upon the
character and action of Cromwell. The first extract is from Book XIII,
the second from Book XV.)

THE KING'S FLIGHT FROM WORCESTER

AS the victory cost the enemy no blood, so after it
there was not much cruelty used to the prisoners
who were taken upon the spot. But very many of those
who ran away were every day knocked in the head by
the country people, and used with barbarity. Towards
the king's menial servants, whereof most were taken,
there was nothing of severity; but, within few days, they
were all discharged and set at liberty.

Though the king could not get a body of horse to
fight, he could have too many to fly with him; and he
had not been many hours from Worcester, when he found
about him near, if not above, four thousand of his horse.

There was David Lesley with all his own equipage, as if he had not fled upon the sudden; so that good order, and regularity, and obedience, might yet have made a hopeful retreat even into Scotland itself. But there was paleness in every man's looks, and jealousy and confusion in their faces; and nothing could worse befall the king, than a safe return into Scotland; which yet he could not reasonably promise to himself in that company. But when the night covered them, he found means to withdraw himself with one or two of his own servants; whom he likewise discharged, when it begun to be light; and after he had made them cut off his hair, he betook himself alone into an adjacent wood, and relied only upon Him for deliverance who alone could, and did miraculously deliver him.

When it was morning, and the troops, which had marched all night, and who knew that when it begun to be dark the king was with them, found now that he was not there, they cared less for each other's company; and all who were English separated themselves, and went into other roads; and wherever twenty horse appeared of the country, which was now awake, and upon their guard to stop and arrest the runaways, the whole body of the Scottish horse would fly, and run several ways; and twenty of them would give themselves prisoners to two country fellows: however, David Lesley reached Yorkshire with above fifteen hundred horse in a body. But the jealousies increased every day; and those of his own country were so unsatisfied with his whole conduct and behaviour, that they did, that is many of them, believe that he was corrupted by Cromwell; and the rest, who did not think so, believed him not to understand his profession, in which he had been bred from his cradle. When he was in his flight, considering one morning with the principal persons which way they should take, some proposed this, and others that way; sir William Armorer asked him, "which way he thought best?" which when he had named, the other said, "he would then go the other; for, he swore, he had betrayed the king and the army all the time"; and so left him.

They were all soon after taken. And it is hard to be believed how very few of that numerous body of horse (for there can be no imagination that any of the foot escaped) returned into Scotland. Upon all the enquiry that was made, when a discovery was made of most of the false and treacherous actions which had been committed by most men, there appeared no cause to suspect that David Lesley had been unfaithful in his charge: though he never recovered any reputation with those of his own country, who wedded the king's interest. And yet it was some vindication to him, that, from the time of his imprisonment, he never received any favour from the Parliament, whom he had served so long; nor from Cromwell, in whose company he had served; but underwent all the severities, and long imprisonment, the rest of his countrymen underwent. The king did not believe him false; and did always think him an excellent officer of horse, to distribute and execute orders, but in no degree capable of commanding in chief. And without doubt he was so amazed in that fatal day, that he performed not the office of a general, or of any competent officer.

It is great pity that there was never a journal made of that miraculous deliverance, in which there might be seen so many visible impressions of the immediate hand of God. When the darkness of the night was over, after the king had cast himself into that wood, he discerned another man, who had gotten upon an oak in the same wood, near the place where the king had rested himself, and had slept soundly. The man upon the tree had first seen the king, and knew him, and came down to him, and was known to the king, being a gentleman of the neighbour county of Staffordshire, who had served his late majesty during the war, and had now been one of the few who resorted to the king after his coming to Worcester. His name was Careless, who had had a command of foot, above the degree of a captain, under the Lord Loughborough. He persuaded the king, since it could not be safe for him to go out of the wood, and that, as soon as it should be fully light, the wood itself would probably be visited by those of the country, who would be searching to find those whom they might make prisoners, that he would get up into that tree where he had been; where the boughs were so thick with leaves, that a man would not be discovered there without a narrower enquiry than people usually make in places which they do not suspect.

The king thought it good counsel; and, with the other's help, climbed into the tree; and then helped his companion to ascend after him; where they sat all that day, and securely saw many who came purposely into the wood to look after them, and heard all their discourse, how they would use the king himself if they could take him. This wood was either in or upon the borders of Staffordshire; and though there was a highway near one side of it, where the king had entered into it, yet it was large, and all other sides of it opened amongst enclosures, and it pleased God that Careless was not unacquainted with the neighbour villages; and it was part of the king's good fortune, that this gentleman, by being a Roman Catholic, was acquainted with those of that profession of all degrees, who had the best opportunities of concealing him; for it must never be denied, that some of that faith had a very great share in his majesty's preservation.

The day being spent in the tree, it was not in the king's power to forget that he had lived two days with eating very little, and two nights with as little sleep; so that, when the night came, he was willing to make some provision for both: and he resolved, with the advice and assistance of his companion, to leave his blessed tree; and when the night was dark, they walked through the wood into those enclosures which were farthest from any highway, and making a shift to get over hedges and ditches, after walking at least eight or nine miles, which were the more grievous to the king by the weight of his boots (for he could not put them off, when he cut off his hair, for want of shoes), before morning they came to a poor cottage, the owner whereof being a Roman Catholic, was known to Careless. He was called up, and as soon as he knew one of them, he easily concluded in what condition they both were; and presently carried them into a little barn, full of hay, which was a better lodging than he had for himself. But when they were there, and had conferred with their host of the news and temper of the country, it was resolved, that the danger would be the greater if they stayed together; and therefore that Careless should presently be gone; and should within two days, send an honest man to the king, to guide him to some other place of security; and in the meantime his majesty should stay upon the hay-mow. The poor man had nothing for him to eat, but promised him good buttermilk the next morning; and so he was once more left alone, his companion, how weary soever, departing from him before day, the poor man of the house knowing no more, than that he was a friend of the captain's, and one of those who had escaped from Worcester. The king slept very well in his lodging, till the time that his host brought him a piece of bread, and a great pot of butter-milk, which he thought

the best food he had ever eaten. The poor man spoke
very intelligently to him of the country, and of the people
who were well or ill affected to the king, and of the great
fear and terror that possessed the hearts of those who
were best affected. He told him, " that he himself lived
by his daily labour, and that what he had brought him
was the fare he and his wife had; and that he feared, if
he should endeavour to procure better, it might draw
suspicion upon him, and people might be apt to think
he had somebody with him that was not of his own
family. However, if he would have him get some meat,
he would do it; but if he could bear this hard diet, he
should have enough of the milk, and some of the butter
that was made with it." The king was satisfied with
his reason, and would not run the hazard for a change
of diet; desired only the man, " that he might have his
company as often, and as much as he could give it
him ", there being the same reason against the poor
man's discontinuing his labour, as the alteration of his
fare.

After he had rested upon this hay-mow, and fed upon
this diet two days and two nights, in the evening before
the third night, another fellow, a little above the condition of his host, came to the house, sent from Careless,
to conduct the king to another house, more out of any
road near which any part of the army was like to march.
It was above twelve miles that he was to go, and was to
use the same caution he had done the first night, not to
go in any common road; which his guide knew well how
to avoid. Here he new dressed himself, changing clothes
with his landlord and putting on those which he usually
wore: he had a great mind to have kept his own shirt;
but he considered, that men are not sooner discovered
by any mark in disguises, than by having fine linen in
ill clothes; and so he parted with his shirt too, and took

the same his poor host had then on. Though he had foreseen that he must leave his boots, and his landlord had taken the best care he could to provide an old pair of shoes, yet they were not easy to him when he first put them on, and, in a short time after, grew very grievous to him. In this equipage he set out from his first lodging in the beginning of the night, under the conduct of this comrade; who guided him the nearest way, crossing over hedges and ditches, that they might be in least danger of meeting passengers. This was so grievous a march, and he was so tired, that he was even ready to despair, and to prefer being taken and suffered to rest, before purchasing his safety at that price. His shoes had, after the walking a few miles, hurt him so much, that he had thrown them away, and walked the rest of the way in his ill stockings, which were quickly worn out; and his feet, with the thorns in getting over hedges, and with the stones in other places, were so hurt and wounded, that he many times cast himself upon the ground, with a desperate and obstinate resolution to rest there till the morning, that he might shift with less torment, what hazard soever he run. But his stout guide still prevailed with him to make a new attempt, sometimes promising that the way should be better, and sometimes assuring him that he had but little farther to go; and in this distress and perplexity, before the morning, they arrived at the house designed; which, though it was better than that which he had left, his lodging was still in the barn, upon straw instead of hay, a place being made as easy in it as the expectation of a guest could dispose it. Here he had such meat and porridge as such people use to have; with which, but especially with the butter and the cheese, he thought himself well feasted; and took the best care he could to be supplied with other, little better, shoes and stockings: and after his feet were enough recovered that he could go, he was conducted from thence to another poor house, within such a distance as put him not to much trouble: for having not yet in his thought which way or by what means to make his escape, all that was designed was only, by shifting from one house to another, to avoid discovery. And being now in that quarter which was more inhabited by the Roman Catholics than most other parts in England, he was led from one to another of that persuasion, and concealed with great fidelity. But he then observed that he was never carried to any gentleman's house, though that country was full of them, but only to poor houses of poor men, which only yielded him rest with very unpleasant sustenance; whether there was more danger in those better houses, in regard of the resort, and the many servants; or whether the owners of great estates were the owners likewise of more fears and apprehensions.

Within few days, a very honest and discreet person, one Mr. Huddlestone, a Benedictine monk, who attended the service of the Roman Catholics in those parts, came to him, sent by Careless; and was a very great assistance and comfort to him. And when the places to which he carried him were at too great a distance to walk, he provided him a horse, and more proper habit than the rags he wore. This man told him, "that the lord Wilmot lay concealed likewise in a friend's house of his"; which his majesty was very glad of; and wished him to contrive some means how they might speak together, which the other easily did; and within a night or two, brought them into one place. Wilmot told the king, "that he had by very good fortune fallen into the house of an honest gentleman, one Mr. Lane, a person of an excellent reputation for his fidelity to the king, but of so universal and general a good name, that, though he had a son, who had been a colonel in the king's service during the late war, and was then upon his way with men to Worcester the very day of the defeat, men of all affections in the country, and of all opinions, paid the old man a very great respect: that he had been very civilly treated, and that the old gentleman had used some diligence to find out where the king was, that he might get him to his house, where he was sure he could conceal him till he might contrive a full deliverance". He told him, "he had withdrawn from that house, and put himself among the Catholics, in hope that he might discover where his majesty was, and having now happily found him, advised him to repair to that house, which stood not near any other".

The king enquired of the monk of the reputation of this gentleman, who told him, "that he had a fair estate, was exceedingly beloved, and the eldest justice of the peace of that county of Stafford; and though he was a very zealous Protestant, yet he lived with so much civility and candour towards the Catholics, that they would all trust him as much as they would do any of their own profession; and that he could not think of any place of so good repose and security for his majesty's repair to". The king, who by this time had as good a mind to eat well as to sleep, liked the proposition, yet thought not fit to surprise the gentleman; but sent Wilmot thither again to assure himself that he might be received there; and was willing that he should know what guest he received; which hitherto was so much concealed, that none of the houses, where he had yet been, knew, or seemed to suspect more than that he was one of the king's party that fled from Worcester. The monk carried him to a house at a reasonable distance, where he was to expect an account from the lord Wilmot; who returned very punctually, with as much assurance of welcome as he could wish. And so they two went together to Mr.

Lane's house; where the king found he was welcome, and conveniently accommodated in such places, as in a large house had been provided to conceal the persons of malignants or to preserve goods of value from being plundered. Here he lodged and eat very well, and begun to hope that he was in present safety. Wilmot returned under the care of the monk, and expected summons, when any farther motion should be thought to be necessary.

In this station the king remained in quiet and blessed security many days, receiving every day information of the general consternation the kingdom was in, out of the apprehension that his person might fall into the hands of his enemies, and of the great diligence they used to enquire for him. He saw the proclamation that was issued out and printed; in which a thousand pounds were promised to any man who would deliver and discover the person of Charles Stuart, and the penalty of high treason declared against those who presumed to harbour or conceal him; by which he saw how much he was beholding to all those who were faithful to him.

It was now time to consider how he might find himself near the sea, from whence he might find some means to transport himself; and he was now near the middle of the kingdom, saving that it was a little more northward, where he was utterly unacquainted with all the ports, and with that coast. In the west he was best acquainted, and that coast was most proper to transport him into France, to which he was most inclined. Upon this matter he communicated with those of this family to whom he was known, that is, with the old gentleman the father, a very grave and venerable person; the colonel, his eldest son, a very plain man in his discourse and behaviour, but of a fearless courage and an integrity superior to any temptation; and a daughter of the house

of a very good wit and discretion, and very fit to bear
any part in such a trust.   It was a benefit as well as an
inconvenience, in those unhappy times, that the affections of all men were almost as well known as their faces,
by the discovery they had made of themselves, in those
sad seasons, in many trials and persecutions: so that
men knew not only the minds of their next neighbours,
and those who inhabited near them, but, upon conference with their friends, could choose fit houses, at any
distance, to repose themselves in security, from one end
of the kingdom to another, without trusting the hospi-
tality of a common inn: and men were very rarely deceived in their confidence upon such occasions, but the
persons with whom they were at any time could conduct
them to another house of the same affection.

Mr. Lane had a niece, or very near kinswoman, who
was married to a gentleman, one Mr. Norton, a person
of eight or nine hundred pounds *per annum*, who lived
within four or five miles of Bristol, which was at least
four or five days' journey from the place where the king
then was, but a place most to be wished for the king to
be in, because he did not only know all that country
very well, but knew many persons also, to whom, in an
extraordinary case, he durst make himself known.   It
was hereupon resolved that Mrs. Lane should visit this
cousin, who was known to be of good affections; and
that she should ride behind the king, who was fitted with
clothes and boots for such a service; and that a servant
of her father's, in his livery, should wait upon her.   A
good house was easily pitched upon for the first night's
lodging, where Wilmot had notice given him to meet.
And in this equipage the king begun his journey; the
colonel keeping him company at a distance with a hawk
upon his fist and two or three spaniels; which, where
there were any fields at hand, warranted him to ride out

of the way, keeping his company still in his eye, and not seeming to be of it. In this manner they came to their first night's lodging; and they need not now contrive to come to their journey's end about the close of the evening, for it was in the month of October far advanced, that the long journeys they made could not be despatched sooner. Here the lord Wilmot found them; and their journeys being then adjusted, he was instructed where he should be every night: so they were seldom seen together in the journey, and rarely lodged in the same house at night. In this manner the colonel hawked two or three days till he had brought them within less than a day's journey of Mr. Norton's house; and then he gave his hawk to the lord Wilmot, who continued the journey in the same exercise.

There was great care taken when they came to any house, that the king might be presently carried into some chamber; Mrs. Lane declaring, "that he was a neighbour's son, whom his father had lent her to ride before her, in hope that he would the sooner recover from a quartan ague, with which he had been miserably afflicted, and was not yet free". And by this artifice she caused a good bed to be still provided for him, and the best meat to be sent; which she often carried herself, to hinder others from doing it. There was no resting in any place till they came to Mr. Norton's, nor anything extraordinary that happened in the way, save that they met many people every day in the way, who were very well known to the king; and the day that they went to Mr. Norton's, they were necessarily to ride quite through the city of Bristol; a place, and people, the king had been so well acquainted with, that he could not but send his eyes abroad to view the great alterations which had been made there, after his departure from thence: and when he rode near the place where the great fort had stood, he could not forbear putting his horse out of the way, and rode with his mistress behind him round it.

They came to Mr. Norton's house sooner than usual, and it being on a holiday, they saw many people about a bowling-green that was before the door; and the first man the king saw was a chaplain of his own, who was allied to the gentleman of the house, and was sitting upon the rails to see how the bowlers played. William, by which name the king went, walked with his horse into the stable, until his mistress could provide for his retreat. Mrs. Lane was very welcome to her cousin, and was presently conducted to her chamber, where she no sooner was than she lamented the condition of "a good youth, who came with her, and whom she had borrowed of his father to ride before her, who was very sick, being newly recovered of an ague"; and desired her cousin, "that a chamber might be provided for him, and a good fire made; for that he would go early to bed, and was not fit to be below stairs". A pretty little chamber was presently made ready, and a fire prepared, and a boy sent into the stable to call William, and to show him his chamber; who was very glad to be there, freed from so much company as was below. Mrs. Lane was put to find some excuse for making a visit at that time of the year, and so many days' journey from her father, and where she had never been before, though the mistress of the house and she had been bred together, and friends as well as kindred. She pretended, "that she was, after a little rest, to go into Dorsetshire to another friend". When it was supper-time, there being broth brought to the table, Mrs. Lane filled a little dish, and desired the butler, who waited at the table, "to carry that dish of porridge to William, and to tell him that he should have some meat sent to him presently". The butler carried the porridge into the chamber, with a napkin and spoon, and bread, and spoke kindly to the young man, who was willing to be eating.

The butler, looking narrowly upon him, fell upon his knees, and with tears told him, "he was glad to see his majesty". The king was infinitely surprised, yet recollected himself enough to laugh at the man, and to ask him, "what he meant?" The man had been falconer to sir Thomas Jermyn, and made it appear that he knew well enough to whom he spoke, repeating some particulars, which the king had not forgot. Whereupon the king conjured him "not to speak of what he knew, so much as to his master, though he believed him a very honest man". The fellow promised, and faithfully kept his word, and the king was the better waited upon during the time of his abode there.

Dr. Gorges, the king's chaplain, being a gentleman of a good family, near that place, and allied to Mr. Norton, supped with them; and being a man of a cheerful conversation, asked Mrs. Lane many questions concerning William, of whom he saw she was so careful by sending up meat to him, "how long his ague had been gone? and whether he had purged since it left him?" and the like, to which she gave such answers as occurred. The doctor, from the final prevalence of the parliament, had, as many others of that function had done, declined his profession, and pretended to study physic. As soon as supper was done, out of good nature, and without telling any body, he went to see William. The king saw him coming into the chamber, and withdrew to the inside of the bed, that he might be farthest from the candle; and the doctor came, and sat down by him, felt his pulse, and asked him many questions, which he answered in as few words as was possible, and expressing great inclination to go to his bed; to which the doctor left him, and went to Mrs. Lane, and told her "that he had been with

William, and that he would do well"; and advised her'
what she should do if his ague returned. The next
morning the doctor went away, so that the king saw him
no more; of which he was right glad. The next day the
lord Wilmot came to the house with his hawk, to see
Mrs. Lane, and so conferred with William; who was to
consider what he was to do. They thought it necessary
to rest some days, till they were informed what port lay
most convenient for them, and what person lived nearest
to it, upon whose fidelity they might rely: 'and the king
gave him directions to enquire after some persons, and
some other particulars, of which when he should be fully
instructed, he should return again to him. In the mean
time Wilmot lodged at a house not far from Mr. Norton's,
to which he had been recommended.

After some days' stay here, and communication between the king and the lord Wilmot by letters, the king
came to know that Colonel Francis Windham lived
within little more than a day's journey of the place where
he was; of which he was very glad; for besides the inclination he had to his eldest brother, whose wife had
been his nurse, this gentleman had behaved himself very
well during the war, and had been governor of Dunstar
Castle, where the king had lodged when he was in the
west. After the end of the war, and when all other places
were surrendered in that county, he likewise surrendered
that, upon fair conditions, and made his peace, and afterwards married a wife with a competent fortune, and lived
quietly, without any suspicion of having lessened his
affection towards the king.

The king sent Wilmot to him, and acquainted him
where he was, and that "he would gladly speak with him".
It was not hard for him to choose a good place where
to meet, and thereupon the day was appointed. After
the king had taken his leave of Mrs. Lane, who remained

with her cousin Norton, the king, and the lord Wilmot, met the colonel; and, in the way, he encountered, in a town through which they passed, Mr. Kirton, a servant of the king's, who well knew the lord Wilmot, who had no other disguise than the hawk, but took no notice of him, nor suspected the king to be there; yet that day made the king more wary of having him in his company upon the way. At the place of meeting they rested only one night, and then the king went to the colonel's house; where he rested many days, whilst the colonel projected at what place the king might embark, and how they might procure a vessel to be ready there; which was not easy to find; there being so great a caution in all the ports, and so great a fear possessing those who were honest, that it was hard to procure any vessel that was outward bound to take in any passenger.

There was a gentleman, one Mr. Ellison, who lived near Lyme, in Dorsetshire, who was well known to Colonel Windham, having been a captain in the king's army, and was still looked upon as a very honest man. With him the colonel consulted, how they might get a vessel to be ready to take in a couple of gentlemen, friends of his, who were in danger to be arrested, and transport them into France. Though no man would ask who the persons were, yet every man suspected who they were; at least they concluded that it was some of Worcester party. Lyme was generally as malicious and disaffected a town to the king's interest, as any town in England could be; yet there was in it a master of a bark, of whose honesty this captain was very confident. This man was lately returned from France, and had unladen his vessel, when Ellison asked him, "when he would make another voyage?" And he answered, "as soon as he could get lading for his ship". The other asked, "whether he would undertake to carry over a couple of gentlemen, and land them in France, if he might be as well paid for his voyage as he used to be when he was freighted by the merchants ". In conclusion, he told him, " he should receive fifty pounds for his fare ". The large recompense had that effect, that the man undertook it; though he said " he must make his provision very secretly; for that he might be well suspected for going to sea again without being freighted, after he was so newly returned ". Colonel Windham, being advertised of this, came together with the lord Wilmot to the captain's house, from whence the lord and the captain rid to a house near Lyme, where the master of the bark met them; and the lord Wilmot being satisfied with the discourse of the man, and his wariness in foreseeing suspicions which would arise, it was resolved, that on such a night, which, upon consideration of the tides, was agreed upon, the man should draw out his vessel from the pier, and, being at sea, should come to such a point about a mile from the town, where his ship should remain upon the beach when the water was gone; which would take it off again about break of day the next morning. There was very near that point, even in view of it, a small inn, kept by a man who was reputed honest, to which the cavaliers of the country often resorted; and London road passed that way; so that it was seldom without resort. Into that inn the two gentlemen were to come in the beginning of the night, that they might put themselves on board. All things being thus concerted, and good earnest given to the master, the lord Wilmot and the colonel returned to the colonel's house, above a day's journey from the place, the captain undertaking every day to look that the master should provide, and, if anything fell out contrary to expectation, to give the colonel notice at such a place, where they intended the king should be the day before he was to embark.

The king, being satisfied with these preparations, came, at the time appointed, to that house where he was to hear that all went as it ought to do; of which he received assurance from the captain; who found that the man had honestly put his provisions on board, and had his company ready, which were but four men; and that the vessel should be drawn out that night: so that it was fit for the two persons to come to the aforesaid inn, and the captain conducted them within sight of it; and then went to his own house, not distant a mile from it; the colonel remaining still at the house where they had lodged the night before, till he might hear the news of their being embarked.

They found many passengers in the inn; and so were to be contented with an ordinary chamber, which they did not intend to sleep long in. But as soon as there appeared any light, Wilmot went out to discover the bark, of which there was no appearance. In a word, the sun arose, and nothing like a ship in view. They sent to the captain, who was as much amazed; and he sent to the town; and his servant could not find the master of the bark, which was still in the pier. They suspected the captain, and the captain suspected the master. However, it being past ten of the clock, they concluded it was not fit for them to stay longer there, and so they mounted their horses again to return to the house where they had left the colonel, who, they knew, resolved to stay there till he was assured that they were gone.

The truth of the disappointment was this: the man meant honestly, and made all things ready for his departure; and the night he was to go out with his vessel, he had stayed in his own house, and slept two or three hours; and the time of the tide being come, that it was necessary to be on board, he took out of a cupboard some linen, and other things, which he used to carry with him to sea.

His wife had observed, that he had been for some days fuller of thoughts than he used to be, and that he had been speaking with seamen, who used to go with him, and that some of them had carried provisions on board the bark; of which she had asked her husband the reason; who had told her, " that he was promised freight speedily, and therefore he would make all things ready ". She was sure that there was yet no lading in the ship, and therefore, when she saw her husband take all those materials with him, which was a sure sign that he meant to go to sea, and it being late in the night, she shut the door, and swore he should not go out of his house. He told her, " he must go, and was engaged to go to sea that night; for which he should be well paid ". His wife told him, " she was sure he was doing somewhat that would undo him, and she was resolved he should not go out of his house; and if he should persist in it, she would tell the neighbours, and carry him before the mayor to be examined, that the truth might be found out ". The poor man, thus mastered by the passion and violence of his wife, was forced to yield to her, that there might be no farther noise; and so went into his bed.

And it was very happy that the king's jealousy hastened him from that inn. It was the solemn fast day, which was observed in those times principally to inflame the people against the king, and all those who were loyal to him; and there was a chapel in that village, over against that inn, where a weaver, who had been a soldier, used to preach, and utter all the villainy imaginable against the old order of government; and he was then in chapel preaching to his congregation, when the king went from thence, and telling the people, " that Charles Stuart was lurking somewhere in that country, and that they would merit from God Almighty, if they could find him out ". The passengers, who had lodged in the inn that night, had, as soon as they were up, sent for a smith to visit their horses, it being a hard frost.   The smith, when he had done what he was sent for, according to the custom of that people, examined the feet of the other two horses, to find more work.   When he had observed them, he told the host of the house " that one of those horses had travelled far; and that he was sure that his four shoes had been made in four several counties ", which, whether his skill was able to discover or no, was very true.   The smith going to the sermon told this story to some of his neighbours; and so it came to the ears of the preacher, when his sermon was done.   Immediately he sent for an officer, and searched the inn, and inquired for those horses; and being informed that they were gone, he caused horses to be sent to follow them, and to make inquiry after the two men who rid those horses, and positively declared, " that one of them was Charles Stuart ".

When they came again to the colonel, they presently concluded that they were to make no longer stay in those parts, nor any more to endeavour to find a ship upon that coast; and, without any farther delay, they rode back to the colonel's house; where they arrived in the night. Then they resolved to make their next attempt more southward in Hampshire and Sussex, where colonel Windham had no interest.   They must pass through all Wiltshire before they came thither; which would require many days' journey: and they were first to consider what honest houses there were in' or near the way, where they might securely repose; and it was thought very dangerous for the king to ride through any great town as Salisbury, or Winchester, which might probably lie in their way.

There was between that and Salisbury a very honest gentleman, colonel Robert Philips, a younger brother of a very good family, which had always been very loyal; and he had served the king during the war. The king was resolved to trust him; and so sent the lord Wilmot to a place from whence he might send to Mr. Philips to come to him, and when he had spoken with him, Mr. Philips should come to the king, and Wilmot was to stay in such a place as they two should agree. Mr. Philips accordingly came to the colonel's house; which he could do without suspicion, they being nearly allied. The ways were very full of soldiers; which were sent now from the army to their quarters, and many regiments of horse and foot were assigned for the west; of which division Desborough was major-general. These marches were like to last for many days, and it would not be fit for the king to stay so long in that place. Thereupon, he resorted to his old security of taking a woman behind him, a kinswoman of colonel Windham, whom he carried in that manner to a place not far from Salisbury; to which colonel Philips conducted him. In this journey he passed through the middle of a regiment of horse; and, presently after, met Desborough walking down a hill with three or four men with him; who had lodged in Salisbury the night before; all that road being full of soldiers.

The next day, upon the plains, Dr. Hinchman, one of the prebends of Salisbury, met the king, the lord Wilmot and Philips then leaving him to go to the sea-coast to find a vessel, the doctor conducting the king to a place called Heale, three miles from Salisbury, belonging then to serjeant Hyde, who was afterwards chief-justice of the king's bench, and then in the possession of the widow of his elder brother; a house that stood alone from neighbours, and from any highway; where, coming in late in the evening, he supped with some gentlemen who accidentally were in the house; which could not

well be avoided.   But, the next morning, he went early
from thence, as if he had continued his journey; and the
widow, being trusted with the knowledge of her guest,
sent her servants out of the way; and, at an hour appointed, received him again, and accommodated him in
a little room, which had been made since the beginning
of the troubles for the concealment of delinquents, the
seat always belonging to a malignant family.   Here he
lay concealed, without the knowledge of some gentlemen
who lived in the house, and of others who daily resorted
thither, for many days, the widow herself only attending
him with such things as were necessary, and bringing
him such letters as the doctor received from the lord
Wilmot and colonel Philips.   A vessel being at last
provided upon the coast of Sussex, and notice thereof
sent to Dr. Hinchman, he sent to the king to meet him
at Stonehenge upon the plains three miles from Heale;
whither the widow took care to direct him; and being
there met, he attended him to the place where colonel
Philips received him.   He, the next day, delivered him
to the lord Wilmot; who went with him to a house in
Sussex, recommended by colonel Gunter, a gentleman of
that country, who had served the king in the war; who
met him there; and had provided a little bark at Bright-
helmstone, a small fisher-town; where he went early on
board, and, by God's blessing, arrived safely in Normandy.

The earl of Southampton, who was then at his house
at Titchfield in Hampshire, had been advertised of the
king's being in the west, and of his missing his passage at
Lyme, and sent a trusty gentleman to those faithful persons in the country, who, he thought, were most like to
be employed for his escape if he came into those parts,
to let them know, "that he had a ship ready, and if the
king came to him, he should be safe"; which advertise-

ment came to the king the night before he embarked,
and when his vessel was ready. But his majesty ever
acknowledged the obligation with great kindness, he
being the only person of that condition who had the
courage to solicit such danger, though all good men
heartily wished his deliverance. It was about the end
of November, that the king landed in Normandy, in a
small creek; from whence he got to Rouen, and then
gave notice to the queen of his arrival, and freed his
subjects in all places from their dismal apprehensions.

THE CHARACTER OF CROMWELL

He was one of those men, *quos vituperare ne inimici
quidem possunt, nisi ut simul laudent*; for he could never
have done half that mischief without great parts of
courage, industry, and judgement. He must have had
a wonderful understanding in the natures and humours
of men, and as great a dexterity in applying them; who,
from a private and obscure birth (though of a good
family), without interest or estate, alliance or friendship,
could raise himself to such a height, and compound
and knead such opposite and contradictory tempers,
humours, and interests into a consistence, that contributed to his designs, and to their own destruction;
whilst himself grew insensibly powerful enough to cut
off those by whom he had climbed, in the instant that
they projected to demolish their own building. What
Velleius Paterculus said of Cinna may very justly be
said of him, *ausum eum, quæ nemo auderet bonus; per-
fecisse, quæ a nullo, nisi fortissimo, perfici possent*. Without doubt, no man with more wickedness ever attempted
anything, or brought to pass what he desired more
wickedly, more in the face and contempt of religion,
and moral honesty; yet wickedness as great as his could

never have accomplished those trophies, without the assistance of a great spirit, an admirable circumspection and sagacity, and a most magnanimous resolution.

When he appeared first in the parliament, he seemed to have a person in no degree gracious, no ornament of discourse, none of those talents which use to reconcile the affections of the stander by: yet as he grew into place and authority, his parts seemed to be raised, as if he had had concealed faculties, till he had occasion to use them; and when he was to act the part of a great man, he did it without any indecency, notwithstanding the want of custom.

After he was confirmed and invested protector by the humble petition and advice, he consulted with very few upon any action of importance, nor communicated any enterprise he resolved upon, with more than those who were to have principal parts in the execution of it; nor with them sooner than was absolutely necessary. What he once resolved, in which he was not rash, he would not be dissuaded from, nor endure any contradiction of his power and authority; but extorted obedience from them who were not willing to yield it.

When he had laid some very extraordinary tax upon the city, one Cony, an eminent fanatic, and one who had heretofore served him very notably, positively refused to pay his part; and loudly dissuaded others from submitting to it, "as an imposition notoriously against the law, and the property of the subject, which all honest men were bound to defend". Cromwell sent for him, and cajoled him with the memory of "the old kindness, and friendship, that had been between them; and that of all men he did not expect this opposition from him, in a matter that was so necessary for the good of the commonwealth". But it was always his fortune to meet with the most rude and obstinate behaviour from those who had formerly been absolutely governed by him; and they commonly put him in mind of some expressions and sayings of his own, in cases of the like nature: so this man remembered him, how great an enemy he had expressed himself to such grievances, and had declared "that all who submitted to them, and paid illegal taxes, were more to blame, and greater enemies to their country, than they who had imposed them; and that the tyranny of princes could never be grievous, but by the tameness and stupidity of the people".

When Cromwell saw that he could not convert him, he told him, "that he had a will as stubborn as his, and he would try which of them two should be master". Thereupon, with some terms of reproach and contempt, he committed the man to prison; whose courage was nothing abated by it; but as soon as the term came, he brought his habeas corpus in the king's bench, which they then called the upper bench. Maynard, who was of council with the prisoner, demanded his liberty with great confidence, both upon the illegality of the commitment, and the illegality of the imposition, as being laid without any lawful authority. The judges could not maintain or defend either, and enough declared what their sentence would be; and therefore the protector's attorney required a farther day, to answer what had been urged. Before that day, Maynard was committed to the Tower, for presuming to question or make doubt of his authority; and the judges were sent for, and severely reprehended for suffering that license; when they, with all humility, mentioned the law and Magna Charta, Cromwell told them, "their *magna farta* should not control his actions; which he knew were for the safety of the commonwealth". He asked them, "who made them judges? whether they had any authority to sit there, but what he gave them? and if his authority were at an end, they knew well enough what would become of themselves; and therefore advised them to be more tender of that which could only preserve them"; and so dismissed them with caution, "that they should not suffer the lawyers to prate what it would not become them to hear".

Thus he subdued a spirit that had been often troublesome to the most sovereign power, and made Westminster Hall as obedient, and subservient to his commands, as any of the rest of his quarters. In all other matters, which did not concern the life of his jurisdiction, he seemed to have great reverence for the law, rarely interposing between party and party. As he proceeded with this kind of indignation and haughtiness with those who were refractory, and dared to contend with his greatness, so towards all who complied with his good pleasure, and courted his protection, he used a wonderful civility, generosity, and bounty.

To reduce three nations, which perfectly hated him, to an entire obedience to all his dictates; to awe and govern those nations by an army that was indevoted to him, and wished his ruin, was an instance of a very prodigious address. But his greatness at home was but a shadow of the glory he had abroad. It was hard to discover which feared him most, France, Spain, or the Low Countries, where his friendship was current at the value he put upon it. As they did all sacrifice their honour and their interest to his pleasure, so there is nothing he could have demanded, that either of them would have denied him. To manifest which, there needs only two instances. The first is, when those of the valley of Lucerne had unwarily rebelled against the duke of Savoy, which gave occasion to the pope, and the neighbour princes of Italy, to call and solicit for their extirpation, and their prince positively resolved upon it,

Cromwell sent his agent to the duke of Savoy, a prince with whom he had no correspondence or commerce, and so engaged the cardinal, and even terrified the pope himself, without so much as doing any grace to the English Roman Catholics (nothing being more usual than his saying, "that his ships in the Mediterranean should visit Civita Vecchia; and that the sound of his cannon should be heard in Rome"), that the duke of Savoy thought it necessary to restore all that he had taken from them, and did renew all those privileges they had formerly enjoyed, and newly forfeited.

The other instance of his authority was yet greater, and more incredible. In the city of Nismes, which is one of the fairest in the province of Languedoc, and where those of the religion do most abound, there was a great faction at that season when the consuls (who are the chief magistrates) were to be chosen. Those of the reformed religion had the confidence to set up one of themselves for that magistracy; which they of the Roman religion resolved to oppose with all their power. The dissension between them made so much noise, that the intendant of the province, who is the supreme minister in all civil affairs throughout the whole province, went thither to prevent any disorder that might happen. When the day of election came, those of the religion possessed themselves with many armed men of the town-house, where the election was to be made. The magistrates sent to know what their meaning was; to which they answered, "they were there to give their voices for the choice of the new consuls, and to be sure that the election should be fairly made". The bishop of the city, the intendant of the province, with all the officers of the church, and the present magistrates of the town, went together in their robes to be present at the election, without any suspicion that there would be any force used.

When they came near the gate of the town-house, which was shut, and they supposed would be opened when they came, they within poured out a volley of musket-shot upon them, by which the dean of the church, and two or three of the magistrates of the town, were killed upon the place, and very many others wounded; whereof some died shortly after. In this confusion, the magistrates put themselves into as good a posture to defend themselves as they could, without any purpose of offending the other, till they should be better provided; in order to which they sent an express to the court with a plain relation of the whole matter of fact, "and that there appeared to be no manner of combination with those of the religion in other places of the province; but that it was an insolence in those of the place, upon the presumption of their great numbers, which were little inferior to those of the Catholics". The court was glad of the occasion, and resolved that this provocation, in which other places were not involved, and which nobody could excuse, should warrant all kind of severity in that city, even to the pulling down their temples, and expelling many of them for ever out of the city; which, with the execution and forfeiture of many of the principal persons, would be a general mortification to all of the religion in France; with whom they were heartily offended; and a part of the army was forthwith ordered to march towards Nismes, to see this executed with the utmost rigour.

Those of the religion in the town were quickly sensible into what condition they had brought themselves; and sent, with all possible submission, to the magistrates to excuse themselves, and to impute what had been done to the rashness of particular men, who had no order for what they did. The magistrates answered, "that they were glad they were sensible of their miscarriage; but they could say nothing upon the subject till the king's

pleasure should be known; to whom they had sent a full
relation of all that had passed". The others very well
knew what the king's pleasure would be, and forthwith
sent an express, one Moulins, a Scotchman, who had
lived many years in that place and in Montpelier, to
Cromwell to desire his protection and interposition. The
express made so much haste, and found so good a recep-
tion the first hour he came, that Cromwell, after he had
received the whole account, bade him "refresh himself
after so long a journey, and he would take such care of
his business that by the time he came to Paris, he should
find it despatched"; and, that night, sent away another
messenger to his ambassador Lockhart; who, by the time
Moulins came thither, had so far prevailed with the
cardinal, that orders were sent to stop the troops, which
were upon their march towards Nismes; and, within few
days after, Moulins returned with a full pardon and am-
nesty from the king, under the great seal of France, so
fully confirmed with all circumstances, that there was
never farther mention made of it, but all things passed as
if there had never been any such thing. So that nobody
can wonder, that his memory remains still in those parts,
and with those people, in great veneration. He would
never suffer himself to be denied anything he ever asked
of the cardinal, alleging, "that the people would not be
otherwise satisfied"; which the cardinal bore very heavily,
and complained of to those with whom he would be free.
One day he visited madam Turenne, and when he took
his leave of her, she, according to her custom, besought
him to continue gracious to the churches. Whereupon
the cardinal told her, "that he knew not how to behave
himself; if he advised the king to punish and suppress
their insolence, Cromwell threatened him to join with
the Spaniard; and if he showed any favour to them, at
Rome they accounted him an heretic".

He was not a man of blood, and totally declined Machiavel's method; which prescribes, upon any alteration of government, as a thing absolutely necessary, to cut off all the heads of those, and extirpate their families, who are friends to the old one. It was confidently reported, that, in the council of officers, it was more than once proposed "that there might be a general massacre of all the royal party, as the only expedient to secure the government", but that Cromwell would never consent to it; it may be, out of too much contempt of his enemies. In a word, as he had all the wickedness against which damnation is denounced, and for which hell-fire is prepared, so he had some virtues which have caused the memory of some men in all ages to be celebrated, and he will be looked upon by posterity as a brave bad man.

4. DAVID HUME

(Hume's *History of England* is doubtless little read now either by students of history or of English literature; but it may be doubted whether this neglect is deserved or wise. No one, it is true, must go to the book either for unquestioned accuracy or for unprejudiced comment. Hume was a philosopher who turned his attention to history, and his equipment for his new task was, according to modern standards, insufficient. But Hume's intellectual greatness is such that his reflections on history claim attention, and his literary style and method of arrangement and presentation are throughout admirable. Nor is the *History* nearly so superficial as it has sometimes been represented. He was made librarian to the Advocates of Edinburgh in 1752, and had thus constant access to the best collection of books in Scotland: the extent of his task and the absence of arrangement in the national records would have made it impossible for him to use manuscript materials even if he had desired to do so. The value of his work varies considerably. The early part is naturally the weakest, while that which deals with the Stuart period has usually been considered as most vigorous in point of style, and founded upon the widest reading. The passage that follows, dealing as it does with the trial of Charles I and the character of Cromwell, has been chosen not only for its intrinsic interest, but also because it affords an interesting contrast with Clarendon on the one hand and Gardiner on the other. It will be interesting also to compare it with Carlyle's treatment of the same subject (*Cromwell's Letters and Speeches*, Letter LXXXVI). Hume's work gave offence to the dominant Whig party in England by its strong Tory sympathies. Something of them may be observed in this passage; but they do not find their strongest expression until the Revolution of 1688 comes up for treatment.)

THE TRIAL OF KING CHARLES I

THE pomp, the dignity, the ceremony of this transaction corresponded to the greatest conception that is suggested in the annals of human kind; the delegates of a great people sitting in judgment upon their supreme magistrate, and trying him for his misgovernment and breach of trust. The solicitor, in the name of the commons, represented, that Charles Stuart, being admitted king of England, and *entrusted* with a limited power; yet nevertheless, from a wicked design to erect an unlimited and tyrannical government, had traitorously and maliciously levied war against the present parliament, and the people, whom they represented, and was therefore impeached as a tyrant, traitor, murderer, and a public and implacable enemy to the commonwealth. After the charge was finished, the president directed his discourse to the king, and told him that the court expected his answer.

The king, though long detained a prisoner, and now produced as a criminal, sustained, by his magnanimous courage, the majesty of a monarch. With great temper and dignity, he declined the authority of the court, and refused to submit himself to their jurisdiction. He represented, that having been engaged in treaty with his two houses of parliament, and having finished almost every article, he had expected to be brought to his capital in another manner, and ere this time to have been restored to his power, dignity, revenue, as well as to his personal liberty: that he could not now perceive any appearance of the upper house, so essential a member of the constitution; and had learned, that even the commons, whose authority was pretended, were subdued by lawless force, and were bereaved of their liberty: that he himself was their "native hereditary king"; nor was the whole authority of the state, though free and united, entitled to try him, who derived his dignity from the Supreme Majesty of heaven: that, admitting those extravagant principles which levelled all orders of men, the court could plead no power delegated by the people; unless the consent of every individual, down to the meanest and most ignorant peasant, had been previously asked and obtained: that he acknowledged, without scruple, that he had a *trust* committed to him, and one most sacred and inviolable; he was entrusted with the liberties of his people, and would not now betray them by recognizing a power founded on the most atrocious violence and usurpation: that having taken arms, and frequently exposed his life in defence of public liberty, of the constitution, of the fundamental laws of the kingdom, he was willing in this last and most solemn scene, to seal with his blood those precious rights for which, though in vain, he had so long contended: that those who arrogated a title to sit as his judges, were born his subjects, and born subjects to those laws which determined, "that the king can do no wrong": that he was not reduced to the necessity of sheltering himself under this general maxim, which guards every English monarch, even the least deserving; but was able, by the most satisfactory reasons, to justify those measures in which he had been engaged: that to the whole world, and even to them, his pretended judges, he was desirous, if called upon in another manner, to prove the integrity of his conduct, and assert the justice of those defensive arms to which, unwillingly and unfortunately, he had had recourse; but that, in order to preserve a uniformity of conduct, he must at present forego the apology of his innocence; lest, by ratifying an authority no better founded than that of robbers and pirates, he be justly branded as the betrayer, instead of being applauded as the martyr of the constitution.

The president, in order to support the majesty of the people, and maintain the superiority of his court above the prisoner, still inculcated, that he must not decline the authority of his judges; that they overruled his objections; that they were delegated by the people, the only source of every lawful power; and that kings themselves acted but in trust from that community which had invested this high court of justice with its jurisdiction.

Even according to those principles, which, in his present situation, he was perhaps obliged to adopt, his behaviour in general will appear not a little harsh and barbarous; but when we consider him as a subject, and one, too, of no high character, addressing himself to his unfortunate sovereign, his style will be esteemed to the last degree audacious and insolent.

Three times was Charles produced before the court, and as often declined their jurisdiction. On the fourth, the judges having examined some witnesses, by whom it was proved that the king had appeared in arms against the forces commissioned by the parliament, they pronounced sentence against him. He seemed very anxious at this time to be admitted to a conference with the two houses; and it was supposed, that he intended to resign the crown to his son: but the court refused compliance, and considered that request as nothing but a delay of justice.

It is confessed, that the king's behaviour, during this last scene of his life, does honour to his memory; and that, in all appearances before his judges, he never forgot his part, either as a prince or as a man. Firm and intrepid, he maintained, in each reply, the utmost perspicuity and justness both of thought and expression: mild and equable, he rose into no passion at that unusual authority which was assumed over him. His soul, without effort or affectation, seemed only to remain in the situation familiar to it, and to look down with contempt on all the efforts of human malice and iniquity. The soldiers, instigated by their superiors, were brought, though with difficulty, to cry aloud for justice. " Poor souls!" said the king to one of his attendants; "for a little money they would do as much against their commanders." Some of them were permitted to go the utmost length of brutal insolence, and to spit in his face, as he was conducted

along the passage to the court.   To excite a sentiment
of pity was the only effect which this inhuman insult
was able to produce upon him.

The people, though under the rod of lawless, unlimited
power, could not forbear, with the most ardent prayers,
pouring forth their wishes for his preservation; and in
his present distress, they avowed him, by their generous
tears, for their monarch, whom, in their misguided fury,
they had before so violently rejected.   The king was
softened at this moving scene, and expressed his gratitude
for their dutiful affection.   One soldier, too, seized by
contagious sympathy, demanded from heaven a blessing
on oppressed and fallen majesty: his officer, overhearing
the prayer, beat him to the ground in the king's presence.
"The punishment, methinks, exceeds the offence": this
was the reflection which Charles formed on that occasion.

As soon as the intention of trying the king was known
in foreign countries, so enormous an action was exclaimed
against by the general voice of reason and humanity;
and all men, under whatever form of government they
were born, rejected this example, as the utmost effort of
undisguised usurpation, and the most heinous insult on
law and justice.   The French ambassador, by orders from
his court, interposed in the king's behalf: the Dutch
employed their good offices: the Scots exclaimed and
protested against the violence: the queen, the prince,
wrote pathetic letters to the parliament.   All solicitations
were found fruitless with men whose resolutions were
fixed and irrevocable.

Four of Charles's friends, persons of virtue and dignity,
Richmond, Hertford, Southampton, Lindesey, applied to
the commons.   They represented, that they were the
king's counsellors, and had concurred by their advice in
all those measures which were now imputed as crimes to
their royal master: that, in the eye of the law, and ac-

cording to the dictates of common reason, they alone were guilty, and were alone exposed to censure for every blameable action of the prince; and that they now presented themselves, in order to save, by their own punishment, that precious life which it became the commons themselves, and every subject, with the utmost hazard, to protect and defend. Such a generous effort tended to their honour, but contributed nothing towards the king's safety.

The people remained in that silence and astonishment which all great passions, when they have not an opportunity of exerting themselves, naturally produce in the human mind. The soldiers, being incessantly plied with prayers, sermons, and exhortations, were wrought up to a degree of fury, and imagined, that in the acts of the most extreme disloyalty towards their prince consisted their greatest merit in the eye of heaven.

Three days were allowed the king between his sentence and his execution. This interval he passed with great tranquillity, chiefly in reading and devotion. All his family that remained in England were allowed access to him. It consisted only of the princess Elizabeth and the duke of Gloucester; for the duke of York had made his escape. Gloucester was little more than an infant: the princess, notwithstanding her tender years, showed an advanced judgment; and the calamities of her family had made a deep impression upon her. After many pious consolations and advices, the king gave her in charge to tell the queen, that during the whole course of his life he had never once, even in thought, failed in his fidelity towards her; and that his conjugal tenderness and his life should have an equal duration.

To the young duke, too, he could not forbear giving some advice, in order to season his mind with early principles of loyalty and obedience towards his brother, who was so soon to be his sovereign. Holding him on his knee, he said, " Now they will cut off thy father's head ". At these words the child looked very steadfastly upon him. " Mark, child, what I say: they will cut off my head! and perhaps make thee a king; but, mark what I say: thou must not be a king, as long as thy brothers Charles and James are alive. They will cut off thy brothers' heads, when they can catch them! And thy head too will they cut off at last! Therefore, I charge thee, do not be made a king by them!" The duke, sighing, replied, " I will be torn in pieces first!" So determined an answer, from one of such tender years, filled the king's eyes with tears of joy and admiration.

Every night during this interval the king slept as sound as usual; though the noise of workmen employed in framing the scaffold, and other preparations for his execution, continually resounded in his ears. The morning of the fatal day he rose early; and calling Herbert, one of his attendants, he bade him employ more than usual care in dressing him, and preparing him for so great and joyful a solemnity. Bishop Juxon, a man endowed with the same mild and steady virtues by which the king himself was so much distinguished, assisted him in his devotions, and paid the last melancholy duties to his friend and sovereign.

The street before Whitehall was the place destined for the execution; for it was intended, by choosing that very place, in sight of his own palace, to display more evidently the triumph of popular justice over royal majesty. When the king came upon the scaffold, he found it so surrounded with soldiers, that he could not expect to be heard by any of the people: he addressed, therefore, his discourse to the few persons who were about him; particularly colonel Tomlinson, to whose care he had lately been committed, and upon whom, as upon many others, his amiable deportment had wrought an entire conversion. He justified his own innocence in the late fatal wars; and observed, that he had not taken arms till after the parliament had enlisted forces; nor had he any other object in his warlike operations, than to preserve that authority entire which his predecessors had transmitted to him. He threw not, however, the blame upon the parliament; but was more inclined to think, that ill instruments had interposed, and raised in them fears and jealousies with regard to his intentions. Though innocent towards his people, he acknowledged the equity of his execution in the eyes of his Maker; and observed, that an unjust sentence which he had suffered to take effect, was now punished by an unjust sentence upon himself. He forgave all his enemies, even the chief instruments of his death; but exhorted them and the whole nation, to return to the ways of peace, by paying obedience to their lawful sovereign, his son and successor. When he was preparing himself for the block, bishop Juxon called to him: "There is, sir, but one stage more, which, though turbulent and troublesome, is yet a very short one. Consider, it will soon carry you a great way; it will carry you from earth to heaven; and there you shall find, to your great joy, the prize to which you hasten, a crown of glory." "I go", replied the king, "from a corruptible to an incorruptible crown; where no disturbance can have place." At one blow was his head severed from his body. A man in a vizor performed the office of executioner: another, in a like disguise, held up to the spectators the head streaming with blood, and cried aloud, "This is the head of a traitor!"

It is impossible to describe the grief, indignation, and astonishment which took place, not only among the spectators, who were overwhelmed with a flood of sorrow, but throughout the whole nation, as soon as the report of this fatal execution was conveyed to them. Never monarch, in the full triumph of success and victory, was more dear to his people, than his misfortunes and magnanimity, his patience and piety, had rendered this unhappy prince. In proportion to their former delusions, which had animated them against him, was the violence of their return to duty and affection; while each reproached himself, either with active disloyalty towards him, or with too indolent defence of his oppressed cause.   On weaker minds, the effect of these complicated passions was prodigious. Women are said to have cast forth the untimely fruit of their womb: others fell into convulsions, or sunk into such a melancholy as attended them to their grave: nay some, unmindful of themselves, as though they could not or would not survive their beloved prince, it is reported, suddenly fell down dead.   The very pulpits were bedewed with unsuborned tears; those pulpits which had formerly thundered out the most violent imprecations and anathemas against him.   And all men united in their detestation of those hypocritical parricides, who, by sanctified pretences, had so long disguised their treasons, and in this last act of iniquity had thrown an indelible stain upon the nation.

A fresh instance of hypocrisy was displayed the very day of the king's death.   The generous Fairfax, not content with being absent from the trial, had used all the interest which he yet retained to prevent the execution of the fatal sentence; and had even employed persuasion with his own regiment, though none else should follow him, to rescue the king from his disloyal murderers.   Cromwell and Ireton, informed of this intention, endeavoured to convince him, that the Lord had rejected the king; and they exhorted him to seek by prayer some direction from heaven on this important occasion: but they concealed from him that they had already signed the warrant for the execution. Harrison was the person appointed to join in prayer with the unwary general. By agreement, he prolonged his doleful cant till intelligence arrived, that the fatal blow was struck. He then rose from his knees, and insisted with Fairfax that this event was a miraculous and providential answer, which heaven had sent to their devout supplications.

It being remarked, that the king, the moment before he stretched out his neck to the executioner, had said to Juxon, with a very earnest accent, the single word, "Remember", great mysteries were supposed to be concealed under that expression; and the generals vehemently insisted with the prelate, that he should inform them of the king's meaning. Juxon told them, that the king having frequently charged him to inculcate on his son the forgiveness of his murderers, had taken this opportunity, in the last moment of his life, when his commands, he supposed, would be regarded as sacred and inviolable, to reiterate that desire; and that his mild spirit thus terminated its present course by an act of benevolence towards his greatest enemies.

The character of this prince, as that of most men, if not of all men, was mixed; but his virtues predominated extremely above his vices, or more properly speaking, his imperfections; for scarce any of his faults rose to that pitch as to merit the appellation of vices. To consider him in the most favourable light, it may be affirmed, that his dignity was free from pride, his humanity from weakness, his bravery from rashness, his temperance from austerity, his frugality from avarice: all these virtues in him maintained their proper bounds, and merited unreserved praise. To speak the most harshly of him, we may affirm, that many of his good qualities were attended with some latent frailty, which, though seemingly inconsiderable, was able, when seconded by the extreme

malevolence of his fortune, to disappoint them of all
their influence: his beneficent disposition was clouded by
a manner not very gracious; his virtue was tinctured with
superstition; his good sense was disfigured by a deference
to persons of capacity inferior to his own; and his moderate temper exempted him not from hasty and precipitate
resolutions.   He deserves the epithet of a good, rather
than of a great man; and was more fitted to rule in a
regular established government, than either to give way
to the encroachments of a popular assembly, or finally to
subdue their pretensions.   He wanted suppleness and
dexterity sufficient for the first measure: he was not endowed with the vigour requisite for the second.   Had he
been born an absolute prince, his humanity and good
sense had rendered his reign happy and his memory
precious: had the limitations on prerogative been in his
time quite fixed and certain, his integrity had made him
regard as sacred the boundaries of the constitution.   Unhappily, his fate threw him into a period, when the
precedents of many former reigns savoured strongly of
arbitrary power, and the genius of the people ran violently
towards liberty.   And if his political prudence was not
sufficient to extricate him from so perilous a situation, he
may be excused; since, even after the event, when it is
commonly easy to correct all errors, one is at a loss to
determine what conduct, in his circumstances, could have
maintained the authority of the crown, and preserved the
peace of the nation.   Exposed, without revenue, without
arms, to the assault of furious, implacable, and bigoted
factions, it was never permitted him, but with the most
fatal consequences, to commit the smallest mistake; a
condition too rigorous to be imposed on the greatest
human capacity.

Some historians have rashly questioned the good faith
of this prince; but, for this reproach, the most malignant

scrutiny of his conduct, which in every circumstance is now thoroughly known, affords not any reasonable foundation. On the contrary, if we consider the extreme difficulties to which he was so frequently reduced, and compare the sincerity of his professions and declarations, we shall avow, that probity and honour ought justly to be numbered among his most shining qualities. In every treaty, those concessions which he thought he could not in conscience maintain, he never could, by any motive or persuasion, be induced to make. And though some violations of the petition of right may be imputed to him, these are more to be ascribed to the necessity of his situation, and to the lofty ideas of royal prerogative, which, from former established precedents, he had imbibed, than to any failure in the integrity of his principles.

This prince was of a comely presence; of a sweet, but melancholy aspect. His face was regular, handsome, and well complexioned; his body strong, healthy, and justly proportioned; and, being of a middle stature, he was capable of enduring the greatest fatigues. He excelled in horsemanship and other exercises; and he possessed all the exterior, as well as many of the essential qualities, which form an accomplished prince.

The tragical death of Charles begat a question, whether the people, in any case, were entitled to judge and punish their sovereign; and most men, regarding chiefly the atrocious usurpation of the pretended judges, and the merit of the virtuous prince who suffered, were inclined to condemn the republican principle as highly seditious and extravagant; but there still were a few who, abstracting from the particular circumstances of this case, were able to consider the question in general, and were inclined to moderate, not contradict the prevailing sentiment. Such might have been their reasoning. If

ever, on any occasion, it were laudable to conceal truth
from the populace, it must be confessed that the doctrine
of resistance affords such an example; and that all speculative reasoners ought to observe, with regard to this
principle, the same cautious silence which the laws, in
every species of government, have ever prescribed to
themselves. Government is instituted in order to restrain
the fury and injustice of the people; and being always
founded on opinion, not on force, it is dangerous to
weaken, by these speculations, the reverence which the
multitude owe to authority, and to instruct them before-
hand, that the case can ever happen when they may be
freed from their duty of allegiance. Or should it be
found impossible to restrain the license of human dis-
quisitions, it must be acknowledged, that the doctrine of
obedience ought alone to be *inculcated*; and that the
exceptions, which are rare, ought seldom or never to be
mentioned in popular reasonings and discourses. Nor is
there any danger that mankind, by this prudent reserve,
should universally degenerate into a state of abject servi-
tude. When the exception really occurs, even though it
be not previously expected and descanted on, it must,
from its very nature, be so obvious and undisputed, as to
remove all doubt, and overpower the restraint, however
great, imposed by teaching the general doctrine of obedience. But between resisting a prince and dethroning
him, there is a wide interval; and the abuses of power
which can warrant the latter violence, are greater and
more enormous than those which will justify the former.
History, however, supplies us with examples even of this
kind; and the reality of the supposition, though for the
future it ought ever to be little looked for, must, by all
candid enquirers, be acknowledged in the past. But
between dethroning a prince and punishing him, there is
another very wide interval; and it were not strange, if

even men of the most enlarged thought should question, whether human nature could ever, in any monarch, reach that height of depravity, as to warrant, in revolted subjects, this last act of extraordinary jurisdiction. That illusion, if it be an illusion, which teaches us to pay a sacred regard to the persons of princes, is so salutary, that to dissipate it by the formal trial and punishment of a sovereign, will have more pernicious effects upon the people, than the example of justice can be supposed to have a beneficial influence upon princes, by checking their career of tyranny. It is dangerous also, by these examples, to reduce princes to despair, or bring matters to such extremities against persons endowed with great power, as to leave them no resource but in the most violent and most sanguinary counsels. This general position being established, it must, however, be observed, that no reader, almost of any party or principle, was ever shocked, when he read in ancient history that the Roman senate voted Nero, their absolute sovereign, to be a public enemy, and, even without trial, condemned him to the severest and most ignominious punishment; a punishment from which the meanest Roman citizen was, by the laws, exempted. The crimes of that bloody tyrant are so enormous, that they break through all rules; and extort a confession, that such a dethroned prince is no longer superior to his people, and can no longer plead, in his own defence, laws which were established for conducting the ordinary course of administration. But when we pass from the case of Nero to that of Charles, the great disproportion, or rather total contrariety of character immediately strikes us; and we stand astonished, that, among a civilized people, so much virtue could ever meet with so fatal a catastrophe. History, the great mistress of wisdom, furnishes examples of all kinds; and every prudential, as well as moral precept, may be authorized by those events which her enlarged mirror is able to present to us. From the memorable revolutions which passed in England during this period, we may naturally deduce the same useful lesson which Charles himself in his later years inferred; that it is dangerous for princes, even from the appearance of necessity, to assume more authority than the laws have allowed them. But it must be confessed, that these events furnish us with another instruction, no less natural, and no less useful, concerning the madness of the people, the furies of fanaticism, and the danger of mercenary armies.

5. EDWARD GIBBON

(For the character of Gibbon's work see Introduction. His treatment of Julian is chosen as a thoroughly representative passage of his work at its best. Julian was usually a great hero with the sceptical writers of the eighteenth century: they rejoiced to find a pagan emperor preaching toleration while the contemporary Christians were practising persecution, and declaring the infinite value of the classical learning which the triumph of the Christian Church was soon to overwhelm. There was a great temptation, therefore, to regard Julian with undiscriminating hero-worship, and to misunderstand the circumstances of his time. Gibbon has been saved by his historical sense and his unenthusiastic nature from treating Julian as Voltaire treated him.

The character of this book makes it necessary to omit the notes, which are, as has been said in the preface, an important and interesting feature of Gibbon's work. But a student who desires to make himself acquainted with the full literary quality of Gibbon's work must not omit to turn to them.)

JULIAN

JULIAN was not insensible of the advantages of freedom. From his studies he had imbibed the spirit of ancient sages and heroes; his life and fortunes had depended on the caprice of a tyrant; and, when he ascended the throne, his pride was sometimes mortified by the reflection that the slaves who would not dare to censure his defects were not worthy to applaud his virtues. He sincerely abhorred the system of Oriental despotism which Diocletian, Constantine, and the patient habits of fourscore years, had established in the empire. A motive of superstition prevented the execution of the design which Julian had frequently meditated, of relieving his head from the weight of a costly diadem; but he absolutely refused the titles of *Dominus*, or *Lord*, a word which was grown so familiar to the ears of the Romans, that they no longer remembered its servile and humiliating origin. The office, or rather the name, of consul was cherished by a prince who contemplated with reverence the ruins of the republic; and the same behaviour which had been assumed by the prudence of Augustus was adopted by Julian from choice and inclination. On the calends of January, at break of day, the new consuls, Mamertinus and Nevitta, hastened to the palace to salute the emperor. As soon as he was informed of their approach, he leaped from his throne, eagerly advanced to meet them, and compelled the blushing magistrates to receive the demonstrations of his affected humility. From the palace they proceeded to the senate. The emperor, on foot, marched before their litters, and the gazing multitude admired the image of ancient times, or secretly blamed a conduct which, in their eyes, degraded the majesty of the purple. But the behaviour of Julian was uniformly supported. During the games of the Circus he had, imprudently or designedly, performed the manumission of a slave in the presence of the consul. The moment he was reminded that he had trespassed on the jurisdiction of *another* magistrate, he condemned himself to pay a fine of ten pounds of gold, and embraced this public occasion of declaring to the world that he was subject, like the rest of his fellow-citizens, to the laws, and even to the forms, of the republic. The spirit of his administration, and his regard for the place of his nativity, induced Julian to confer on the senate of Constantinople the same honours, privileges, and authority which were still enjoyed by the senate of ancient Rome. A legal fiction was introduced and gradually established, that one-half of the national council had migrated into the East, and the despotic successors of Julian, accepting the title of Senators, acknowledged themselves the members of a respectable body which was permitted to represent the majesty of the Roman name. From Constantinople the attention of the monarch was extended to the municipal senates of the provinces. He abolished, by repeated edicts, the unjust and pernicious exemptions which had withdrawn so many idle citizens from the service of their country; and by imposing an equal distribution of public duties, he restored the strength, the splendour, or, according to the glowing expression of Libanius, the soul of the expiring cities of his empire. The venerable age of Greece excited the most tender compassion in the mind of Julian, which kindled into rapture when he recollected the gods, the heroes, and the men superior to heroes and to gods, who had bequeathed to the latest posterity the monuments of their genius or the example of their virtues. He relieved the distress and restored the beauty of the cities of Epirus and Peloponnesus. Athens acknowledged him for her benefactor, Argos for her deliverer. The pride of Corinth, again rising from her ruins with the honours of a Roman colony, exacted a tribute from the adjacent republics for the purpose of defraying the games of the Isthmus, which were celebrated in the amphitheatre with the hunting of bears and panthers. From this tribute the cities of Elis, of Delphi, and of Argos, which had inherited from their remote ancestors the sacred office of perpetuating the Olympic, the Pythian, and the Nemean games, claimed a just exemption. The immunity of Elis and Delphi was respected by the Corinthians, but the poverty of Argos tempted the insolence of oppression, and the feeble complaints of its deputies were silenced by the decree of a provincial magistrate, who seems to have consulted only the interest of the capital in which he resided. Seven years after this sentence Julian allowed the cause to be referred to a superior tribunal, and his eloquence was interposed, most probably with success, in the defence of a city which had been the royal seat of Agamemnon, and had given to Macedonia a race of kings and conquerors.

The laborious administration of military and civil affairs, which were multiplied in proportion to the extent of the empire, exercised the abilities of Julian; but he frequently assumed the two characters of Orator and of Judge, which are almost unknown to the modern sovereigns of Europe. The arts of persuasion, so diligently cultivated by the first Cæsars, were neglected by the military ignorance and Asiatic pride of their successors, and, if they condescended to harangue the soldiers, whom they feared, they treated with silent disdain the senators, whom they despised. The assemblies of the senate, which Constantius had avoided, were considered by Julian as the place where he could exhibit with the most propriety the maxims of a republican and the talents of a rhetorician. He alternately practised, as in a school of declamation, the several modes of praise, of censure, of exhortation; and his friend Libanius has remarked that the study of Homer taught him to imitate the simple, concise style of Menelaus, the copiousness of Nestor, whose words descended like the flakes of a winter's snow, or the pathetic and forcible eloquence of Ulysses. The functions of a judge, which are sometimes incompatible with those of a prince, were exercised by Julian not only as a duty, but as an amusement; and although he might have trusted the integrity and discernment of his Prætorian præfects, he often placed himself by their side on the seat of judgment. The acute penetration of his mind was agreeably occupied in detecting and defeating the chicanery of the advocates, who laboured to disguise the truth of facts and to pervert the sense of the laws. He sometimes forgot the gravity of his station, asked indiscreet or unseasonable questions, and betrayed, by the loudness of his voice and the agitation of his body, the earnest vehemence with which he maintained his opinion against the judges, the advocates, and their clients. But his knowledge of his own temper prompted him to encourage, and even to solicit, the reproof of his friends and ministers: and whenever they ventured to oppose the irregular sallies of his passions, the spectators could observe the shame as well as the gratitude of their monarch. The decrees of Julian were almost always founded on the principles of justice, and he had the firmness to resist the two most dangerous temptations which assault the tribunal of a sovereign under the specious forms of compassion and equity. He decided the merits of the cause without weighing the circumstances of the parties; and the poor, whom he wished to relieve, were condemned to satisfy the just demands of a noble and wealthy adversary. He carefully distinguished the judge from the legislator; and though he meditated a necessary reformation of the Roman jurisprudence, he pronounced sentence according to the strict and literal interpretation of those laws which the magistrates were bound to execute and the subjects to obey.

The generality of princes, if they were stripped of their purple and cast naked into the world, would immediately sink to the lowest rank of society, without a hope of emerging from their obscurity. But the personal merit of Julian was, in some measure, independent of his fortune. Whatever had been his choice of life, by the force of intrepid courage, lively wit, and intense application, he would have obtained, or at least he would have deserved, the highest honours of his profession, and Julian might have raised himself to the rank of minister or general of the state in which he was born a private citizen. If the jealous caprice of power had disappointed his expectations, if he had prudently declined the paths of greatness, the employment of the same talents in studious solitude would have placed beyond the reach of kings his present happiness and his immortal fame. When we inspect with minute, or perhaps malevolent, attention the portrait of Julian, something seems wanting to the grace and perfection of the whole figure. His genius was less powerful and sublime than that of Cæsar, nor did he possess the consummate prudence of Augustus. The virtues of Trajan appear more steady and natural, and the philosophy of Marcus is more simple and consistent. Yet Julian sustained adversity with firmness, and prosperity with moderation. After an interval of one hundred and twenty years from the death of Alexander Severus, the Romans beheld an emperor who made no distinction between his duties and his pleasures, who laboured to relieve the distress and to revive the spirit of his subjects, and who endeavoured always to connect authority with merit, and happiness with virtue. Even faction, and religious faction, was constrained to acknowledge the superiority of his genius in peace as well as in war, and to confess, with a sigh, that the apostate Julian was a lover of his country, and that he deserved the empire of the world.

The character of Apostate has injured the reputation of Julian; and the enthusiasm which clouded his virtues has exaggerated the real and apparent magnitude of his faults. Our partial ignorance may represent him as a philosophic monarch, who studied to protect, with an equal hand, the religious factions of the empire, and to allay the theological fever which had inflamed the minds of the people from the edicts of Diocletian to the exile of Athanasius. A more accurate view of the character and conduct of Julian will remove this favourable prepossession for a prince who did not escape the general contagion of the times. We enjoy the singular advantage of comparing the pictures which have been delineated by his fondest admirers and his implacable enemies. The actions of Julian are faithfully related by a judicious and candid historian, the impartial spectator of his life and death. The unanimous evidence of his contemporaries is confirmed by the public and private declarations of the emperor himself; and his various writings express the uniform tenor of his religious sentiments, which policy would have prompted him to dissemble rather than to affect. A devout and sincere attachment for the gods of Athens and Rome constituted the ruling passion of Julian; the powers of an enlightened understanding were betrayed and corrupted by the influence of superstitious prejudice; and the phantoms which existed only in the mind of the emperor had a real and pernicious effect on the government of the empire. The vehement zeal of the Christians, who despised the worship, and overturned the altars, of those fabulous deities, engaged their votary in a state of irreconcilable hostility with a very numerous party of his subjects; and he was sometimes tempted, by the desire of victory or the shame of a repulse, to violate the laws of prudence, and even of justice. The triumph of the party which he deserted and opposed has fixed a stain of infamy on the name of Julian; and the unsuccessful apostate has been overwhelmed with a torrent of pious invectives, of which the signal was given by the sonorous trumpet of Gregory Nazianzen. The interesting nature of the events which were crowded into the short reign of this active emperor deserves a just and circumstantial narrative. His motives, his counsels, and his actions, as far as they are connected with the history of religion, will be the subject of the present chapter.

The cause of his strange and fatal apostasy may be derived from the early period of his life when he was left an orphan in the hands of the murderers of his family.

The names of Christ and of Constantius, the ideas of slavery and of religion, were soon associated in a youthful imagination, which was susceptible of the most lively impressions. The care of his infancy was entrusted to Eusebius, bishop of Nicomedia, who was related to him on the side of his mother; and till Julian reached the twentieth year of his age, he received from his Christian preceptors the education not of a hero but of a saint. The emperor, less jealous of a heavenly than of an earthly crown, contented himself with the imperfect character of a catechumen, while he bestowed the advantages of baptism on the nephews of Constantine. They were even admitted to the inferior offices of the ecclesiastical order; and Julian publicly read the Holy Scriptures in the church of Nicomedia. The study of religion, which they assiduously cultivated, appeared to produce the fairest fruits of faith and devotion. They prayed, they fasted, they distributed alms to the poor, gifts to the clergy, and oblations to the tombs of the martyrs; and the splendid monument of St. Mamas, at Cæsarea, was erected, or at least was undertaken, by the joint labour of Gallus and Julian. They respectfully conversed with the bishops who were eminent for superior sanctity, and solicited the benediction of the monks and hermits who had introduced into Cappadocia the voluntary hardships of the ascetic life. As the two princes advanced towards the years of manhood, they discovered, in their religious sentiments, the difference of their characters. The dull and obstinate understanding of Gallus embraced, with implicit zeal, the doctrines of Christianity, which never influenced his conduct, or moderated his passions. The mild disposition of the younger brother was less repugnant to the precepts of the Gospel; and his active curiosity might have been gratified by a theological system which explains the mysterious essence of the Deity, and opens the boundless prospect of invisible and future worlds. But the independent spirit of Julian refused to yield the passive and unresisting obedience which was required, in the name of religion, by the haughty ministers of the church. Their speculative opinions were imposed as positive laws, and guarded by the terrors of eternal punishments; but while they prescribed the rigid formulary of the thoughts, the words, and the actions of the young prince; whilst they silenced his objections, and severely checked the freedom of his inquiries, they secretly provoked his impatient genius to disclaim the authority of his ecclesiastical guides. He was educated in Lesser Asia, amidst the scandals of the Arian controversy. The fierce contest of the Eastern bishops, the incessant alterations of their creeds, and the profane motives which appeared to actuate their conduct, insensibly strengthened the prejudice of Julian that they neither understood nor believed the religion for which they so fiercely contended. Instead of listening to the proofs of Christianity with that favourable attention which adds weight to the most respectable evidence, he heard with suspicion, and disputed with obstinacy and acuteness, the doctrines for which he already entertained an invincible aversion. Whenever the young princes were directed to compose declamations on the subject of the prevailing controversies, Julian always declared himself the advocate of Paganism, under the specious excuse that, in the defence of the weaker cause, his learning and ingenuity might be more advantageously exercised and displayed.

As soon as Gallus was invested with the honours of the purple, Julian was permitted to breathe the air of freedom, of literature, and of Paganism. The crowd of sophists, who were attracted by the taste and liberality of their royal pupil, had formed a strict alliance between the learning and the religion of Greece; and the poems of Homer, instead of being admired as the original productions of human genius, were seriously ascr_ted to the heavenly aspiration of Apollo and the muses. The deities of Olympus, as they are painted by the immortal bard, imprint themselves on the minds which are the least addicted to superstitious credulity. Our familiar knowledge of their names and characters, their forms and attributes, *seems* to bestow on those airy beings a real and substantial existence; and the.pleasing enchantment produces an imperfect and momentary assent of the imagination to those fables which are the most repugnant to our reason and experience. In the age of Julian every circumstance contributed to prolong and fortify the illusion—the magnificent temples of Greece and Asia; the works of those artists who had expressed, in painting or in sculpture, the divine conceptions of the poet; the pomp of festivals and sacrifices; the successful arts of divination; the popular traditions of oracles and prodigies; and the ancient practice of two thousand years. The weakness of polytheism was, in some measure, excused by the moderation of its claims; and the devotion of the pagans was not incompatible with the most licentious scepticism. Instead of an indivisible and regular system, which occupies the whole extent of the believing mind, the mythology of the Greeks was composed of a thousand loose and flexible parts, and the servant of the gods was at liberty to define the degree and measure of his religious faith. The creed which Julian adopted for his own use was of the largest dimensions; and, by a strange contradiction, he disdained the salutary yoke of the Gospel, whilst he made a voluntary offering of his reason on the altars of Jupiter and Apollo. One of the orations of Julian is consecrated to the honour of Cybele, the mother of the gods, who required from her effeminate priests the bloody sacrifice so rashly performed by the madness of the Phrygian boy. The pious emperor condescends to relate, without a blush and without a smile, the voyage of the goddess from the shores of Pergamus to the mouth of the Tiber; and the stupendous miracle which convinced the senate and people of Rome that the lump of clay which their ambassadors had transported over the seas was endowed with life, and sentiment, and divine power. For the truth of this prodigy he appeals to the public monuments of the city; and censures, with some acrimony, the sickly and affected taste of those men who impertinently derided the sacred traditions of their ancestors.

But the devout philosopher, who sincerely embraced, and warmly encouraged, the superstition of the people, reserved for himself the privilege of a liberal interpretation, and silently withdrew from the foot of the altars into the sanctuary of the temple. The extravagance of the Grecian mythology proclaimed, with a clear and audible voice, that the pious inquirer, instead of being scandalized or satisfied with the literal sense, should diligently explore the occult wisdom, which had been disguised, by the prudence of antiquity, under the mask of folly and of fable. The philosophers of the Platonic school, Plotinus, Porphyry, and the divine Iamblichus, were admired as the most skilful masters of this allegorical science, which laboured to soften and harmonize the deformed features of Paganism. Julian himself, who was directed in the mysterious pursuit by Ædesius, the venerable successor of Iamblichus, aspired to the possession of a treasure which he esteemed, if we may credit his solemn asseverations, far above the empire of the world. It was indeed a treasure which derived its value only from opinion; and every artist who flattered himself that he had extracted the precious ore from the surrounding dross claimed an equal right of stamping the name and figure the most agreeable to his peculiar fancy. The fable of Atys and Cybele had already been explained by Porphyry; but his labours served only to animate the pious industry of Julian, who invented and published his own allegory of that ancient and mystic tale. This freedom of interpretation, which might gratify the pride of the Platonists, exposed the vanity of their art. Without a tedious detail the modern reader could not form a just idea of the strange allusions, the forced etymologies, the solemn trifling, and the impenetrable obscurity of these sages, who professed to reveal the system of the universe. As the traditions of Pagan mythology were variously related, the sacred interpreters were at liberty to select the most convenient circumstances; and as they translated an arbitrary cipher, they could extract from *any* fable *any* sense which was adapted to their favourite system of religion and philosophy. The lascivious form of a naked Venus was tortured into the discovery of some moral precept, or some physical truth; and the castration of Atys explained the revolution of the sun between the tropics, or the separation of the human soul from vice and error.

The theological system of Julian appears to have contained the sublime and important principles of natural religion. But as the faith which is not founded on revelation must remain destitute of any firm assurance, the disciple of Plato imprudently relapsed into the habits of vulgar superstition; and the popular and philosophic notion of the Deity seems to have been confounded in the practice, the writings, and even in the mind of Julian. The pious emperor acknowledged and adored the Eternal Cause of the universe, to whom he ascribed all the perfections of an infinite nature, invisible to the eyes and inaccessible to the understanding of feeble mortals. The Supreme God had created, or rather, in the Platonic language, had generated, the gradual succession of dependent spirits, of gods, of dæmons, of heroes, and of men; and every being which derived its existence immediately from the First Cause received the inherent gift of immortality. That so precious an advantage might not be lavished upon unworthy objects, the Creator had intrusted to the skill and power of the inferior gods the office of forming the human body, and of arranging the beautiful harmony of the animal, the vegetable, and the mineral kingdoms. To the conduct of these divine ministers he delegated the temporal government of this lower world; but their imperfect administration is not exempt from discord or error. The earth and its inhabitants are divided among them, and the characters of Mars or Minerva, of Mercury or Venus, may be distinctly traced in the laws and manners of their peculiar votaries. As long as our immortal souls are confined in a mortal prison, it is our interest, as well as our duty, to solicit the favour, and to deprecate the wrath, of the powers of heaven; whose pride is gratified by the devotion of mankind, and whose grosser parts may be supposed to derive some nourishment from the fumes of sacrifice. The inferior gods might sometimes condescend to animate the statues, and to inhabit the temples, which were dedicated to their honour. They might occasionally visit the earth, but the heavens were the proper throne and symbol of their glory. The invariable order of the sun, moon, and stars was hastily admitted by Julian as a proof of their *eternal* duration; and their eternity was a sufficient evidence that they were the workmanship, not of an inferior deity, but of the Omnipotent King. In the system of the Platonists the visible was a type of the invisible world. The celestial bodies, as they were informed by a divine spirit, might be considered as the objects the most worthy of religious worship. The Sun, whose genial influence pervades and sustains the universe, justly claimed the adoration of mankind as the bright representative of the Logos, the lively, the rational, the beneficent image of the intellectual Father.

In every age the absence of genuine inspiration is supplied by the strong illusions of enthusiasm and the mimic arts of imposture. If, in the time of Julian, these arts had been practised only by the pagan priests, for the support of an expiring cause, some indulgence might perhaps be allowed to the interest and habits of the sacerdotal character. But it may appear a subject of surprise and scandal that the philosophers themselves should have contributed to abuse the superstitious credulity of mankind, and that the Grecian mysteries should have been supported by the magic or theurgy of the modern Platonists. They arrogantly pretended to control the order of nature, to explore the secrets of futurity, to command the service of the inferior dæmons, to enjoy the view and conversation of the superior gods, and, by disengaging the soul from her material bands, to re-unite that immortal particle with the Infinite and Divine Spirit.

The devout and fearless curiosity of Julian tempted the philosophers with the hopes of an easy conquest, which, from the situation of their young proselyte, might be productive of the most important consequences. Julian imbibed the first rudiments of the Platonic doctrines from the mouth of Ædesius, who had fixed at Pergamus his wandering and persecuted school. But as the declining strength of that venerable sage was unequal to the ardour, the diligence, the rapid conception of his pupil, two of his most learned disciples, Chrysanthes and Eusebius, supplied, at his own desire, the place of their aged master. These philosophers seem to have prepared and distributed their respective parts; and they artfully contrived, by dark hints and affected disputes, to excite the impatient hopes of the *aspirant* till they delivered him into the hands of their associate Maximus, the boldest and most skilful master of the Theurgic science. By his hands Julian was secretly initiated at Ephesus in the twentieth year of his age. His residence at Athens confirmed this unnatural alliance of philosophy and superstition. He obtained the privilege of a solemn initiation into the mysteries of Eleusis, which, amidst the general decay of the Grecian worship, still retained some vestiges of their primæval sanctity; and such was the zeal of Julian that he afterwards invited the Eleusinian pontiff to the court of Gaul, for the sole purpose of consummating, by mystic rites and sacrifices, the great work of his sanctification. As these ceremonies were performed in the depths of caverns and in the silence of the night, and as the inviolable secret of the mysteries was preserved by the discretion of the initiated, I shall not presume to describe the horrid sounds and fiery apparitions which were presented to the senses or the imagination of the credulous aspirant, till the visions of comfort and knowledge broke upon him in a blaze of celestial light. In the caverns of Ephesus and Eleusis the mind of Julian was penetrated with sincere, deep, and unalterable enthusiasm; though he might sometimes exhibit the vicissitudes of pious fraud and hyprocrisy which may be observed, or at least suspected, in the characters of the most conscientious fanatics. From that moment he consecrated his life to the service of the gods; and while the occupations of war, of government, and of study seemed to claim the whole measure of his time, a stated portion of the hours of the night was invariably reserved for the exercise of private devotion. The temperance which adorned the severe manners of the soldier and the philosopher was connected with some strict and frivolous rules of religious abstinence; and it was in honour of Pan or Mercury, of Hecate or Isis, that Julian, on particular days, denied himself the use of some particular food, which might have been offensive to his tutelar deities. By these voluntary fasts he prepared his senses and his understanding for the frequent and familiar visits with which he was honoured by the celestial powers. Notwithstanding the modest silence of Julian himself, we may learn from his faithful friend, the orator Libanius, that he lived in a perpetual intercourse with the gods and goddesses; that they descended upon earth to enjoy the conversation of their favourite hero; that they gently interrupted his slumbers by touching his hand or his hair; that they warned him of every impending danger, and conducted him, by their infallible wisdom, in every action of his life; and that he had acquired such an intimate knowledge of his heavenly guests, as readily to distinguish the voice of Jupiter from that of Minerva, and the form of Apollo from the figure of Hercules. These sleeping or waking visions, the ordinary effects of abstinence and fanaticism, would almost degrade the emperor to the level of an Egyptian monk. But the useless lives of Antony or Pachomius were consumed in these vain occupations. Julian could break from the dream of superstition to arm himself for battle; and after vanquishing in the field the enemies of Rome, he calmly retired into his tent to dictate the wise and salutary laws of an empire, or to indulge his genius in the elegant pursuits of literature and philosophy.

The important secret of the apostasy of Julian was intrusted to the fidelity of the *initiated*, with whom he was united by the sacred ties of friendship and religion. The pleasing rumour was cautiously circulated among the adherents of the ancient worship; and his future greatness became the object of the hopes, the prayers, and the predictions of the Pagans in every province of the empire. From the zeal and virtues of their royal proselyte they fondly expected the cure of every evil and the restoration of every blessing; and instead of disapproving of the ardour of their pious wishes, Julian ingenuously confessed that he was ambitious to attain a situation in which he might be useful to his country and to his religion. But this religion was viewed with an hostile eye by the successor of Constantine, whose capricious passions alternately saved and threatened the life of Julian. The arts of magic and divination were strictly prohibited under a despotic government which condescended to fear them; and if the Pagans were reluctantly indulged in the exercise of their superstition, the rank of Julian would have excepted him from the general toleration. The apostate soon became the presumptive heir of the monarchy, and his death could alone have appeased the just apprehensions of the Christians. But the young prince, who aspired to the glory of a hero rather than of a martyr, consulted his safety by dissembling his religion; and the easy temper of polytheism permitted him to join in the public worship of a sect which he inwardly despised. Libanius has considered the hypocrisy of his friend as a subject, not of censure, but of praise. "As the statues of the gods," says that orator, "which have been defiled with filth, are again placed in a magnificent temple, so the beauty of truth was seated in the mind of Julian after it had been purified from the errors and follies of his education. His sentiments were changed; but as it would have been dangerous to have avowed his sentiments, his conduct still continued the same. Very different from the ass in Æsop, who disguised himself with a lion's hide, our lion was obliged to conceal himself under the skin of an ass; and, while he embraced the dictates of reason, to obey the laws of prudence and necessity." The dissimulation of Julian lasted above ten years, from his secret initiation at Ephesus to the beginning of the civil war, when he declared himself at once the implacable enemy of Christ and of Constantius. This state of constraint might contribute to strengthen his devotion; and as soon as he had satisfied the obligation of assisting, on solemn festi vals, at the assemblies of the Christians, Julian returned, with the impatience of a lover, to burn his free and volun· tary incense on the domestic chapels of Jupiter and Mercury. But as every act of dissimulation must be painful to an ingenuous spirit, the profession of Christianity increased the aversion of Julian for a religion which oppressed the freedom of his mind, and compelled him to hold a conduct repugnant to the noblest attributes of human nature—sincerity and courage.

The inclination of Julian might prefer the gods of Homer and of the Scipios to the new faith which his uncle had established in the Roman empire, and in which he himself had been sanctified by the sacrament of baptism. But, as a philosopher, it was incumbent on him to justify his dissent from Christianity, which was supported by the number of its converts, by the chain of prophecy, the splendour of miracles, and the weight of evidence. The elaborate work which he composed amidst the preparations of the Persian war contained the substance of those arguments which he had long revolved in his mind. Some fragments have been transcribed and preserved by his adversary, the vehement Cyril of Alexandria; and they exhibit a very singular mixture of wit and learning, of sophistry and fanaticism. The elegance of the style and the rank of the author recommended his writings to the public attention; and in the impious list of the enemies of Christianity the celebrated name of Porphyry was effaced by the superior merit or reputation of Julian. The minds of the faithful were either seduced, or scandalized, or alarmed; and the Pagans, who some-

times presumed to engage in the unequal dispute, derived, from the popular work of their Imperial missionary, an inexhaustible supply of fallacious objections. But
in the assiduous prosecution of these theological studies
the emperor of the Romans imbibed the illiberal prejudices and passions of a polemic divine. He contracted
an irrevocable obligation to maintain and propagate his
religious opinions; and whilst he secretly applauded the
strength and dexterity with which he yielded the weapons
of controversy, he was tempted to distrust the sincerity,
or to despise the understandings, of his antagonists, who
could obstinately resist the force of reason and eloquence.

The Christians, who beheld with horror and indignation the apostasy of Julian, had much more to fear from
his power than from his arguments. The Pagans, who
were conscious of his fervent zeal, expected, perhaps with
impatience, that the flames of persecution should be
immediately kindled against the enemies of the gods;
and that the ingenious malice of Julian would invent
some cruel refinements of death and torture which had
been unknown to the rude and inexperienced fury of his
predecessors. But the hopes, as well as the fears, of the
religious factions were apparently disappointed by the
prudent humanity of a prince who was careful of his own
fame, of the public peace, and of the rights of mankind.
Instructed by history and reflection, Julian was persuaded
that, if the diseases of the body may sometimes be cured
by salutary violence, neither steel nor fire can eradicate
the erroneous opinions of the mind. The reluctant
victim may be dragged to the foot of the altar; but the
heart still abhors and disclaims the sacrilegious act of the
hand. Religious obstinacy is hardened and exasperated
by oppression; and, as soon as the persecution subsides,
those who have yielded are restored as penitents, and
those who have resisted are honoured as saints and

martyrs.   If Julian adopted the unsuccessful cruelty of
Diocletian and his colleagues, he was sensible that he
should stain his memory with the name of tyrant, and
add new glories to the catholic church, which had derived
strength and increase from the severity of the Pagan
magistrates.   Actuated by these motives, and apprehen-
sive of disturbing the repose of an unsettled reign, Julian
surprised the world by an edict which was not unworthy
of a statesman or a philosopher.   He extended to all the
inhabitants of the Roman world the benefits of a free
and equal toleration; and the only hardship which he
inflicted on the Christians was to deprive them of the
power of tormenting their fellow - subjects, whom they
stigmatized with the odious titles of idolaters and heretics.
The Pagans received a gracious permission, or rather an
express order, to open ALL their temples; and they were
at once delivered from the oppressive laws and arbitrary
vexations which they had sustained under the reign of
Constantine and of his sons.   At the same time, the
bishops and clergy who had been banished by the Arian
monarch were recalled from exile, and restored to their
respective churches; the Donatists, the Novatians, the
Macedonians, the Eunomians, and those who, with a
more prosperous fortune, adhered to the doctrine of the
council of Nice.   Julian, who understood and derided
their theological disputes, invited to the palace the leaders
of the hostile sects, that he might enjoy the agreeable
spectacle of their furious encounters.   The clamour of
controversy sometimes provoked the emperor to exclaim,
"Hear me! the Franks have heard me, and the
'Alemanni'"; but he soon discovered that he was now
engaged with more obstinate and implacable enemies;
and though he exerted the powers of oratory to persuade
them to live in concord, or at least in peace, he was
perfectly satisfied, before he dismissed them from his

presence, that he had nothing to dread from the union of the Christians. The impartial Ammianus has ascribed this affected clemency to the desire of fomenting the intestine divisions of the church; and the insidious design of undermining the foundations of Christianity was inseparably connected with the zeal which Julian professed to restore the ancient religion of the empire.

THE LAST CAMPAIGN AND DEATH OF JULIAN

As it became necessary to transport the Roman army over the Tigris, another labour presented itself, of less toil, but of more danger, than the preceding expedition. The stream was broad and rapid, the ascent steep and difficult; and the entrenchments which had been formed on the ridge of the opposite bank were lined with a numerous army of heavy cuirassiers, dexterous archers, and huge elephants; who (according to the extravagant hyperbole of Libanius) could trample with the same ease a field of corn or a legion of Romans. In the presence of such an enemy the construction of a bridge was impracticable; and the intrepid prince, who instantly seized the only possible expedient, concealed his design, till the moment of execution, from the knowledge of the barbarians, of his own troops, and even of his generals themselves. Under the specious pretence of examining the state of the magazines, fourscore vessels were gradually unladen; and a select detachment, apparently destined for some secret expedition, was ordered to stand to their arms on the first signal. Julian disguised the silent anxiety of his own mind with smiles of confidence and joy; and amused the hostile nations with the spectacle of military games, which he insultingly celebrated under the walls of Coche. The day was consecrated to pleasure; but, as soon as the hour of supper was past, the emperor

summoned the generals to his tent, and acquainted them
that he had fixed that night for the passage of the Tigris.
They stood in silent and respectful astonishment; but
when the venerable Sallust assumed the privilege of his
age and experience, the rest of the chiefs supported with
freedom the weight of his prudent remonstrances. Julian
contented himself with observing that conquest and
safety depended on the attempt; that, instead of diminishing, the number of their enemies would be increased by
successive reinforcements; and that a longer delay would
neither contract the breadth of the stream nor level the
height of the bank.   The signal was instantly given, and
obeyed: the most impatient of the legionaries leaped into
five vessels that lay nearest to the bank; and, as they
plied their oars with intrepid diligence, they were lost
after a few moments in the darkness of the night.   A
flame arose on the opposite side; and Julian, who too
clearly understood that his foremost vessels in attempting
to land had been fired by the enemy, dexterously con-
verted their extreme danger into a presage of victory.
"Our fellow-soldiers", he eagerly exclaimed, "are already
masters of the bank: see — they make the appointed
signal; let us hasten to emulate and assist their courage."
The united and rapid motion of a great fleet broke the
violence of the current, and they reached the eastern
shore of the Tigris with sufficient speed to extinguish
the flames and rescue their adventurous companions.
The difficulties of a steep and lofty ascent were increased
by the weight of armour and the darkness of the night.
A shower of stones, darts, and fire was incessantly discharged on the heads of the assailants; who, after an
arduous struggle, climbed the bank and stood victorious
upon the rampart.   As soon as they possessed a more
equal field, Julian, who with his light infantry had led
the attack, darted through the ranks a skilful and ex-

perienced eye: his bravest soldiers, according to the precepts of Homer, were distributed in the front and rear; and all the trumpets of the Imperial army sounded to battle. The Romans, after sending up a military shout, advanced in measured steps to the animating notes of martial music; launched their formidable javelins, and rushed forwards with drawn swords to deprive the barbarians, by a closer onset, of the advantage of their missile weapons. The whole engagement lasted about twelve hours; till the gradual retreat of the Persians was changed into a disorderly flight, of which the shameful example was given by the principal leaders and the Surenas himself. They were pursued to the gates of Ctesiphon; and the conquerors might have entered the dismayed city, if their general, Victor, who was dangerously wounded with an arrow, had not conjured them to desist from a rash attempt, which must be fatal if it were not successful. On *their* side the Romans acknowledged the loss of only seventy-five men; while they affirmed that the barbarians had left on the field of battle two thousand five hundred, or even six thousand, of their bravest soldiers. The spoil was such as might be expected from the riches and luxury of an Oriental camp; large quantities of silver and gold, splendid arms and trappings, and beds and tables of massive silver. The victorious emperor distributed, as the rewards of valour, some honourable gifts, civic, and mural, and naval crowns; which he, and perhaps he alone, esteemed more precious than the wealth of Asia. A solemn sacrifice was offered to the god of war, but the appearances of the victims threatened the most inauspicious events; and Julian soon discovered, by less ambiguous signs, that he had now reached the term of his prosperity.

On the second day after the battle the domestic guards, the Jovians and Herculians, and the remaining troops, which composed near two-thirds of the whole army, were securely wafted over the Tigris. While the Persians beheld from the walls of Ctesiphon the desolation of the adjacent country, Julian cast many an anxious look towards the north, in full expectation that, as he himself had victoriously penetrated to the capital of Sapor, the march and junction of his lieutenants, Sebastian and Procopius, would be executed with the same courage and diligence. His expectations were disappointed by the treachery of the Armenian king, who permitted, and most probably directed, the desertion of his auxiliary troops from the camp of the Romans; and by the dissensions of the two generals, who were incapable of forming or executing any plan for the public service. When the emperor had relinquished the hope of this important reinforcement, he condescended to hold a council of war, and approved, after a full debate, the sentiment of those generals who dissuaded the siege of Ctesiphon, as a fruitless and pernicious undertaking. It is not easy for us to conceive by what arts of fortification a city thrice besieged and taken by the predecessors of Julian could be rendered impregnable against an army of sixty thousand Romans, commanded by a brave and experienced general, and abundantly supplied with ships, provisions, battering-engines, and military stores. But we may rest assured, from the love of glory, and contempt of danger, which formed the character of Julian, that he was not discouraged by any trivial or imaginary obstacles. At the very time when he declined the siege of Ctesiphon, he rejected, with obstinacy and disdain, the most flattering offers of a negotiation of peace. Sapor, who had been so long accustomed to the tardy ostentation of Constantius, was surprised by the intrepid diligence of his successor. As far as the confines of India and Scythia, the satraps of the distant provinces were ordered to assemble their troops, and to march, without delay, to the assistance of their monarch. But their preparations were dilatory, their motions slow; and before Sapor could lead an army into the field, he received the melancholy intelligence of the devastation of Assyria, the ruin of his palaces, and the slaughter of his bravest troops, who defended the passage of the Tigris. The pride of royalty was humbled in the dust; he took his repasts on the ground; and the disorder of his hair expressed the grief and anxiety of his mind. Perhaps he would not have refused to purchase, with one half of his kingdom, the safety of the remainder; and he would have gladly subscribed himself, in a treaty of peace, the faithful and dependent ally of the Roman conqueror. Under the pretence of private business, a minister of rank and confidence was secretly despatched to embrace the knees of Hormisdas, and to request, in the language of a suppliant, that he might be introduced into the presence of the emperor. The Sassanian prince, whether he listened to the voice of pride or humanity, whether he consulted the sentiments of his birth or the duties of his situation, was equally inclined to promote a salutary measure which would terminate the calamities of Persia, and secure the triumph of Rome. He was astonished by the inflexible firmness of a hero who had remembered, most unfortunately for himself and for his country, that Alexander had uniformly rejected the propositions of Darius. But as Julian was sensible that the hope of a safe and honourable peace might cool the ardour of his troops, he earnestly requested that Hormisdas would privately dismiss the minister of Sapor, and conceal this dangerous temptation from the knowledge of the camp.

The honour, as well as interest, of Julian, forbade him to consume his time under the impregnable walls of Ctesiphon; and as often as he defied the barbarians, who defended the city, to meet him on the open plain, they prudently replied that, if he desired to exercise his valour, he might seek the army of the Great King. He felt the insult, and he accepted the advice. Instead of confining his servile march to the banks of the Euphrates and Tigris, he resolved to imitate the adventurous spirit of Alexander, and boldly to advance into the inland provinces, till he forced his rival to contend with him, perhaps in the plains of Arbela, for the empire of Asia. The magnanimity of Julian was applauded and betrayed by the arts of a noble Persian, who, in the cause of his country, had generously submitted to act a part full of danger, of falsehood, and of shame. With a train of faithful followers, he deserted to the Imperial camp; exposed, in a specious tale, the injuries which he had sustained; exaggerated the cruelty of Sapor, the discontent of the people, and the weakness of the monarchy; and confidently offered himself as the hostage and guide of the Roman march. The most rational grounds of suspicion were urged, without effect, by the wisdom and experience of Hormisdas; and the credulous Julian, receiving the traitor into his bosom, was persuaded to issue a hasty order, which, in the opinion of mankind, appeared to arraign his prudence and to endanger his safety. He destroyed in a single hour the whole navy, which had been transported above five hundred miles, at so great an expense of toil, of treasure, and of blood. Twelve, or, at the most, twenty-two, small vessels were saved, to accompany, on carriages, the march of the army, and to form occasional bridges for the passage of the rivers. A supply of twenty days' provisions was reserved for the use of the soldiers; and the rest of the magazines, with a fleet of eleven hundred vessels, which rode at anchor in the Tigris, were abandoned to the flames by the absolute command of the emperor. The Christian bishops, Gregory and Augustin, insult the madness of the apostate, who executed, with his own hands, the sentence of divine justice. Their authority, of less weight, perhaps, in a military question, is confirmed by the cool judgment of an experienced soldier, who was himself spectator of the conflagration, and who could not disapprove the reluctant murmurs of the troops. Yet there are not wanting some specious, and perhaps solid, reasons, which might justify the resolution of Julian. The navigation of the Euphrates never ascended above Babylon, nor that of the Tigris above Opis. The distance of the last-mentioned city from the Roman camp was not very considerable; and Julian must soon have renounced the vain and impracticable attempt of forcing upwards a great fleet against the stream of a rapid river, which in several places was embarrassed by natural or artificial cataracts. The power of sails and oars was insufficient; it became necessary to tow the ships against the current of the river; the strength of twenty thousand soldiers was exhausted in this tedious and servile labour; and if the Romans continued to march along the banks of the Tigris, they could only expect to return home without achieving any enterprise worthy of the genius or fortune of their leader. If, on the contrary, it was advisable to advance into the inland country, the destruction of the fleet and magazines was the only measure which could save that valuable prize from the hands of the numerous and active troops which might suddenly be poured from the gates of Ctesiphon. Had the arms of Julian been victorious, we should now admire the conduct as well as the courage of a hero who, by depriving his soldiers of the hopes of a retreat, left them only the alternative of death or conquest.

The cumbersome train of artillery and wagons, which retards the operations of a modern army, was in a great measure unknown in the camps of the Romans. Yet, in every age, the subsistence of sixty thousand men must have been one of the most important cares of a prudent general; and that subsistence could only be drawn from his own or from the enemy's country. Had it been possible for Julian to maintain a bridge of communication on the Tigris, and to preserve the conquered places of Assyria, a desolated province could not afford any large or regular supplies in a season of the year when the lands were covered by the inundation of the Euphrates, and the unwholesome air was darkened with swarms of innumerable insects. The appearance of the hostile country was far more inviting. The extensive region that lies between the river Tigris and the mountains of Media was filled with villages and towns; and the fertile soil, for the most part, was in a very improved state of cultivation. Julian might expect that a conqueror who possessed the two forcible instruments of persuasion, steel and gold, would easily procure a plentiful subsistence from the fears or avarice of the natives. But on the approach of the Romans this rich and smiling prospect was instantly blasted. Wherever they moved, the inhabitants deserted the open villages and took shelter in the fortified towns; the cattle were driven away; the grass and ripe corn were consumed with fire; and, as soon as the flames had subsided which interrupted the march of Julian, he beheld the melancholy face of a smoking and naked desert. This desperate but effectual method of defence can only be executed by the enthusiasm of a people who prefer their independence to their property; or by the rigour of an arbitrary government, which consults the public safety without submitting to their inclinations the liberty of choice. On the present occasion the zeal and obedience of the Persians seconded the commands of Sapor; and the emperor was soon reduced to the scanty stock of provisions which continually

wasted in his hands. Before they were entirely consumed
he might still have reached the wealthy and unwarlike
cities of Ecbatana or Susa by the effort of a rapid and
well-directed march; but he was deprived of this last
resource by his ignorance of the roads and by the perfidy
of his guides. The Romans wandered several days in
the country to the eastward of Bagdad; the Persian de-
serter, who had artfully led them into the snare, escaped
from their resentment; and his followers, as soon as they
were put to the torture, confessed the secret of the conspiracy. The visionary conquests of Hyrcania and India,
which had so long amused, now tormented, the mind of
Julian. Conscious that his own imprudence was the
cause of the public distress, he anxiously balanced the
hopes of safety or success without obtaining a satisfactory
answer either from gods or men. At length, as the only
practicable measure, he embraced the resolution of direct-
ing his steps towards the banks of the Tigris, with the
design of saving the army by a hasty march to the confines of Corduene, a fertile and friendly province, which
acknowledged the sovereignty of Rome. The desponding
troops obeyed the signal of the retreat, only seventy days
after they had passed the Chaboras with the sanguine
expectation of subverting the throne of Persia.

As long as the Romans seemed to advance into the
country, their march was observed and insulted from a
distance by several bodies of Persian cavalry, who, showing themselves, sometimes in loose and sometimes in
closer order, faintly skirmished with the advanced guards.
These detachments were, however, supported by a much
greater force; and the heads of the columns were no
sooner pointed towards the Tigris than a cloud of dust
arose on the plain. The Romans, who now aspired only
to the permission of a safe and speedy retreat, endeavoured to persuade themselves that this formidable ap-

pearance was occasioned by a troop of wild asses, or perhaps by the approach of some friendly Arabs. They halted, pitched their tents, fortified their camp, passed the whole night in continual alarms; and discovered at the dawn of day that they were surrounded by an army of Persians. This army, which might be considered only as the van of the barbarians, was soon followed by the main body of cuirassiers, archers, and elephants, commanded by Meranes, a general of rank and reputation. He was accompanied by two of the king's sons and many of the principal satraps; and fame and expectation exaggerated the strength of the remaining powers, which slowly advanced under the conduct of Sapor himself. As the Romans continued their march, their long array, which was forced to bend or divide, according to the varieties of the ground, afforded frequent and favourable opportunities to their vigilant enemies. The Persians repeatedly charged with fury; they were repeatedly repulsed with firmness; and the action at Marouga, which almost deserved the name of a battle, was marked by a considerable loss of satraps and elephants, perhaps of equal value in the eyes of their monarch. These splendid advantages were not obtained without an adequate slaughter on the side of the Romans: several officers of distinction were either killed or wounded; and the emperor himself, who on all occasions of danger inspired and guided the valour of his troops, was obliged to expose his person and exert his abilities. The weight of offensive and defensive arms, which still constituted the strength and safety of the Romans, disabled them from making any long or effectual pursuit; and as the horsemen of the East were trained to dart their javelins and shoot their arrows at full speed and in every possible direction, the cavalry of Persia were never more formidable than in the moment of a rapid and disorderly flight. But the most certain and irreparable loss of the Romans was that of time. The hardy veterans, accustomed to the cold climate of Gaul and Germany, fainted under the sultry heat of an Assyrian summer; their vigour was exhausted by the incessant repetition of march and combat; and the progress of the army was suspended by the precautions of a slow and dangerous retreat in the presence of an active enemy. Every day, every hour, as the supply diminished, the value and price of subsistence increased in the Roman camp. Julian, who always contented himself with such food as a hungry soldier would have disdained, distributed for the use of the troops the provisions of the Imperial household, and whatever could be spared from the sumpter-horses of the tribunes and generals. But this feeble relief served only to aggravate the sense of the public distress; and the Romans began to entertain the most gloomy apprehensions that, before they could reach the frontiers of the empire, they should all perish, either by famine or by the sword of the barbarians.

While Julian struggled with the almost insuperable difficulties of his situation, the silent hours of the night were still devoted to study and contemplation. Whenever he closed his eyes in short and interrupted slumbers, his mind was agitated with painful anxiety; nor can it be thought surprising that the Genius of the empire should once more appear before him, covering with a funereal veil his head and his horn of abundance, and slowly retiring from the Imperial tent. The monarch started from his couch, and, stepping forth to refresh his wearied spirits with the coolness of the midnight air, he beheld a fiery meteor, which shot athwart the sky, and suddenly vanished. Julian was convinced that he had seen the menacing countenance of the god of war; the council which he summoned, of Tuscan Haruspices, unanimously pronounced that he should abstain from action; but on this occasion necessity and reason were more prevalent than superstition; and the trumpets sounded at the break of day.   The army marched through a hilly country; and the hills had been secretly occupied by the Persians. Julian led the van with the skill and attention of a consummate general; he was alarmed by the intelligence that his rear was suddenly attacked.   The heat of the weather had tempted him to lay aside his cuirass; but he snatched a shield from one of his attendants, and hastened, with a sufficient reinforcement, to the relief of the rear-guard.   A similar danger recalled the intrepid prince to the defence of the front; and, as he galloped between the columns, the centre of the left was attacked, and almost overpowered, by a furious charge of the Persian cavalry and elephants.   This huge body was soon defeated by the well-timed evolution of the light infantry, who aimed their weapons, with dexterity and effect, against the backs of the horsemen and the legs of the elephants. The barbarians fled: and Julian, who was foremost in every danger, animated the pursuit with his voice and gestures.   His trembling guards, scattered and oppressed by the disorderly throng of friends and enemies, reminded their fearless sovereign that he was without armour, and conjured him to decline the fall of the impending ruin. As they exclaimed, a cloud of darts and arrows was discharged from the flying squadrons; and a javelin, after razing the skin of his arm, transpierced the ribs, and fixed in the inferior part of the liver.   Julian attempted to draw the deadly weapon from his side; but his fingers were cut by the sharpness of the steel, and he fell senseless from his horse.   His guards flew to his relief, and the wounded emperor was gently raised from the ground, and conveyed out of the tumult of the battle into an adjacent tent.   The report of the melancholy event passed from rank to rank; but the grief of the Romans inspired them with invincible valour, and the desire of revenge. The bloody and obstinate conflict was maintained by the two armies till they were separated by the total darkness of the night. The Persians derived some honour from the advantage which they obtained against the left wing, where Anatolius, master of the offices, was slain, and the præfect Sallust very narrowly escaped. But the event of the day was adverse to the barbarians. They abandoned the field; their two generals, Meranes and Nohordates, fifty nobles or satraps, and a multitude of their bravest soldiers: and the success of the Romans, if Julian had survived, might have been improved into a decisive and useful victory.

The first words that Julian uttered, after his recovery from the fainting fit into which he had been thrown by loss of blood, were expressive of his martial spirit. He called for his horse and arms, and was impatient to rush into the battle. His remaining strength was exhausted by the painful effort; and the surgeons, who examined his wound, discovered the symptoms of approaching death. He employed the awful moments with the firm temper of a hero and a sage; the philosophers who had accompanied him in this fatal expedition compared the tent of Julian with the prison of Socrates; and the spectators, whom duty, or friendship, or curiosity had assembled round his couch, listened with respectful grief to the funeral oration of their dying emperor. "Friends and fellow-soldiers, the seasonable period of my departure is now arrived, and I discharge, with the cheerfulness of a ready debtor, the demands of nature. I have learned from philosophy how much the soul is more excellent than the body; and that the separation of the nobler substance should be the subject of joy rather than of affliction. I have learned from religion that an early death has often been the reward of piety; and I accept, as a favour of the gods, the mortal stroke that secures me from the danger of disgracing a character which has hitherto been supported by virtue and fortitude. I die without remorse, as I have lived without guilt. I am pleased to reflect on the innocence of my private life; and I can affirm with confidence that the supreme authority, that emanation of the Divine Power, has been preserved in my hands pure and immaculate. Detesting the corrupt and destructive maxims of despotism, I have considered the happiness of the people as the end of government. Submitting my actions to the laws of prudence, of justice, and of moderation, I have trusted the event to the care of Providence. Peace was the object of my counsels, as long as peace was consistent with the public welfare; but when the imperious voice of my country summoned me to arms, I exposed my person to the dangers of war, with the clear foreknowledge (which I had acquired from the art of divination) that I was destined to fall by the sword. I now offer my tribute of gratitude to the Eternal Being, who has not suffered me to perish by the cruelty of a tyrant, by the secret dagger of conspiracy, or by the slow tortures of lingering disease. He has given me, in the midst of an honourable career, a splendid and glorious departure from this world; and I hold it equally absurd, equally base, to solicit, or to decline, the stroke of fate.—Thus much I have attempted to say; but my strength fails me, and I feel the approach of death.—I shall cautiously refrain from any word that may tend to influence your suffrages in the election of an emperor. My choice might be imprudent or injudicious; and if it should not be ratified by the consent of the army, it might be fatal to the person whom I should recommend. I shall only, as a good citizen, express my hope that the Romans may be

blessed with the government of a virtuous sovereign."
After this discourse, which Julian pronounced in a firm
and gentle tone of voice, he distributed, by a military
testament, the remains of his private fortune; and making
some enquiry why Anatolius was not present, he understood, from the answer of Sallust, that Anatolius was
killed; and bewailed, with amiable inconsistency, the
loss of his friend. At the same time he reproved the
immoderate grief of the spectators; and conjured them
not to disgrace, by unmanly tears, the fate of a prince
who in a few moments would be united with heaven and
with the stars. The spectators were silent; and Julian
entered into a metaphysical argument with the philosophers Priscus and Maximus on the nature of the soul.
The efforts which he made, of mind as well as body,
most probably hastened his death. His wound began
to bleed with fresh violence; his respiration was embarrassed by the swelling of the veins; he called for a
draught of cold water; and, as soon as he had drunk
it, expired without pain, about the hour of midnight.
Such was the end of that extraordinary man, in the
thirty-second year of his age, after a reign of one year
and about eight months from the death of Constantius.
In his last moments he displayed, perhaps with some
ostentation, the love of virtue and of fame, which had
been the ruling passions of his life.

6. LORD MACAULAY

(Macaulay is here represented by three passages which illustrate his
highest qualities as a writer of history. It has already been maintained
in the Introduction to this book that he does not, at least in his *History*,
convey to his readers a clear sense of historical perspective and the continuity of human development: and that his view of the causes of things
is superficial except in what concerns politics. His special strength is
to be found, firstly, in brilliant historical narrative, in which he has no
equal among English writers of history; and, secondly, in the incom-
parable lucidity of his discussion of political questions. Criticism is
possible, indeed, on both points: for his narratives, which cannot be too
highly praised as isolated episodes, are apt by their very brilliance of
colouring to blind his readers to their real place and importance in the
whole story; and his political discussions are perhaps too strongly influenced by the ideas and atmosphere of the House of Commons.

But Macaulay's gifts are so great that he would triumph over far
more serious defects than can be charged against him. His reputation
has passed through a period of detraction, and now ranks among the
highest with both English and Continental critics.)

THE CHARACTER OF HALIFAX

AMONG the statesmen of those times Halifax was, in
genius, the first. His intellect was fertile, subtle,
and capacious. His polished, luminous, and animated
eloquence, set off by the silver tones of his voice, was
the delight of the House of Lords. His conversation
overflowed with thought, fancy, and wit. His political
tracts well deserve to be studied for their literary merit,
and fully entitle him to a place among English classics.
To the weight derived from talents so great and various
he united all the influence which belongs to rank and
ample possessions. Yet he was less successful in politics
than many who enjoyed smaller advantages. Indeed,

those intellectual peculiarities which make his writings valuable, frequently impeded him in the contests of active life. For he always saw passing events, not in the point of view in which they commonly appear to one who bears a part in them, but in the point of view in which, after the lapse of many years, they appear to the philosophic historian. With such a turn of mind, he could not long continue to act cordially with any body of men. All the prejudices, all the exaggerations, of both the great parties in the state moved his scorn. He despised the mean arts and unreasonable clamour of demagogues. He despised still more the doctrines of divine right and passive obedience. He sneered impartially at the bigotry of the Churchman and at the bigotry of the Puritan. He was equally unable to comprehend how any man should object to Saints' days and surplices, and how any man should persecute any other man for objecting to them. In temper he was what, in our time, is called a Conservative: in theory he was a Republican. Even when his dread of anarchy and his disdain for vulgar delusions led him to side for a time with the defenders of arbitrary power, his intellect was always with Locke and Milton. Indeed, his jests upon hereditary monarchy were sometimes such as would have better become a member of the Calf's Head Club than a Privy Councillor of the Stuarts. In religion he was so far from being a zealot that he was called by the uncharitable an atheist; but this imputation he vehemently repelled; and in truth, though he sometimes gave scandal by the way in which he exerted his rare powers both of reasoning and of ridicule on serious subjects, he seems to have been by no means unsusceptible of religious impressions.

He was the chief of those politicians whom the two great parties contemptuously called Trimmers. Instead of quarrelling with this nickname, he assumed it as a title of honour, and vindicated, with great vivacity, the dignity of the appellation. Everything good, he said, trims between extremes. The temperate zone trims between the climate in which men are roasted and the climate in which they are frozen. The English Church trims between the Anabaptist madness and the Papist lethargy. The English constitution trims between Turkish despotism and Polish anarchy. Virtue is nothing but a just temper between propensities any one of which, if indulged to excess, becomes vice. Nay, the perfection of the Supreme Being himself consists in the exact equilibrium of attributes, none of which could preponderate without disturbing the whole moral and physical order of the world. Thus Halifax was a Trimmer on principle. He was also a Trimmer by the constitution both of his head and of his heart. His understanding was keen, sceptical, inexhaustibly fertile in distinctions and objections; his taste refined, his sense of the ludicrous exquisite; his temper placid and forgiving, but fastidious, and by no means prone either to malevolence or to enthusiastic admiration. Such a man could not long be constant to any band of political allies.

He had greatly distinguished himself in opposition, and had thus drawn on himself the royal displeasure, which was indeed so strong that he was not admitted into the Council of Thirty without much difficulty and long altercation. As soon, however, as he had obtained a footing at court, the charms of his manner and of his conversation made him a favourite. He was seriously alarmed by the violence of the public discontent. He thought that liberty was for the present safe, and that order and legitimate authority were in danger. He therefore, as was his fashion, joined himself to the weaker side. Perhaps his conversion was not wholly disinterested. For study and reflection, though they had emancipated him from many vulgar prejudices, had left him a slave to vulgar desires. Money he did not want; and there is no evidence that he ever obtained it by any means which, in that age, even severe censors considered as dishonourable; but rank and power had strong attractions for him. He pretended, indeed, that he considered titles and great offices as baits which could allure none but fools, that he hated business, pomp, and pageantry, and that his dearest wish was to escape from the bustle and glitter of Whitehall to the quiet woods which surrounded his ancient mansion in Nottinghamshire; but his conduct was not a little at variance with his professions. In truth he wished to command the respect at once of courtiers and of philosophers, to be admired for attaining high dignities, and to be at the same time admired for despising them.

THE TRIAL OF THE BISHOPS

This scandalous apostasy (of Sunderland) could not but heighten the interest with which the nation looked forward to the day when the fate of the seven brave confessors of the English Church was to be decided. To pack a jury was now the great object of the King. The crown lawyers were ordered to make strict enquiry as to the sentiments of the persons who were registered in the freeholders' book. Sir Samuel Astry, Clerk of the Crown, whose duty it was, in cases of this description, to select the names, was summoned to the palace, and had an interview with James in the presence of the Chancellor. Sir Samuel seems to have done his best. For, among the forty-eight persons whom he nominated, were said to be several servants of the King, and several Roman Catholics. But as the counsel for the Bishops had a right to strike off twelve, these persons were removed.

The crown lawyers also struck off twelve. The list was thus reduced to twenty-four. The first twelve who answered to their names were to try the issue.

On the twenty-ninth of June, Westminster Hall, Old and New Palace Yard, and all the neighbouring streets to a great distance were thronged with people. Such an auditory had never before and has never since been assembled in the Court of King's Bench. Thirty-five temporal peers of the realm were counted in the crowd.

All the four Judges of the Court were on the Bench. Wright, who presided, had been raised to his high place over the heads of many abler and more learned men solely on account of his unscrupulous servility. Allibone was a Papist, and owed his situation to that dispensing power, the legality of which was now in question. Holloway had hitherto been a serviceable tool of the government. Even Powell, whose character for honesty stood high, had borne a part in some proceedings which it is impossible to defend. He had, in the great case of Sir Edward Hales, with some hesitation, it is true, and after some delay, concurred with the majority of the bench, and had thus brought on his character a stain which his honourable conduct on this day completely effaced.

The counsel were by no means fairly matched. The government had required from its law officers services so odious and disgraceful that all the ablest jurists and advocates of the Tory party had, one after another, refused to comply, and had been dismissed from their employments. Sir Thomas Powis, the Attorney-General, was scarcely of the third rank in his profession. Sir William Williams, the Solicitor-General, had great abilities and dauntless courage: but he wanted discretion; he loved wrangling; he had no command over his temper; and he was hated and despised by all political parties. The most conspicuous assistants of the Attorney and

Solicitor were Serjeant Trinder, a Roman Catholic, and Sir Bartholomew Shower, Recorder of London, who had some legal learning, but whose fulsome apologies and endless repetitions were the jest of Westminster Hall. The government had wished to secure the services of Maynard: but he had plainly declared that he could not in conscience do what was asked of him.

On the other side were arrayed almost all the eminent forensic talents of the age. Sawyer and Finch, who, at the time of the accession of James, had been Attorney and Solicitor General, and who, during the persecution of the Whigs in the late reign, had served the crown with but too much vehemence and success, were of counsel for the defendants. With them were joined two persons who, since age had diminished the activity of Maynard, were reputed the two best lawyers that could be found in the Inns of Court; Pemberton, who had, in the time of Charles the Second, been Chief-Justice of the King's Bench, who had been removed from his high place on account of his humanity and moderation, and who had resumed his practice at the bar; and Pollexfen, who had long been at the head of the Western circuit, and who, though he had incurred much unpopularity by holding briefs for the crown at the Bloody Assizes, and particularly by appearing against Alice Lisle, was known to be at heart a Whig, if not a Republican. Sir Creswell Levinz was also there, a man of great knowledge and experience, but of singularly timid nature. He had been removed from the bench some years before, because he was afraid to serve the purposes of the government. He was now afraid to appear as the advocate of the Bishops, and had at first refused to receive their retainer: but it had been intimated to him by the whole body of attorneys who employed him that, if he declined this brief, he should never have another.

Sir George Treby, an able and zealous Whig, who had been Recorder of London under the old charter, was on the same side. Sir John Holt, a still more eminent Whig lawyer, was not retained for the defence, in consequence, it should seem, of some prejudice conceived against him by Sancroft, but was privately consulted on the case by the Bishop of London. The junior counsel for the Bishops was a young barrister named John Somers. He had no advantages of birth or fortune; nor had he yet had any opportunity of distinguishing himself before the eyes of the public: but his genius, his industry, his great and various accomplishments, were well known to a small circle of friends; and, in spite of his Whig opinions, his pertinent and lucid mode of arguing and the constant propriety of his demeanour, had already secured to him the ear of the Court of King's Bench. The importance of obtaining his services had been strongly represented to the Bishops by Johnstone; and Pollexfen, it is said, had declared that no man in Westminster Hall was so well qualified to treat a historical and constitutional question as Somers.

The jury was sworn. It consisted of persons of highly respectable station. The foreman was Sir Roger Langley, a baronet of old and honourable family. With him were joined a knight and ten esquires, several of whom are known to have been men of large possessions. There were some Nonconformists in the number; for the Bishops had wisely resolved not to show any distrust of the Protestant Dissenters. One name excited considerable alarm, that of Michael Arnold. He was brewer to the palace; and it was apprehended that the government counted on his voice. The story goes that he complained bitterly of the position in which he found himself. "Whatever I do," he said, "I am sure to be half ruined. If I say Not Guilty, I shall brew no more for the King;

and if I say Guilty, I shall brew no more for anybody else."

The trial then commenced, a trial which, even when coolly perused after the lapse of more than a century and a half, has all the interest of a drama. The advocates contended on both sides with far more than professional keenness and vehemence; the audience listened with as much anxiety as if the fate of every one of them was to be decided by the verdict; and the turns of fortune were so sudden and amazing that the multitude repeatedly passed in a single minute from anxiety to exultation, and back again from exultation to still deeper anxiety.

The information charged the Bishops with having written or published, in the county of Middlesex, a false, malicious, and seditious libel. The Attorney and Solicitor first tried to prove the writing. For this purpose several persons were called to speak to the hands of the Bishops. But the witnesses were so unwilling that hardly a single plain answer could be extracted from any of them. Pemberton, Pollexfen, and Levinz contended that there was no evidence to go to the jury. Two of the Judges, Holloway and Powell, declared themselves of the same opinion; and the hopes of the spectators rose high. All at once the crown lawyers announced their intention to take another line. Powis, with shame and reluctance which he could not dissemble, put into the witness-box Blathwayt, a Clerk of the Privy Council, who had been present when the King interrogated the Bishops. Blathwayt swore that he had heard them own their signatures. His testimony was decisive. "Why," said Judge Holloway to the Attorney, "when you had such evidence, did not you produce it at first, without all this waste of time?" It soon appeared why the counsel for the crown had been unwilling, without absolute necessity, to resort to this mode of proof. Pemberton stopped Blathwayt,

subjected him to a searching cross-examination, and insisted upon having all that had passed between the King
and the defendants fully related. " That is a pretty thing
indeed," cried Williams. "Do you think", said Powis,
"that you are at liberty to ask our witnesses any imperti-
nent question that comes into your heads?" The advocates of the Bishops were not men to be so put down.
" He is sworn", said Pollexfen, "to tell the truth and the
whole truth; and an answer we must and will have."
The witness shuffled, equivocated, pretended to misunderstand the questions, implored the protection of the
Court. But he was in hands from which it was not easy
to escape. At length the Attorney again interposed.
" If ", he said, "you persist in asking such a question, tell
us, at least, what use you mean to make of it." Pemberton, who, through the whole trial, did his duty manfully
and ably, replied without hesitation: " My Lords, I will
answer Mr. Attorney. I will deal plainly with the Court.
If the Bishops owned this paper under a promise from
His Majesty that their confession should not be used
against them, I hope that no unfair advantage will be
taken of them." "You put on His Majesty what I dare
hardly name," said Williams. "Since you will be so
pressing, I demand, for the King, that the question may
be recorded." "What do you mean, Mr. Solicitor?" said
Sawyer, interposing. "I know what I mean," said the
apostate; "I desire that the question may be recorded
in Court." "Record what you will. I am not afraid of
you, Mr. Solicitor," said Pemberton. Then came a loud
and fierce altercation, which Wright could with difficulty
quiet. In other circumstances, he would probably have
ordered the question to be recorded, and Pemberton to
be committed. But on this great day the unjust Judge
was overawed. He often cast a side glance towards the
thick rows of Earls and Barons by whom he was watched,

and before whom, in the next Parliament, he might stand at the bar. He looked, a bystander said, as if all the peers present had halters in their pockets. At length Blathwayt was forced to give a full account of what had passed. It appeared that the King had entered into no express covenant with the Bishops. But it appeared also that the Bishops might not unreasonably think that there was an implied engagement. Indeed, from the unwillingness of the crown lawyers to put the Clerk of the Council into the witness-box, and from the vehemence with which they objected to Pemberton's cross-examination, it is plain that they were themselves of this opinion.

However, the handwriting was now proved. But a new and serious objection was raised. It was not sufficient to prove that the Bishops had written the alleged libel. It was necessary to prove also that they had written it in the county of Middlesex. And not only was it out of the power of the Attorney and Solicitor to prove this, but it was in the power of the defendants to prove the contrary. For it so happened that Sancroft had never once left the palace at Lambeth from the time when the Order in Council appeared till after the petition was in the King's hands. The whole case for the prosecution had therefore completely broken down; and the audience, with great glee, expected a speedy acquittal.

The crown lawyers then changed their ground again, abandoned altogether the charge of writing a libel, and undertook to prove that the Bishops had published a libel in the county of Middlesex. The difficulties were great. The delivery of the petition to the King was undoubtedly, in the eye of the law, a publication. But how was this delivery to be proved? No person had been present at the audience in the royal closet, except the King and the defendants. The King could not well be sworn. It was therefore only by the admissions of the defendants that the fact of publication could be established. Blathwayt was again examined, but in vain. He well remembered, he said, that the Bishops owned their hands; but he did not remember that they owned the paper which lay on the table of the Privy Council to be the same paper which they had delivered to the King, or that they were even interrogated on that point. Several other official men who had been in attendance on the Council were called, and among them Samuel Pepys, Secretary of the Admiralty; but none of them could remember that anything was said about the delivery. It was to no purpose that Williams put leading questions till the counsel on the other side declared that such twisting, such wiredrawing, was never seen in a court of justice, and till Wright himself was forced to admit that the Solicitor's mode of examination was contrary to all rule. As witness after witness answered in the negative, roars of laughter and shouts of triumph, which the Judges did not even attempt to silence, shook the hall.

It seemed that at length this hard fight had been won. The case for the crown was closed. Had the counsel for the Bishops remained silent, an acquittal was certain; for nothing which the most corrupt and shameless Judge could venture to call legal evidence of publication had been given. The Chief-Justice was beginning to charge the jury, and would undoubtedly have directed them to acquit the defendants; but Finch, too anxious to be perfectly discreet, interfered, and begged to be heard. " If you will be heard," said Wright, " you shall be heard; but you do not understand your own interests." The other counsel for the defence made Finch sit down, and begged the Chief-Justice to proceed. He was about to do so, when a messenger came to the Solicitor-General with news that Lord Sunderland could prove the publication, and would come down to the court immediately.

Wright maliciously told the counsel for the defence that they had only themselves to thank for the turn which things had taken. The countenances of the great multitude fell. Finch was, during some hours, the most unpopular man in the country. Why could he not sit still, as his betters, Sawyer, Pemberton, and Pollexfen, had done? His love of meddling, his ambition to make a fine speech, had ruined everything.

Meanwhile the Lord President was brought in a sedan-chair through the hall. Not a hat moved as he passed; and many voices cried out "Popish dog". He came into court pale and trembling, with eyes fixed on the ground, and gave his evidence in a faltering voice. He swore that the Bishops had informed him of their intention to present a petition to the King, and that they had been admitted into the royal closet for that purpose. This circumstance, coupled with the circumstance that, after they left the closet, there was in the King's hands a petition signed by them, was such proof as might reasonably satisfy a jury of the fact of the publication.

Publication in Middlesex was then proved. But was the paper thus published a false, malicious, and seditious libel? Hitherto the matter in dispute had been whether a fact which everybody well knew to be true could be proved according to technical rules of evidence; but now the contest became one of deeper interest. It was necessary to enquire into the limits of prerogative and liberty, into the right of the King to dispense with statutes, into the right of the subject to petition for the redress of grievances. During three hours the counsel for the petitioners argued with great force in defence of the fundamental principles of the constitution, and proved from the Journals of the House of Commons that the Bishops had affirmed no more than the truth when they represented to the King that the dispensing power which he claimed had been repeatedly declared illegal by Parliament. Somers rose last. He spoke little more than five minutes: but every word was full of weighty matter; and when he sate down his reputation as an orator and a constitutional lawyer was established. He went through the expressions which were used in the information to describe the offence imputed to the Bishops, and showed that every word, whether adjective or substantive, was altogether inappropriate. The offence imputed was a false, a malicious, a seditious libel. False the paper was not; for every fact which it set forth had been shown from the journals of Parliament to be true. Malicious the paper was not; for the defendants had not sought an occasion of strife, but had been placed by the government in such a situation that they must either oppose themselves to the royal will, or violate the most sacred obligations of conscience and honour. Seditious the paper was not; for it had not been scattered by the writers among the rabble, but delivered privately into the hands of the King alone; and a libel it was not, but a decent petition such as, by the laws of England, nay, by the laws of imperial Rome, by the laws of all civilized states, a subject who thinks himself aggrieved may with propriety present to the sovereign.

The Attorney replied shortly and feebly. The Solicitor spoke at great length and with great acrimony, and was often interrupted by the clamours and hisses of the audience. He went so far as to lay it down that no subject or body of subjects, except the Houses of Parliament, had a right to petition the King. The galleries were furious; and the Chief-Justice himself stood aghast at the effrontery of this venal turncoat.

At length Wright proceeded to sum up the evidence. His language showed that the awe in which he stood of the government was tempered by the awe with which the audience, so numerous, so splendid, and so strongly excited, had impressed him. He said that he would give no opinion on the question of the dispensing power; that it was not necessary for him to do so; that he could not agree with much of the Solicitor's speech; that it was the right of the subject to petition; but that the particular petition before the Court was improperly worded, and was, in the contemplation of law, a libel. Allibone was of the same mind, but, in giving his opinion, showed such gross ignorance of law and history as brought on him the contempt of all who heard him. Holloway evaded the question of the dispensing power, but said that the petition seemed to him to be such as subjects who think themselves aggrieved are entitled to present, and therefore no libel. Powell took a bolder course. He avowed that, in his judgment, the Declaration of Indulgence was a nullity, and that the dispensing power, as lately exercised, was utterly inconsistent with all law. If these encroachments of prerogative were allowed, there was an end of Parliaments. The whole legislative authority would be in the King. "That issue, gentlemen," he said, " I leave to God and to your consciences."

It was dark before the jury retired to consider of their verdict. The night was a night of intense anxiety. Some letters are extant which were despatched during that period of suspense, and which have therefore an interest of a peculiar kind. " It is very late," wrote the Papal Nuncio; " and the decision is not yet known. The Judges and the culprits have gone to their own homes. The jury remain together. To-morrow we shall learn the event of this great struggle."

The solicitor for the Bishops sate up all night with a body of servants on the stairs leading to the room where the jury was consulting. It was absolutely necessary to watch the officers who watched the doors; for those officers were supposed to be in the interest of the crown, and might, if not carefully observed, have furnished a courtly juryman with food, which would have enabled him to starve out the other eleven. Strict guard was therefore kept. Not even a candle to light a pipe was permitted to enter. Some basins of water for washing were suffered to pass at about four in the morning. The jurymen, raging with thirst, soon lapped up the whole. Great numbers of people walked the neighbouring streets till dawn. Every hour a messenger came from Whitehall to know what was passing. Voices, high in altercation, were repeatedly heard within the room; but nothing certain was known.

At first nine were for acquitting and three for convicting. Two of the minority soon gave way: but Arnold was obstinate. Thomas Austin, a country gentleman of great estate, who had paid close attention to the evidence and speeches, and had taken full notes, wished to argue the question. Arnold declined. He was not used, he doggedly said, to reasoning and debating. His conscience was not satisfied: and he should not acquit the Bishops. "If you come to that," said Austin, "look at me. I am the largest and strongest of the twelve; and before I find such a petition as this a libel, here 1 will stay till I am no bigger than a tobacco pipe." It was six in the morning before Arnold yielded. It was soon known that the jury were agreed: but what the verdict would be was still a secret.

At ten the Court again met. The crowd was greater than ever. The jury appeared in their box; and there was a breathless stillness.

Sir Samuel Astry spoke. "Do you find the defendants, or any of them, guilty of the misdemeanour whereof they are impeached, or not guilty?" Sir Roger Langley answered, "Not Guilty". As the words were uttered,

Halifax sprang up and waved his hat. At that signal, benches and galleries raised a shout. In a moment ten thousand persons who crowded the great hall, replied with a still louder shout, which made the old oaken roof crack; and in another moment the innumerable throng without set up a third huzza, which was heard at Temple Bar. The boats which covered the Thames gave an answering cheer. A peal of gunpowder was heard on the water, and another, and another; and so, in a few moments, the glad tidings went flying past the Savoy and the Friars to London Bridge, and to the forest of masts below. As the news spread, streets and squares, market-places and coffee-houses, broke forth into acclamations. Yet were the acclamations less strange than the weeping. For the feelings of men had been wound up to such a point that at length the stern English nature, so little used to outward signs of emotion, gave way, and thousands sobbed aloud for very joy. Meanwhile, from the outskirts of the multitude, horsemen were spurring off to bear along all the great roads intelligence of the victory of our Church and nation. Yet not even that astounding explosion could awe the bitter and intrepid spirit of the Solicitor. Striving to make himself heard above the din, he called on the Judges to commit those who had violated, by clamour, the dignity of a court of justice. One of the rejoicing populace was seized. But the tribunal felt that it would be absurd to punish a single individual for an offence common to hundreds of thousands, and dismissed him with a gentle reprimand.

It was vain to think of passing at that moment to any other business. Indeed the roar of the multitude was such that, during half an hour, scarcely a word could be heard in the court. Williams got to his coach amidst a tempest of hisses and curses. Cartwright, whose curiosity was ungovernable, had been guilty of the folly and indecency of coming to Westminster in order to hear the decision. He was recognized by his sacerdotal garb and by his corpulent figure, and was hooted through the hall. "Take care", said one, "of the wolf in sheep's clothing." "Make room", cried another, "for the man with the Pope in his belly."

The acquitted prelates took refuge in the nearest chapel from the crowd which implored their blessing. Many churches were open on that morning throughout the capital; and many pious persons repaired thither. The bells of all the parishes of the City and liberties were ringing. The jury meanwhile could scarcely make their way out of the hall. They were forced to shake hands with hundreds. "God bless you!" cried the people; "God prosper your families! you have done like honest good-natured gentlemen: you have saved us all to-day." As the noblemen who had attended to support the good cause drove off, they flung from their carriage windows handfuls of money, and bade the crowd drink to the health of the King, the Bishops, and the jury.

The Attorney went with the tidings to Sunderland, who happened to be conversing with the Nuncio. "Never," said Powis, "within man's memory, have there been such shouts and such tears of joy as to-day." The King had that morning visited the camp on Hounslow Heath. Sunderland instantly sent a courier thither with the news. James was in Lord Feversham's tent when the express arrived. He was greatly disturbed, and exclaimed in French, "So much the worse for them". He soon set out for London. While he was present, respect prevented the soldiers from giving a loose to their feelings; but he had scarcely quitted the camp when he heard a great shouting behind him. He was surprised, and asked what that uproar meant. "Nothing," was the answer: "the soldiers are glad that the Bishops are acquitted." "Do

you call that nothing?" said James. And then he repeated, "So much the worse for them".

THE NATIONAL DEBT

During the interval between the Restoration and the
Revolution the riches of the nation had been rapidly
increasing. Thousands of busy men found every Christmas
that, after the expenses of the year's housekeeping had
been defrayed out of the year's income, a surplus remained; and how that surplus was to be employed
was a question of some difficulty. In our time, to in-
vest such a surplus, at something more than three per
cent, on the best security that has ever been known in
the world, is the work of a few minutes. But, in the
seventeenth century, a lawyer, a physician, a retired merchant, who had saved some thousands and who wished
to place them safely and profitably, was often greatly
embarrassed. Three generations earlier, a man who had
accumulated wealth in a trade or a profession generally
purchased real property or lent his savings on mortgage.
But the number of acres in the kingdom had remained
the same; and the value of those acres, though it had
greatly increased, had by no means increased so fast as
the quantity of capital which was seeking for employment.
Many, too, wished to put their money where they could
find it at an hour's notice, and looked about for some
species of property which could be more readily trans-
ferred than a house or a field. A capitalist might lend
on bottomry or on personal security: but, if he did so,
he ran a great risk of losing interest and principal.
There were a few joint-stock companies, among which
the East India Company held the foremost place; but
the demand for the stock of such companies was far
greater than the supply. Indeed the cry for a new East

India Company was chiefly raised by persons who had
found difficulty in placing their savings at interest on
good security.   So great was that difficulty that the
practice of hoarding was common.   We are told that the
father of Pope the poet, who retired from business in the
City about the time of the Revolution, carried to a retreat
in the country a strong-box containing near twenty thousand pounds, and took out from time to time what was
required for household expenses; and it is highly probable
that this was not a solitary case.   At present the quantity
of coin which is hoarded by private persons is so small
that it would, if brought forth, make no perceptible
addition to the circulation.   But, in the earlier part of
the reign of William the Third, all the greatest writers on
currency were of opinion that a very considerable mass
of gold and silver was hidden in secret drawers and
behind wainscots.

The natural effect of this state of things was that a
crowd of projectors, ingenious and absurd, honest and
knavish, employed themselves in devising new schemes
for the employment of redundant capital.   It was about
the year 1688 that the word stockjobber was first heard
in London.   In the short space of four years a crowd of
companies, every one of which confidently held out to
subscribers the hope of immense gains, sprang into existence: the Insurance Company, the Paper Company, the
Lutestring Company, the Pearl Fishery Company, the
Glass Bottle Company, the Alum Company, the Blythe
Coal Company, the Swordblade Company.   There was
a Tapestry Company, which would soon furnish pretty
hangings for all the parlours of the middle class and for
all the bedchambers of the higher.   There was a Copper
Company, which proposed to explore the mines of England, and held out a hope that they would prove not less
valuable than those of Potosi.   There was a Diving Com-

pany, which undertook to bring up precious effects from shipwrecked vessels, and which announced that it had laid in a stock of wonderful machines resembling complete suits of armour. In front of the helmet was a huge glass eye like that of Polyphemus; and out of the crest went a pipe through which the air was to be admitted. The whole process was exhibited on the Thames. Fine gentlemen and fine ladies were invited to the show, were hospitably regaled, and were delighted by seeing the divers in their panoply descend into the river, and return laden with old iron and ship's tackle. There was a Greenland Fishing Company, which could not fail to drive the Dutch whalers and herring-busses out of the Northern Ocean. There was a Tanning Company, which promised to furnish leather superior to the best that was brought from Turkey or Russia. There was a society which undertook the office of giving gentlemen a liberal education on low terms, and which assumed the sounding name of the Royal Academies Company. In a pompous advertisement it was announced that the directors of the Royal Academies Company had engaged the best masters in every branch of knowledge, and were about to issue twenty thousand tickets at twenty shillings each. There was to be a lottery; two thousand prizes were to be drawn; and the fortunate holders of the prizes were to be taught, at the charge of the Company, Latin, Greek, Hebrew, French, Spanish, conic sections, trigonometry, heraldry, japanning, fortification, book-keeping, and the art of playing the theorbo. Some of these companies took large mansions and printed their advertisements in gilded letters. Others, less ostentatious, were content with ink, and met at coffee-houses in the neighbourhood of the Royal Exchange. Jonathan's and Garraway's were in a constant ferment with brokers, buyers, sellers, meetings of directors, meetings of proprietors. Time bargains soon came into fashion. Extensive combinations were formed, and monstrous fables were circulated, for the purpose of raising or depressing the price of shares. Our country witnessed for the first time those phenomena with which a long experience has made us familiar. A mania of which the symptoms were essentially the same with those of the mania of 1720, of the mania of 1825, of the mania of 1845, seized the public mind. An impatience to be rich, a contempt for those slow but sure gains which are the proper reward of industry, patience, and thrift, spread through society. The spirit of the cogging dicers of Whitefriars took possession of the grave Senators of the City, Wardens of Trades, Deputies, Aldermen. It was much easier and much more lucrative to put forth a lying prospectus announcing a new stock, to persuade ignorant people that the dividends could not fall short of twenty per cent, and to part with five thousand pounds of this imaginary wealth for ten thousand solid guineas, than to load a ship with a well-chosen cargo for Virginia or the Levant. Every day some new bubble was puffed into existence, rose buoyant, shone bright, burst, and was forgotten.

The new form which covetousness had taken furnished the comic poets and satirists with an excellent subject; nor was that subject the less welcome to them because some of the most unscrupulous and most successful of the new race of gamesters were men in sad-coloured clothes and lank hair, men who called cards the Devil's books, men who thought it a sin and a scandal to win or lose twopence over a backgammon board. It was in the last drama of Shadwell that the hypocrisy and knavery of the speculators was, for the first time, exposed to public ridicule. He died in November, 1692, just before his *Stockjobbers* came on the stage; and the epilogue was spoken by an actor dressed in deep mourning. The

best scene is that in which four or five stern Nonconformists, clad in the full Puritan costume, after discussing
the prospects of the Mousetrap Company and the Flea-
killing Company, examine the question whether the godly
may lawfully hold stock in a Company for bringing over
Chinese rope-dancers. "Considerable men have shares,"
says one austere person in cropped hair and bands;
"but verily I question whether it be lawful or not."
These doubts are removed by a stout old Roundhead
colonel who had fought at Marston Moor, and who re-
minds his weaker brother that the saints need not themselves see the rope-dancing, and that, in all probability,
there will be no rope-dancing to see. "The thing", he
says, "is like to take. The shares will sell well: and
then we shall not care whether the dancers come over or
no." It is important to observe that this scene was
exhibited and applauded before one farthing of the
national debt had been contracted. So ill-informed were
the numerous writers who, at a later period, ascribed to
the national debt the existence of stockjobbing and of
all the immoralities connected with stockjobbing. The
truth is, that society had, in the natural course of its
growth, reached a point at which it was inevitable that
there should be stockjobbing whether there were a
national debt or not, and inevitable also that, if there
were a long and costly war, there should be a national
debt.

How, indeed, was it possible that a debt should not
have been contracted, when one party was impelled by
the strongest motives to borrow, and another was impelled by equally strong motives to lend? A moment
had arrived at which the government found it impossible,
without exciting the most formidable discontents, to raise
by taxation the supplies necessary to defend the liberty
and independence of the nation; and, at that very moment,

numerous capitalists were looking round them in vain for
some good mode of investing their savings, and for want
of such a mode were keeping their wealth locked up, or
were lavishing it on absurd projects. Riches sufficient to
equip a navy which would sweep the German Ocean and
Atlantic of French privateers, riches sufficient to maintain an army which might retake Namur and avenge the
disaster of Steinkirk, were lying idle, or were passing away
from the owners into the hands of sharpers. A statesman might well think that some part of the wealth which
was daily buried or squandered might, with advantage
to the proprietor, to the tax-payer, and to the State, be
attracted into the Treasury. Why meet the extraordinary
charge of a year of war by seizing the chairs, the tables,
the beds of hard-working families, by compelling one
country gentleman to cut down his trees before they
were ready for the axe, another to let the cottages on
his land fall to ruin, a third to take away his hopeful son
from the University, when Change Alley was swarming
with people who did not know what to do with their
money and who were pressing everybody to borrow it?

It was often asserted at a later period by Tories, who
hated the national debt most of all things, and who hated
Burnet most of all men, that Burnet was the person who
first advised the government to contract a national debt.
But this assertion is proved by no trustworthy evidence,
and seems to be disproved by the Bishop's silence. Of
all men he was the least likely to conceal the fact that an
important fiscal revolution had been his work. Nor was
the Board of Treasury at that time one which much
needed, or was likely much to regard, the counsels of a
divine. At that board sate Godolphin, the most prudent
and experienced, and Montague, the most daring and
inventive of financiers. Neither of these eminent men
could be ignorant that it had long been the practice of

the neighbouring states to spread over many years of peace the excessive taxation which was made necessary by one year of war. In Italy this practice had existed through several generations. France had, during the war which began in 1672 and ended in 1679, borrowed not less than thirty millions of our money. Sir William Temple, in his interesting work on the Batavian federation, had told his countrymen that, when he was ambassador at the Hague, the single province of Holland, then ruled by the frugal and prudent De Witt, owed about five millions sterling, for which interest at four per cent was always ready to the day, and that, when any part of the principal was paid off, the public creditor received his money with tears, well knowing that he could find no other investment equally secure. The wonder is not that England should have at length imitated the example both of her enemies and of her allies, but that the fourth year of her arduous and exhausting struggle against Lewis should have been drawing to a close before she resorted to an expedient so obvious.

On the fifteenth of December, 1692, the House of Commons resolved itself into a Committee of Ways and Means. Somers took the chair. Montague proposed to raise a million by way of loan: the proposition was approved; and it was ordered that a bill should be brought in. The details of the scheme were much discussed and modified; but the principle appears to have been popular with all parties. The moneyed men were glad to have a good opportunity of investing what they had hoarded. The landed men, hard pressed by the load of taxation, were ready to consent to anything for the sake of present ease. No member ventured to divide the House. On the twentieth of January the bill was read a third time, carried up to the Lords by Somers, and passed by them without any amendment.

By this memorable law new duties were imposed on beer and other liquors. These duties were to be kept in the Exchequer separate from all other receipts, and were to form a fund on the credit of which a million was to be raised by life annuities. As the annuitants dropped off, their annuities were to be divided among the survivors, till the number of survivors was reduced to seven. After that time, whatever fell in was to go to the public. It was therefore certain that the eighteenth century would be far advanced before the debt would be finally extinguished; and, in fact, long after King George the Third was on the throne, a few aged men were receiving large incomes from the State, in return for a little money which had been advanced to King William on their account when they were children. The rate of interest was to be ten per cent till the year 1700, and after that year seven per cent. The advantages offered to the public creditor by this scheme may seem great, but were not more than sufficient to compensate him for the risk which he ran. It was not impossible that there might be a counter-revolution; and it was certain that if there were a counter-revolution, those who had lent money to William would lose both interest and principal.

Such was the origin of that debt which has since become the greatest prodigy that ever perplexed the sagacity and confounded the pride of statesmen and philosophers. At every stage in the growth of that debt the nation has set up the same cry of anguish and despair. At every stage in the growth of that debt it has been seriously asserted by wise men that bankruptcy and ruin were at hand. Yet still the debt went on growing, and still bankruptcy and ruin were as remote as ever. When the great contest with Lewis the Fourteenth was finally terminated by the Peace of Utrecht, the nation owed about fifty millions; and that debt was considered, not merely by the rude multitude, not merely by fox-hunting squires and coffee-house orators, but by acute and profound thinkers, as an encumbrance which would permanently cripple the body politic. Nevertheless trade flourished: wealth increased: the nation became richer and richer. Then came the war of the Austrian Succession; and the debt rose to eighty millions. Pamphleteers, historians, and orators pronounced that now, at all events, our case was desperate. Yet the signs of increasing prosperity, signs which could neither be counterfeited nor concealed, ought to have satisfied observant and reflecting men that a debt of eighty millions was less to the England which was governed by Pelham than a debt of fifty millions had been to the England which was governed by Oxford. Soon war again broke forth; and, under the energetic and prodigal administration of the first William Pitt, the debt rapidly swelled to a hundred and forty millions. As soon as the first intoxication of victory was over, men of theory and men of business almost unanimously pronounced that the fatal day had now really arrived. The only statesman, indeed, active or speculative, who was too wise to share in the general delusion was Edmund Burke. David Hume, undoubtedly one of the most profound political economists of his time, declared that our madness had exceeded the madness of the Crusaders. Richard Cœur de Lion and St. Lewis had not gone in the face of arithmetical demonstration. It was impossible to prove by figures that the road to Paradise did not lie through the Holy Land: but it was possible to prove by figures that the road to national ruin was through the national debt. It was idle, however, now to talk about the road: we had done with the road: we had reached the goal: all was over: all the revenues of the island north of Trent and west of Reading were mortgaged. Better for us to have been conquered by

Prussia or Austria than to be saddled with the interest of a hundred and forty millions. And yet this great philosopher,—for such he was,—had only to open his eyes, and to see improvement all around him, cities increasing, cultivation extending, marts too small for the crowd of buyers and sellers, harbours insufficient to contain the shipping, artificial rivers joining the chief inland seats of industry to the chief seaports, streets better lighted, houses better furnished, richer wares exposed to sale in statelier shops, swifter carriages rolling along smoother roads. He had, indeed, only to compare the Edinburgh of his boyhood with the Edinburgh of his old age. His prediction remains to posterity, a memorable instance of the weakness from which the strongest minds are not exempt. Adam Smith saw a little, and but a little further. He admitted that, immense as the pressure was, the nation did actually sustain it and thrive under it in a way which nobody could have foreseen. But he warned his countrymen not to repeat so hazardous an experiment. The limit had been reached. Even a small increase might be fatal. Not less gloomy was the view which George Grenville, a minister eminently diligent and practical, took of our financial situation. The nation must, he conceived, sink under a debt of a hundred and forty millions, unless a portion of the load were borne by the American colonies. The attempt to lay a portion of the load on the American colonies produced another war. That war left us with an additional hundred millions of debt, and without the colonies whose help had been represented as indispensable. Again England was given over; and again the strange patient persisted in becoming stronger and more blooming in spite of all the diagnostics and prognostics of State physicians. As she had been visibly more prosperous with a debt of one hundred and forty millions than with a debt of fifty millions, so she was visibly more prosperous with a debt of two hundred and forty millions than with a debt of one hundred and forty millions. Soon, however, the wars which sprang from the French Revolution, and which far exceeded in cost any that the world had ever seen, tasked the powers of public credit to the utmost. When the world was again at rest the funded debt of England amounted to eight hundred millions. If the most enlightened man had been told, in 1792, that, in 1815, the interest on eight hundred millions would be duly paid to the day at the Bank, he would have been as hard of belief as if he had been told that the government would be in possession of the lamp of Aladdin or of the purse of Fortunatus. It was in truth a gigantic, a fabulous, debt; and we can hardly wonder that the cry of despair should have been louder than ever. But again that cry was found to have been as unreasonable as ever. After a few years of exhaustion, England recovered herself. Yet like Addison's valetudinarian, who continued to whimper that he was dying of consumption till he became so fat that he was shamed into silence, she went on complaining that she was sunk in poverty till her wealth showed itself by tokens which made her complaints ridiculous. The beggared, the bankrupt, society not only proved able to meet all its obligations, but, while meeting those obligations, grew richer and richer so fast that the growth could almost be discerned by the eye. In every county, we saw wastes recently turned into gardens: in every city, we saw new streets, and squares, and markets, more brilliant lamps, more abundant supplies of water: in the suburbs of every great seat of industry, we saw villas multiplying fast, each embosomed in its gay little paradise of lilacs and roses. While shallow politicians were repeating that the energies of the people were borne down by the weight of the public burdens, the first journey was performed by steam on a railway. Soon the island was intersected by railways. A sum exceeding the whole amount of the national debt at the end of the American war, was, in a few years, voluntarily expended by this ruined people on viaducts, tunnels, embankments, bridges, stations, engines. Meanwhile taxation was almost constantly becoming lighter and lighter: yet still the Exchequer was full. It may be now affirmed without fear of contradiction that we find it as easy to pay the interest of eight hundred millions as our ancestors found it, a century ago, to pay the interest of eighty millions.

It can hardly be doubted that there must have been some great fallacy in the notions of those who uttered, and of those who believed, that long succession of confident predictions, so signally falsified by a long succession of indisputable facts. To point out that fallacy is the office rather of the political economist than of the historian. Here it is sufficient to say that the prophets of evil were under a double delusion. They erroneously imagined that there was an exact analogy between the case of an individual who is in debt to another individual and the case of a society which is in debt to a part of itself: and this analogy led them into endless mistakes about the effect of the system of funding. They were under an error not less serious touching the resources of the country. They made no allowance for the effect produced by the incessant progress of every experimental science, and by the incessant efforts of every man to get on in life. They saw that the debt grew; and they forgot that other things grew as well as the debt.

A long experience justifies us in believing that England may, in the twentieth century, be better able to pay a debt of sixteen hundred millions than she is at the present time to bear her present load. But be this as it may, those who so confidently predicted that she must sink, first under a debt of fifty millions, then under a debt of eighty millions, then under a debt of a hundred and forty millions, then under a debt of two hundred and forty millions, and lastly under a debt of eight hundred millions, were beyond all doubt under a twofold mistake. They greatly overrated the pressure of the burden: they greatly underrated the strength by which the burden was to be borne.

7. THOMAS CARLYLE

(Both the following extracts are taken from Carlyle's *French Revolution*, which is without much question his most remarkable work. The French Revolution was constantly in his thoughts, and its work was almost the pivot of his social and political philosophy. The first extract (Book V, Chap. I) sums up, in language of extraordinary fire and heat, his view of the Revolution, which he always regarded as the death of the old order, not as the beginning of a new one. The strong poetical vein in Carlyle's writing is also seen well here: there are passages which are much nearer to dithyrambic poetry than to ordinary English prose. The second passage, describing the fall and death of Robespierre, is a characteristic illustration of Carlyle's narrative style, which, with all its mannerisms and obscure allusions, fixes the events upon the memory with a force greater even than that of Macaulay.)

THE MEANING OF THE REIGN OF TERROR

WE are now, therefore, got to that black precipitous Abyss; whither all things have long been tending; where, having now arrived on the giddy verge, they hurl down, in confused ruin; headlong, pellmell, down, down; till Sansculottism have consummated itself; and in this wondrous French Revolution, as in a Doomsday, a World have been rapidly, if not born again, yet destroyed and engulfed. Terror has long been terrible: but to the actors themselves it has now become manifest that their appointed course is one of Terror; and they say, Be it so. " *Que la Terreur soit à l'ordre du jour.*"

So many centuries, say only from Hugh Capet downwards, had been adding together, century transmitting it with increase to century, the sum of Wickedness, of Falsehood, Oppression of man by man. Kings were sinners, and Priests were, and People. Open Scoundrels rode triumphant, bediademed, becoronetted, bemitred; or the still fataler species of Secret-Scoundrels, in their fair-sounding formulas, speciosities, respectabilities, hollow within: the race of Quacks was grown many as the sands of the sea. Till at length such a sum of Quackery had accumulated itself as, in brief, the Earth and the Heavens were weary of. Slow seemed the Day of Settlement; coming on, all imperceptible, across the bluster and fanfaronade of Courtierisms, Conquering-Heroisms, Most Christian *Grand Monarque*-isms, Well-beloved Pompadourisms: yet behold it was always coming; behold it has come, suddenly, unlooked for by any man! The harvest of long centuries was ripening and whitening so rapidly of late; and now it is grown *white*, and is reaped rapidly, as it were, in one day. Reaped, in this Reign of Terror; and carried home, to Hades and the Pit! Unhappy sons of Adam: it is ever so; and never do they know it, nor will they know it. With cheerfully smoothed countenances, day after day, and generation after generation, they, calling cheerfully to one another, Well-speed-ye, are at work, *sowing the wind*. And yet, as God lives, they *shall reap the whirl-wind*: no other thing, we say, is possible,—since God is a Truth, and His World is a Truth.

History, however, in dealing with this Reign of Terror, has had her own difficulties. While the Phenomenon continued in its primary state, as mere " Horrors of the French Revolution", there was abundance to be said and shrieked. With and also without profit. Heaven knows, there were terrors and horrors enough: yet that was not all the Phenomenon; nay, more properly, that was not the Phenomenon at all, but rather was the *shadow* of it, the negative part of it. And now, in a new stage of the business, when History, ceasing to shriek, would try rather to include under her old Forms of speech or

speculation this new amazing Thing; that so some ac-
credited scientific Law of Nature might suffice for the
unexpected Product of Nature, and History might get to
speak of it articulately, and draw inferences and profit
from it; in this new stage, History, we must say, babbles
and flounders perhaps in a still painfuler manner. Take,
for example, the latest Form of speech we have seen
propounded on the subject as adequate to it, almost in
these months by our worthy M. Roux, in his *Histoire
Parlementaire.* The latest and strangest: that the French
Revolution was a dead-lift effort, after eighteen hundred
years of preparation, to realize—the Christian Religion!
Unity, Indivisibility, Brotherhood or Death, did indeed
stand printed on all Houses of the Living; also on
Cemeteries, or Houses of the Dead, stood printed, by
order of Procureur Chaumette, *Here is Eternal Sleep*:
but a Christian Religion, realized by the Guillotine and
Death-Eternal, "is suspect to me", as Robespierre was
wont to say, "*m'est suspecte*".

Alas, no, M. Roux! A Gospel of Brotherhood, not
according to any of the Four old Evangelists, and calling
on men to repent, and amend *each his own* wicked existence, that they might be saved; but a Gospel rather, as
we often hint, according to a new Fifth Evangelist, Jean-
Jacques, calling on men to amend *each the whole world's*
wicked existence, and be saved by making the Constitution. A thing different and distant *toto cælo*, as they say:
the whole breadth of the sky, and farther if possible!—It
is thus, however, that History, and indeed all human
Speech and Reason does yet, what Father Adam began
life by doing: strive to *name* the new Things it sees of
Nature's producing,—often helplessly enough.

But what if History were to admit, for once, that all
the Names and Theorems yet known to her fall short?
That this grand Product of Nature was even grand, and

new, in that it came not to range itself under old recorded Laws of Nature at all, but to disclose new ones?
In that case, History, renouncing the pretension to *name*
it at present, will *look* honestly at it, and name what she
can of it! Any approximation to the right Name has
value: were the right Name itself once here, the Thing
is known henceforth; the Thing is then ours, and can
be dealt with.

Now surely not realization, of Christianity or of aught
earthly, do we discern in this Reign of Terror, in this
French Revolution of which it is the consummating.
Destruction rather we discern,—of all that was destruc-
tible. It is as if Twenty-five millions, risen at length into
the Pythian mood, had stood up simultaneously to say,
with a sound which goes through far lands and times,
that this Untruth of an Existence had become insupport-
able. O ye Hypocrisies and Speciosities, Royal mantles,
Cardinal plush-cloaks, ye Credos, Formulas, Respectabilities, fair-painted Sepulchres full of dead men's bones,
—behold, ye appear to us to be altogether a Lie. Yet
our Life is not a Lie; yet our Hunger and Misery is not
a Lie! Behold we lift up, one and all, our Twenty-five
million right-hands; and take the Heavens, and the
Earth, and also the Pit of Tophet to witness, that either
ye shall be abolished, or else we shall be abolished!

No inconsiderable Oath, truly; forming, as has been
often said, the most remarkable transaction in these last
thousand years. Wherefrom likewise there follow, and
will follow, results. The fulfilment of this Oath: that is
to say, the black desperate battle of Men against their
whole Condition and Environment,—a battle, alas, withal,
against the Sin and Darkness that was in themselves as
in others: this is the Reign of Terror. Transcendental
despair was the purport of it, though not consciously so.
False hopes, of Fraternity, Political Millennium, and

what not, we have always seen: but the unseen heart of the whole, the transcendental despair, was not false; neither has it been of no effect. Despair, pushed far enough, completes the circle, so to speak; and becomes a kind of genuine productive hope again.

Doctrine of Fraternity, out of old Catholicism, does, it is true, very strangely in the vehicle of a Jean-Jacques Evangel, suddenly plump down out of its cloud-firmament; and from a theorem determine to make itself a practice. But just so do all creeds, intentions, customs, knowledges, thoughts and things, which the French have, suddenly plump down; Catholicism, Classicism, Sentimentalism, Cannibalism: all *isms* that make up Man in France are rushing and roaring in that gulf; and the theorem has become a practice, and whatsoever cannot swim sinks. Not Evangelist Jean-Jacques alone; there is not a Village Schoolmaster but has contributed his quota; do we not *thou* one another, according to the Free Peoples of Antiquity? The French Patriot, in red Phrygian nightcap of Liberty, christens his poor little red infant Cato,—Censor, or else of Utica. Gracchus has become Babœuf, and edits Newspapers; Mutius Scævola, Cordwainer of that ilk, presides in the Section Mutius-Scævola: and in brief, there is a world wholly jumbling itself, to try what will swim.

Wherefore we will, at all events, call this Reign of Terror a very strange one. Dominant Sansculottism makes, as it were, free arena; one of the strangest temporary states Humanity was ever seen in. A nation of men, full of wants and void of habits! The old habits are gone to wreck because they were old: men, driven forward by Necessity and fierce Pythian Madness, have, on the spur of the instant, to devise for the want the *way* of satisfying it. The Wonted tumbles down; by imitation, by invention, the Unwonted hastily builds itself up.

What the French National head has in it comes out: if not a great result, surely one of the strangest.

Neither shall the Reader fancy that it was all black, this Reign of Terror; far from it. How many hammer-men and squaremen, bakers and brewers, washers and wringers, over this France, must ply their old daily work, let the Government be one of Terror or one of Joy! In this Paris there are Twenty-three Theatres nightly; some count as many as Sixty Places of Dancing. The Play-wright manufactures,—pieces of a strictly Republican character. Ever fresh Novel-garbage, as of old, fodders the Circulating Libraries. The "Cesspool of *Agio*", now in a time of Paper Money, works with a vivacity unexam-pled, unimagined; exhales from itself "sudden fortunes", like Aladdin-Palaces: really a kind of miraculous Fata-Morganas, since you *can* live in them, for a time. Terror is as a sable ground, on which the most variegated ot scenes paints itself. In startling transitions, in colours all intensated, the sublime, the ludicrous, the horrible succeed one another; or rather, in crowding tumult, accompany one another.

Here, accordingly, if anywhere, the "hundred tongues", which the old Poets often clamour for, were of supreme service! In defect of any such organ on our part, let the Reader stir up his own imaginative organ: let us snatch for him this or the other significant glimpse of things, in the fittest sequence we can.

THE FALL AND DEATH OF ROBESPIERRE

Tallien's eyes beamed bright, on the morrow, Ninth of Thermidor, "about nine o'clock", to see that the Conven-tion had actually met. Paris is in rumour; but at least we are met, in Legal Convention here; we have not been snatched seriatim; treated with a *Pride's Purge* at the door. "*Allons*, brave men of the Plain", late Frogs of the Marsh! cried Tallien with a squeeze of the hand, as he passed in; Saint-Just's sonorous voice being now audible from the Tribune, and the game of games begun.

Saint-Just is verily reading that Report of his; green Vengeance, in the shape of Robespierre, watching nigh. Behold, however, Saint-Just has read but few sentences, when interruption rises, rapid *crescendo*; when Tallien starts to his feet, and Billaud, and this man starts and that,—and Tallien, a second time, with his: "Citoyens, at the Jacobins last night, I trembled for the Republic. I said to myself, if the Convention dare not strike the Tyrant, then I myself dare; and with this I will do it, if need be," said he, whisking out a clear-gleaming Dagger, and brandishing it there; the Steel of Brutus, as we call it. Whereat we all bellow, and brandish, impetuous acclaim. "Tyranny! Dictatorship! Triumvirate!" And the *Salut* Committee-men accuse, and all men accuse, and uproar, and impetuously acclaim. And Saint-Just is standing motionless, pale of face; Couthon ejaculating, "Triumvir?" with a look at his paralytic legs. And Robespierre is struggling to speak, but President Thuriot is jingling the bell against him, but the Hall is sounding against him like an Æolus-Hall: and Robespierre is mounting the Tribune-steps and descending again; going and coming, like to choke with rage, terror, desperation:—and mutiny is the order of the day!

O President Thuriot, thou that wert Elector Thuriot, and from the Bastille battlements sawest Saint-Antoine rising like the Ocean-tide, and hast seen much since, sawest thou ever the like of this? Jingle of bell, which thou jinglest against Robespierre, is hardly audible amid the Bedlam storm; and men rage for life. "President of Assassins," shrieks Robespierre, "I demand speech of thee for the last time!" It cannot be had. "To you,

O virtuous men of the Plain," cries he, finding audience one moment, "I appeal to you!" The virtuous men of the Plain sit silent as stones. And Thuriot's bell jingles, and the Hall sounds like Æolus's Hall. Robespierre's frothing lips are grown "blue"; his tongue dry, cleaving to the roof of his mouth. "The blood of Danton chokes him," cry they. "Accusation! Decree of Accusation!" Thuriot swiftly puts that question. Accusation passes; the incorruptible Maximilien is decreed Accused.

"I demand to share my Brother's fate, as I have striven to share his virtues," cries Augustin, the Younger Robespierre: Augustin also is decreed. And Couthon, and Saint-Just, and Lebas, they are all decreed; and packed forth,—not without difficulty, the Ushers almost trembling to obey. Triumvirate and Company are packed forth, into *Salut* Committee-room; their tongue cleaving to the roof of their mouth. You have but to summon the Municipality; to cashier Commandant Henriot, and launch Arrest at him; to regulate formalities; hand Tinville his victims. It is noon: the Æolus-Hall has delivered itself; blows now victorious, harmonious, as one irresistible wind.

And so the work is finished? One thinks so: and yet it is not so. Alas, there is yet but the first-act finished; three or four other acts still to come; and an uncertain catastrophe! A huge City holds in it so many confusions: seven hundred thousand human heads; not one of which knows what its neighbour is doing, nay not what itself is doing.—See, accordingly, about three in the afternoon, Commandant Henriot, how instead of sitting cashiered, arrested, he gallops along the Quais, followed by Municipal Gendarmes, "trampling down several persons"! For the Townhall sits deliberating, openly insurgent: Barriers to be shut; no Gaoler to admit any Prisoner this day;— and Henriot is galloping towards the Tuileries, to deliver

Robespierre. On the Quai de la Ferraillerie, a young Citoyen, walking with his wife, says aloud: "Gendarmes, that man is not your Commandant; he is under arrest." The Gendarmes strike down the young Citoyen with the flat of their swords.

Representatives themselves (as Merlin the Thionviller), who accost him, this puissant Henriot flings into guard-houses. He bursts towards the Tuileries Committee-room, "to speak with Robespierre": with difficulty, the Ushers and Tuileries Gendarmes, earnestly pleading and drawing sabre, seize this Henriot; get the Henriot Gendarmes persuaded not to fight; get Robespierre and Company packed into hackney-coaches, sent off under escort, to the Luxembourg and other Prisons. This, then, *is* the end? May not an exhausted Convention adjourn now, for a little repose and sustenance, "at five o'clock "?

An exhausted Convention did it; and repented it. The end was not come; only the end of the *second-act*. Hark, while exhausted Representatives sit at victuals,— tocsin bursting from all steeples, drums rolling, in the summer evening; Judge Coffinhal is galloping with new Gendarmes, to deliver Henriot from Tuileries Committee-room; and does deliver him! Puissant Henriot vaults on horseback; sets to haranguing the Tuileries Gendarmes; corrupts the Tuileries Gendarmes too; trots off with them to Townhall. Alas, and Robespierre is not in Prison: the Gaoler showed his Municipal order, durst not, on pain of his life, admit any Prisoner; the Robespierre Hackney-coaches, in this confused jangle and whirl of uncertain Gendarmes, have floated safe— into the Townhall! There sit Robespierre and Company, embraced by Municipals and Jacobins in sacred right of Insurrection; redacting Proclamations; sounding tocsins; corresponding with Sections and Mother Society. Is not

here a pretty enough third-act of a *natural* Greek Drama;
catastrophe more uncertain than ever?

The hasty Convention rushes together again, in the
ominous nightfall: President Collot, for the chair is his,
enters with long strides, paleness on his face; claps-on
his hat; says with solemn tone: "Citoyens, armed Vil-
lains have beset the Committee-rooms, and got possession
of them. The hour is come, to die at our post!" "*Oui*,"
answer one and all: "We swear it!" It is no rodomon-
tade, this time, but a sad fact and necessity; unless we *do*
at our posts, we must verily die. Swift therefore, Robespierre, Henriot, the Municipality, are declared Rebels;
put *Hors la Loi*, Out of Law. Better still, we appoint
Barras Commandant of what Armed-force is to be had;
send Missionary Representatives to all Sections and
quarters, to preach, and raise force; will die at least with
harness on our back.

What a distracted City; men riding and running,
reporting and hearsaying; the Hour clearly in travail,—
child not to be *named* till born! The poor Prisoners in
the Luxembourg hear the rumour; tremble for a new
September. They see men making signals to them, on
skylights and roofs, apparently signals of hope; cannot
in the least make out what it is. We observe, however,
in the eventide, as usual, the Death-tumbrils faring
Southeastward, through Saint-Antoine, towards their
Barrier du Trône. Saint-Antoine's tough bowels melt;
Saint-Antoine surrounds the Tumbrils; says, It shall not
be. O Heavens, why should it! Henriot and Gendarmes, scouring the streets that way, bellow, with waved
sabres, that it must. Quit hope, ye poor Doomed! The
Tumbrils move on.

But in this set of Tumbrils there are two other things
notable: one notable person; and one want of a notable
person. The notable person is Lieutenant-Géneral Loise-

rolles, a nobleman by birth and by nature; laying down his life here for his son.   In the Prison of Saint-Lazare, the night before last, hurrying to the Grate to hear the Death-list read, he caught the name of his son.   The son was asleep at the moment.   "I am Loiserolles," cried the old man: at Tinville's bar, an error in the Christian name is little; small objection was made.—The want of the notable person, again, is that of Deputy Paine!   Paine has sat in the Luxembourg since January; and seemed forgotten; but Fouquier had pricked him at last.   The Turnkey, List in hand, is marking with chalk the outer doors of to-morrow's *Fournée*.   Paine's outer door happened to be open, turned back on the wall; the Turnkey marked it on the side next him, and hurried on: another Turnkey came, and shut it; no chalk-mark now visible, the *Fournée* went without Paine.   Paine's life lay not there.—

Our fifth-act, of this natural Greek Drama, with its natural unities, can only be painted in gross; somewhat as that antique Painter, driven desperate, did the *foam*. For through this blessed July night, there is clangour, confusion very great, of marching troops; of Sections going this way, Sections going that; of Missionary Representatives reading Proclamations by torchlight; Missionary Legendre, who has raised force somewhere, emptying out the Jacobins, and flinging their key on the Convention table: "I have locked their door; it shall be Virtue that reopens it".   Paris, we say, is set against itself, rushing confused, as Ocean-currents do; a huge Mahlstrom, sounding there, under cloud of night.   Convention sits permanent on this hand; Municipality most permanent on that.   The poor prisoners hear tocsin and rumour; strive to bethink them of the signals apparently of hope.   Meek continual Twilight streaming up, which will be Dawn and a To-morrow, silvers the Northern hem

of Night; it wends and wends there, that meek brightness, like a silent prophecy, along the great ring-dial of
the Heaven. So still, eternal! and on Earth all is confused shadow and conflict; dissidence, tumultuous gloom
and glare; and " Destiny as yet sits wavering, and shakes
her doubtful urn ".

About three in the morning the dissident Armed-forces
have *met*. Henriot's Armed-force stood ranked in the
Place de Grève; and now Barras's, which he has re-
cruited, arrives there; and they front each other, cannon
bristling against cannon. Citoyens! cries the voice of
Discretion loudly enough, Before coming to bloodshed,
to endless civil-war, hear the Convention Decree read:
" Robespierre and all rebels Out of Law!"—Out of Law?
There is terror in the sound. Unarmed Citoyens disperse
rapidly home. Municipal Cannoneers, in sudden whirl,
anxiously unanimous, range themselves on the Convention side, with shouting. At which shout, Henriot
descends from his upper room, far gone in drink as some
say; finds his Place de Grève empty; the cannons' mouth
turned *towards* him; and on the whole,—that it is now
the catastrophe!

Stumbling in again, the wretched drunk-sobered Henriot announces: "All is lost!" " *Misérable*, it is thou
that hast lost it!" cry they; and fling him, or else he
flings himself, out of window: far enough down; into
masonwork and horror of cesspool; not into death but
worse. Augustin Robespierre follows him; with the
like fate. Saint-Just, they say, called on Lebas to kill
him; who would not. Couthon crept under a table;
attempting to kill himself; not doing it.—On entering
that Sanhedrim of Insurrection, we find all as good as
extinct; undone, ready for seizure. Robespierre was
sitting on a chair, with pistol-shot blown through not
his head but his under-jaw; the suicidal hand had failed.

With prompt zeal, not without trouble, we gather these wrecked Conspirators; fish up even Henriot and Augustin, bleeding and foul; pack them all, rudely enough, into carts; and shall, before sunrise, have them safe under lock and key. Amid shoutings and embracings.

Robespierre lay in an anteroom of the Convention Hall, while his Prison-escort was getting ready; the mangled jaw bound up rudely with bloody linen: a spectacle to men. He lies stretched on a table, a deal-box his pillow; the sheath of the pistol is still clenched convulsively in his hand. Men bully him, insult him: his eyes still indicate intelligence; he speaks no word. "He had on the sky-blue coat he had got made for the Feast of the *Être Suprême*"—O Reader, can thy hard heart hold out against that? His trousers were nankeen; the stockings had fallen down over the ankles. He spake no word more in this world.

And so, at six in the morning, a victorious Convention adjourns. Report flies over Paris as on golden wings; penetrates the Prisons; irradiates the faces of those that were ready to perish: turnkeys and *moutons*, fallen from their high estate, look mute and blue. It is the 28th day of July, called 10th of Thermidor, year 1794.

Fouquier had but to identify; his Prisoners being already Out of Law. At four in the afternoon, never before were the streets of Paris seen so crowded. From the Palais de Justice to the Place de la Révolution, for *thither* again go the Tumbrils this time, it is one dense stirring mass; all windows crammed; the very roofs and ridge-tiles budding forth human Curiosity, in strange gladness. The Death-tumbrils, with their motley Batch of Outlaws, some Twenty-three or so, from Maximilien to Mayor Fleuriot and Simon the Cordwainer, roll on. All eyes are on Robespierre's Tumbril, where he, his jaw bound in dirty linen, with his half-dead Brother and half-dead Henriot, lie shattered; their 'seventeen hours' of agony about to end. The Gendarmes point their swords at him, to show the people which is he. A woman springs on the Tumbril; clutching the side of it with one hand, waving the other Sibyl-like; and exclaims: "The death of thee gladdens my very heart, *m'enivre de joie*"; Robespierre opened his eyes; "*Scélérat,* go down to Hell, with the curses of all wives and mothers!"—At the foot of the scaffold, they stretched him on the ground till his turn came. Lifted aloft, his eyes again opened; caught the bloody axe. Samson wrenched the coat off him; wrenched the dirty linen from his jaw: the jaw fell powerless, there burst from him a cry;—hideous to hear and see. Samson, thou canst not be too quick!

Samson's work done, there bursts forth shout on shout of applause. Shout, which prolongs itself not only over Paris, but over France, but over Europe, and down to this generation. Deservedly, and also undeservedly. O unhappiest Advocate of Arras, wert thou worse than other Advocates? Stricter man, according to his Formula, to his Credo and his Cant, of probities, benevolences, pleasures-of-virtue, and suchlike, lived not in that age. A man fitted, in some luckier settled age, to have become one of those incorruptible barren Pattern-Figures, and have had marble-tablets and funeral-sermons. His poor landlord, the Cabinet-maker in the Rue Saint-Honoré, loved him; his Brother died for him. May God be merciful to him and to us!

This is the end of the Reign of Terror; new glorious *Revolution* named *of Thermidor*; of Thermidor 9th, year 2; which being interpreted into old slave-style means 27th of July, 1794. Terror is ended; and death in the Place de la Révolution, were the "*Tail* of Robespierre" once executed; which service Fouquier, in large Batches, is swiftly managing.

8. SAMUEL RAWSON GARDINER

(This series of extracts fittingly ends with the name of Mr. S. R. Gardiner, who, in no metaphorical sense, devoted his life to the elucidation of the period of the Puritan Revolution. It will be interesting to compare the following passage with the extracts from Hume and Clarendon. The difference in tone and style will be at once apparent; but the ordinary reader will be quite unable to appreciate the immense gulf which separates the substructures on which these three works are reared. Personal experience and enquiry, coupled with the sympathies and antipathies that a troubled political career had planted in his mind, form the material of Clarendon's narrative. Hume wrote from a wide acquaintance with printed books, and the information thus collected passed through the medium of his sceptical philosophy and his Tory prejudices. Mr. S. R. Gardiner's book represents a lifelong toil upon all the material, printed and unprinted, that was to be found in the museums and record offices of England and the Continent. It may be that his work will not take a permanent place in English literature; and, as a narrative of the period, it may, in spite of its high literary qualities, be superseded: but it will always be recognized that it is mainly due to Mr. Gardiner's researches that the history of the sixteenth century is at last rescued from party prejudice and dogmatism.)

THE LAST DAYS OF CHARLES I

AS soon as the fatal sentence had been pronounced, Charles was led back to Cotton House, and then, after a short delay, removed to Whitehall, where he was allowed to spend the night. On Sunday, the 28th, he listened with reverent devotion to the prayers of the Church read to him by Bishop Juxon, who had been allowed to visit him now that he was lying under sentence of death. At five o'clock in the afternoon he was conducted back to St. James's, perhaps in order that the preparations for his execution might not reach his ears.

Words very different from those consolations which Juxon addressed to the King resounded on that Sunday morning in the Chapel of Whitehall, where Hugh Peters preached before the members of the High Court of Justice in justification of those who were seeking the King's death. There was need of all his rude eloquence if those judges who had not yet given their signatures to the death-warrant were to be steeled to the work before them. The protests against any attempt to act on that sentence were many and loud. On the 29th the members of the Assembly of Divines joined in supplicating for the King's life, and on the same day two Dutch ambassadors, who had been specially despatched from the Netherlands for the purpose, made a similar request to the House of Commons. It was also reported that Fairfax had urged the Council of Officers in the same direction, whilst it was no secret that the Prince of Wales had sent a blank sheet of paper, signed and sealed by himself, on which the Parliament might inscribe any terms they pleased. That the vast majority of the English people would have accepted this offer gladly was beyond all reasonable doubt.

It was but a small knot of men—a bare majority, if they were even that, amongst the sitting members of the High Court of Justice itself—who had fixedly determined that there should be no relenting; but they had Cromwell amongst them, and Cromwell's will, when once his mind had been made up, was absolutely inflexible. They had, moreover, behind them the greater part of the rank and file of the army, to whom the shortest issue seemed the best.

The first difficulty encountered by those who were bent on carrying out the sentence of the Court was that of obtaining signatures to the death-warrant in sufficient numbers to give even an appearance of unanimity amongst

the judges.   On Saturday, the 27th, a few more signatures had been added to those obtained on the 26th, but
on the morning of Monday, the 29th, not only were many
still wanting, but there was reason to believe that some of
the judges who had already signed would refuse to repeat
their signatures if called on to do so.   Yet it was impossible to make use of the warrant in its existing condition.
It had been, as there is little doubt, dated on the 26th,
and it presupposed a sentence passed on that day, whereas
it was notorious that no sentence had been passed till
the 27th.   Under these circumstances the natural course
of proceeding would have been to re-copy the warrant
with altered dates and to have it signed afresh.   What
was actually done was to erase the existing date, and to
make such other alterations as were requisite to bring the
whole document into conformity with actual facts.   Of
the names of the three officers finally charged with the
execution of the sentence, Hacker, Huncks, and Phayre,
that of Huncks alone was unaltered.   The names over
which those of Hacker and Phayre were written are now
illegible, but they can hardly fail to have been those of
men who shrank from carrying out the grim duty assigned
to them.

Having by this extraordinary means secured the reten-
tion of the signatures already given, the managers of the
business, whoever they were, applied themselves energeti-
cally to increase the number.   The testimony of those
regicides who pleaded after the Restoration that they had
acted under compulsion must, indeed, be received with
the utmost caution; but there is no reason to doubt that
considerable pressure was put upon those judges who,
having agreed to the sentence, now showed a disinclina-
tion to sign the warrant.   In all the stories by the regicides on their defence Cromwell takes a prominent place,
and it is easy to understand how meanly he must have

thought of men who, after joining in passing the sentence, declined to sign the warrant. When those members of the Court who were also members of Parliament took their places in the House, Cromwell is reported to have called on them to sign without further delay. " Those that are gone in", he said, " shall set their hands. I will have their hands now."

Later in the day, when the warrant lay for signature on a table in the Painted Chamber, the scene grew animated. It is said that Cromwell, whose pent-up feelings some-times manifested themselves in horse-play, drew an inky pen across Marten's face, and that Marten inked Crom-well's face in return. According to another story, which was for a long time accepted as true, Cromwell dragged Ingoldsby to the table, and forced him to sign by grasping his hand with a pen in it. The firmness of Ingoldsby's signature, however, contradicts the latter part of the assertion, though it is possible that some kind of compulsion was previously used to bring him to the point.

On the whole it will be safe to assume that great pressure was put, sometimes in rough military fashion, on those who hung back. On the other hand, there was no evidence given by any of the regicides, when put upon their trial, of any definite threats being used against those who made difficulties about signing. Downes, indeed, who did not sign at all, describes himself as having been frightened into assenting to the judgment, but he had nothing to say about any ill effects resulting to him on account of his refusal to sign.

In one way or another fifty-nine signatures were at last obtained. Nine out of the sixty-seven who had given sentence did not sign; but, on the other hand, Ingoldsby, who signed the warrant, had been absent when the sen-tence was passed.

Meanwhile, Charles was awaiting his certain fate with quiet dignity at St. James's. Ever since the commencement of the trial he had been annoyed by the presence of soldiers drinking and smoking even in his bedroom. Colonel Tomlinson, who had a general superintendence over the arrangements for his personal accommodation, was a man of humanity and discretion, and did his best to check the insolence of the men; but Hacker, who commanded the soldiers, was less considerate. Yet even Hacker was induced, a few nights before the trial was ended, to leave the King's bedchamber free, and this particular form of insult was not repeated.

On the morning of the 29th Charles burnt his papers, including the keys of his ciphered correspondence. His two youngest children were then admitted to see him for the last time. Elizabeth, who had just completed her thirteenth year, was a delicate child, and had taken her father's misfortunes so deeply to heart that during the first days of the trial she was reported to have died of sorrow. Her brother, the little Duke of Gloucester, was still in his tenth year.

Both the children burst into tears when they met their father's eye. Charles took them on his knees, telling his daughter not to sorrow overmuch, as he was about to die a glorious death " for the laws and liberties of this land and for maintaining the true Protestant religion". He then recommended her to "read Bishop Andrewes's *Sermons*, Hooker's *Ecclesiastical Polity*, and Bishop Laud's book against Fisher". As for himself, he added, he had forgiven all his enemies, and hoped that God would also forgive them. He then charged his daughter to let her mother know "that his thoughts had never strayed from her, and that his love should be the same to the last". More followed of the outpourings of a father's heart, ending with an injunction to the girl to forgive those who were now bringing him to the scaffold, but never to trust them, " as they had been most false to him ".

Charles had spoken to Elizabeth as to one come to years of discretion. He addressed his son in language suitable to his younger age. " Sweetheart," he said, " now they will cut off thy father's head; mark, child, what I say: they will cut off my head and perhaps make thee a king; but, mark what I say: you must not be a king so long as your brothers Charles and James do live; for they will cut off your brothers' heads when they can catch them, and cut off thy head too at the last, and therefore, I charge you, do not be made a king by them." " I will sooner be torn in pieces first!" cried the gallant boy, gladdening his father's heart by his words. In the end Charles divided his jewels between the children, retaining only the George cut in onyx and surrounded by diamonds. After many tears and embracings he dismissed them both, returning to prayer in the company of Juxon and Herbert.

On the morning of the 30th, the day appointed for his execution, Charles rose early. Herbert told him that he had dreamt of Laud's coming into the room and kissing his old master's hand. Charles had no thoughts to waste upon dreams, and merely replied " It is remarkable ". " Herbert," he continued, "this is my second marriage-day. I would be as trim to-day as may be; for before night I hope to be espoused to my blessed Jesus." Then turning to things of earth—" Let me have", he said, " a shirt on more than ordinary, by reason the season is so sharp as probably may make me shake, which some observers may imagine proceeds from fear. I would have no such imputation; I fear not death. Death is not terrible to me: I bless my God I am prepared."

After a while Juxon arrived, and as soon as the gifts intended for the children had been set aside, Charles spent half an hour with him in private prayer. Then, in Herbert's presence, the Bishop read the morning service. By a remarkable coincidence the lesson for the day was the twenty-seventh chapter of Matthew, which contains the narrative of the Passion of the Lord. After the close of the service Charles continued in prayer and meditation till Hacker knocked at the door to summon him to Whitehall. Charles at once prepared to obey, and, accompanied by Tomlinson and Juxon, and closely followed by Herbert, walked across St. James's Park between a double row of soldiers. When he arrived at Whitehall, he was allowed to rest for some time. Having eaten a piece of bread and drunk a glass of wine, he betook himself to prayer for the remainder of his allotted time.

In the meanwhile strange preparations were being made on the scaffold, which had been erected in front of the Banqueting House. Charles's refusal to plead before the Court had given rise to an idea that he might also refuse to submit voluntarily to the execution of the sentence which it had pronounced against him. Staples were therefore hammered into the floor of the scaffold to afford a purchase for ropes, by aid of which, if any resistance were offered, the King could be forced down into the prone attitude in which victims were at that time beheaded. The delay in leading out the King was, however, too great to be accounted for by the time required for completing this arrangement, and it is not unlikely that the execution was deliberately postponed till the House had passed an Act forbidding the proclamation of any successor. It was not till two o'clock that Charles was finally summoned to his earthly doom.

When Charles stepped out upon the scaffold—probably

from the central window of the Banqueting House—the only friend who followed him was Juxon, Herbert having begged to be excused from witnessing the painful sight. No other persons were admitted to a place on the scaffold excepting Colonels Hacker and Tomlinson and the two masked figures of the executioner and his assistant. Below was a crowded mass of men and women, who had come, for the most part, with sorrowing hearts, to witness Charles's last moments upon earth. To them he would gladly have confided that last appeal to his subjects which he had been forbidden to make when he was hurried away from the Court; but the ranks of soldiers, horse and foot, drawn up immediately round the foot of the scaffold, rendered all communication impossible. Charles there fore addressed himself to Juxon and Tomlinson, declar ing that not he, but the Parliament, had originated the Civil War. He then prayed that his enemies might be forgiven, and protested against the subjection of the country to the power of the sword. Nothing, he said, would prosper till men gave their dues to God, to the King, and to the people. For their duty to God, he recommended the convocation of a national synod, freely chosen. For their duty to the King, it was not for him to speak. "For the people," he continued, "truly I desire their liberty and freedom as much as anybody whatsoever; but I must tell you that their liberty and freedom consists in having government, those laws by which their lives and their goods may be most their own. It is not their having a share in the government; that is nothing appertaining unto them. A subject and a sovereign are clean different things; and, therefore, until you do that—I mean that you put the people in that liberty—they will never enjoy themselves."

After another protest against the rule of the sword, and a declaration made at Juxon's instance, that he died " a

Christian according to the profession of the Church of England", Charles prepared for death. With the assistance of the executioner, whose features as well as those of his assistant were effectually concealed by a mask, he confined his straggling locks within a white satin nightcap. He then exchanged with Juxon a few words of religious consolation, after which, placing in the Bishop's hands the George which he wore round his neck, he addressed to him the simple word " Remember ", meaning, probably, to impress on him the importance of delivering the messages to the Prince and others with which he had already charged him.

Having bidden the executioner to refrain from striking till he stretched out his hands as a sign that he was ready, Charles laid himself down, placing his neck on the low block provided. After a short delay, he made the signal agreed on. The axe fell, and the kingly head, with its crown of sorrows, dropped upon the scaffold. The executioner caught it up, and, holding it aloft, pronounced the accustomed formula, " Behold the head of a traitor!" A loud groan of horror and displeasure was the answer of the people to the announcement. They, at least, had no part in that day's deed. So hostile was their attitude, that orders were given to two troops of horse to patrol up and down the street in order to disperse the angry crowd.

The King's body was at once placed in a coffin, and covered with a velvet pall. For some days it lay in the chamber at Whitehall in which Charles had spent his last minutes before his summons to the scaffold. It was there carefully embalmed, and when that operation had been accomplished was removed to St. James's. A request that it might be buried in Henry the Seventh's Chapel having been refused, Juxon and Herbert were allowed to inter their dead master in St. George's Chapel at Windsor. The sad procession set out from St. James's on February 7. On the 8th the funeral at Windsor was attended by Richmond, Hertford, Southampton, Lindsay, and Juxon. As the coffin was brought to the chapel snow began to fall, and gave to the pall, as the little company loved to remember, "the colour of innocency". The White King, as men named him—calling to memory the white satin dress in which, unlike his predecessors, he had clothed himself at his coronation, and the omens of disaster which were believed to be connected with the name—was borne to the grave in silence. Juxon had prepared himself to read the burial service from the Book of Common Prayer, but Whichcott, the governor of the Castle, forbade him to use any other form but that of the Directory. The coffin was then lowered into the vault which had been opened to receive it—the same in which Henry VIII and Jane Seymour had been buried more than a century before.

Those who brought Charles to the scaffold strengthened the revulsion of feeling in his favour which had begun to set in ever since it had been clearly brought home to the nation that its choice lay between the rule of the King and the rule of the sword. It is indeed true that the feeling hostile to the army was not created by the execution of Charles, but its intensity was greatly strengthened by the horror caused by the spectacle of sufferings so meekly endured.

Charles's own patience, and the gentleness with which he met harshness and insult, together with his own personal dignity, won hearts which might otherwise have been steeled against his pretensions. The often-quoted lines of Andrew Marvel set forth the impression which Charles's bearing on the scaffold produced on even hostile spectators:—

> " He nothing common did or mean
> Upon that memorable scene,
> But with his keener eye
> The axe's edge did try;
> Nor called the gods, with vulgar spite,
> To vindicate his helpless right;
> But bowed his comely head
> Down, as upon a bed ".

Marvell's verses embodied his own recollections of the external dignity of the man. A little book which, under the title of *Eikon Basiliké*, was issued with calculated timeliness to the world on February 9, the day after the King's funeral, purported to be the product of Charles's own pen, and aimed at being a spiritual revelation of the inmost thoughts of the justest of sovereigns and the most self-denying of martyrs. Its real author, Dr. John Gauden, a nominally Presbyterian divine, caught with great felicity the higher motives which were never absent from Charles's mind, and gave to the narratives and meditations of which the book consisted enough of dramatic veracity to convince all who were prepared to believe it that they had before them the real thoughts of the man who had died because he refused to sacrifice law and religion to an intriguing Parliament and a ruffianly army. The demand for the book was well-nigh unlimited. Edition after edition was exhausted almost as soon as it left the press. The greedily-devoured volumes served to create an ideal image of Charles which went far to make the permanent overthrow of the monarchy impossible.

The ideal thus created had the stronger hold on men's minds because it faithfully reproduced at least one side of Charles's character. The other side—his persistent determination to ignore all opinions divergent from his own, and to treat all by whom they were entertained as knaves or fools—had been abundantly illustrated in the course of the various negotiations which had been carried on from time to time in the course of the Civil War. It finally led to a struggle for the possession of that Negative Voice which, if only the King could succeed in retaining it, would enable him to frustrate all new legislation even when supported by a determined national resolve. On the one side was undoubtedly both law and tradition; on the other side the necessity of shaping legislation by the wishes of the nation, and not by the wishes of a single man or of a single class.

Fortunately, or unfortunately, such abstract considerations seldom admit of direct application to politics. It is at all times hard to discover what the wishes of a nation really are, and least of all can this be done amidst the fears and passions of a revolutionary struggle. Only after long years does a nation make clear its definite resolve, and for this reason wise statesmen—whether monarchial or republican—watch the currents of opinion, and submit to compromises which will enable the national sentiment to make its way without a succession of violent shocks. Charles's fault lay not so much in his claim to retain the Negative Voice as in the absolute disregard of the conditions of the time, and of the feelings and opinions of every class of his subjects with which he happened to disagree. Even if those who opposed Charles in the later stages of his career failed to rally the majority of the people to their side, they were undoubtedly acting in accordance with a permanent national demand for that government of compromise which slowly but irresistibly developed itself in the course of the century.

Nor can it be doubted that, if Charles had, under any conditions, been permitted to reseat himself on the throne, he would quickly have provoked a new resistance. As long as he remained a factor in English politics, govern-

ment by compromise was impossible. His own conception of government was that of a wise prince constantly
interfering to check the madness of the people. In the
Isle of Wight he wrote down with approval the lines in
which Claudian, the servile poet of the Court of Honorius,
declared it to be an error to give the name of slavery to
the service of the best of princes, and asserted that liberty
never had a greater charm than under a pious king. Even
on the scaffold he reminded his subjects that a share
in government was nothing appertaining to the people.
It was the tragedy of Charles's life that he was entirely
unable to satisfy the cravings of those who inarticulately
hoped for the establishment of a monarchy which, while
it kept up the old traditions of the country, and thus
saved England from a blind plunge into an unknown
future, would yet allow the people of the country to be to
some extent masters of their own destiny.

Yet if Charles persistently alienated this large and
important section of his subjects, so also did his most
determined opponents. The very merits of the Independents—their love of toleration and of legal and
political reform, together with their advocacy of demo-
cratic change—raised opposition in a nation which was
prepared for none of these things, and drove them step
by step to rely on armed strength rather than upon the
free play of constitutional action. But for this, it is
probable that the Vote of No Addresses would have
received a practically unanimous support in the Parliament and the nation, and that in the beginning of 1648
Charles would have been dethroned, and a new government of some kind or other established with good hope
of success. As it was, in their despair of constitutional
support, the Independents were led in spite of their
better feelings to the employment of the army as an
instrument of government.

The situation, complicated enough already, had been still further complicated by Charles's duplicity. Men who would have been willing to come to terms with him, despaired of any constitutional arrangement in which he was to be a factor; and men who had long been alienated from him were irritated into active hostility. By these he was regarded with increasing intensity as the one disturbing force with which no understanding was possible and no settled order consistent. To remove him out of the way appeared, even to those who had no thought of punishing him for past offences, to be the only possible road to peace for the troubled nation. It seemed that so long as Charles lived, deluded nations and deluded parties would be stirred up, by promises never intended to be fulfilled, to fling themselves, as they had flung themselves in the Second Civil War, against the new order of things which was struggling to establish itself in England.

Of this latter class Cromwell made himself the mouthpiece. Himself a man of compromises, he had been thrust, sorely against his will, into direct antagonism with the uncompromising king. He had striven long to mediate between the old order and the new, first by restoring Charles as a constitutional king, and afterwards by substituting one of his children for him. Failing in this, and angered by the persistence with which Charles stirred up Scottish armies and Irish armies against England, Cromwell finally associated himself with those who cried out most loudly for the King's blood. No one knew better than Cromwell that it was folly to cover the execution of the King with the semblance of constitutional propriety, and he may well have thought that, though law and constitution had both broken down, the first step to be taken towards their reconstruction was the infliction of the penalty of death upon the man who had shown himself so wanting in that elemental quality of veracity upon which laws and constitutions are built up. All that is known of Cromwell's conduct at the trial— his anger with Downes's scruples, and the pressure which he put upon those who were unwilling to sign the death-warrant—point to his contempt for the legal forms with which others were attempting to cover an action essentially illegal.

Tradition has handed down an anecdote which points to the same explanation of the workings of Cromwell's mind. "The night after King Charles was beheaded," it is said, "my Lord Southampton and a friend of his got leave to sit up by the body in the Banqueting House at Whitehall. As they were sitting very melancholy there, about two o'clock in the morning they heard the tread of somebody coming very slowly upstairs. By and by the door opened, and a man entered very much muffled up in his cloak, and his face quite hid in it. He approached the body, considered it very attentively for some time, and then, shaking his head, sighed out the words, 'Cruel necessity!' He then departed in the same slow and concealed manner as he had come. Lord Southampton used to say that he could not distinguish anything of his face, but that by his voice and gait he took him to be Oliver Cromwell."

Whether the necessity really existed or was but the tyrant's plea is a question upon the answer to which men have long differed, and will probably continue to differ. All can perceive that with Charles's death the main obstacle to the establishment of a constitutional system was removed. Personal rulers might indeed reappear, and Parliament had not yet so displayed its superiority as a governing power to make Englishmen anxious to dispense with monarchy in some form or other. The monarchy, as Charles understood it, had disappeared